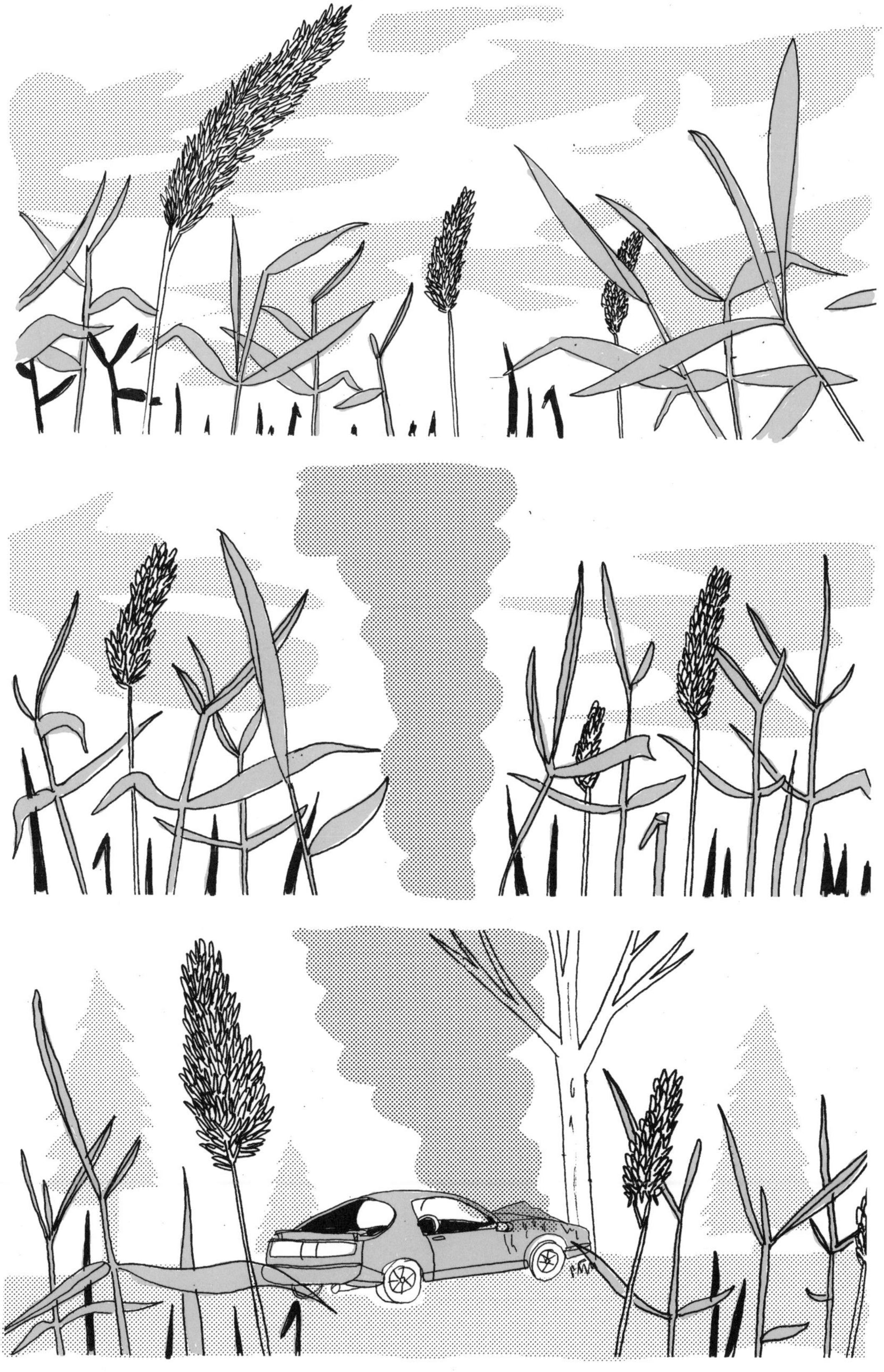

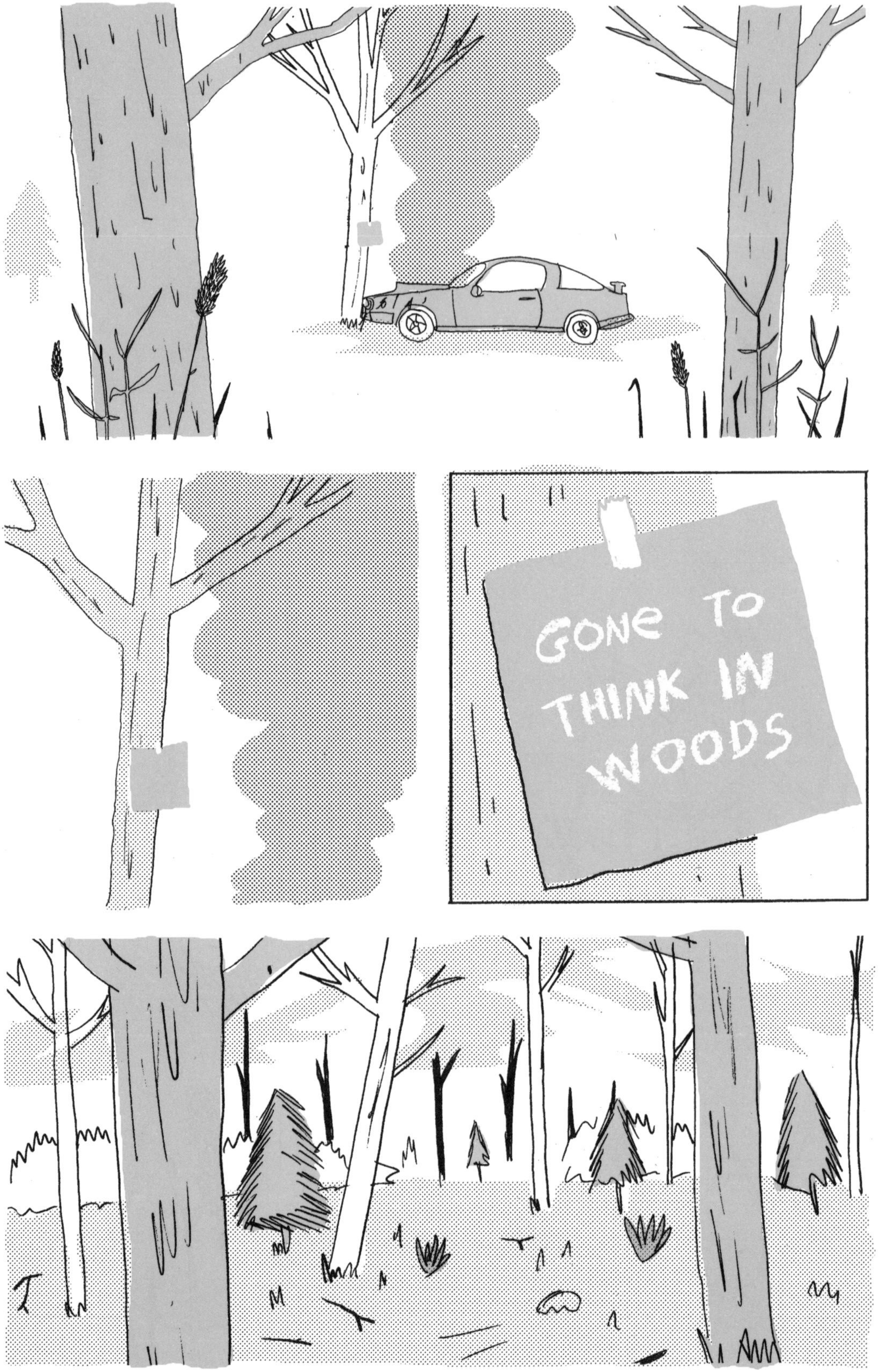
GONE TO
THINK IN
WOODS

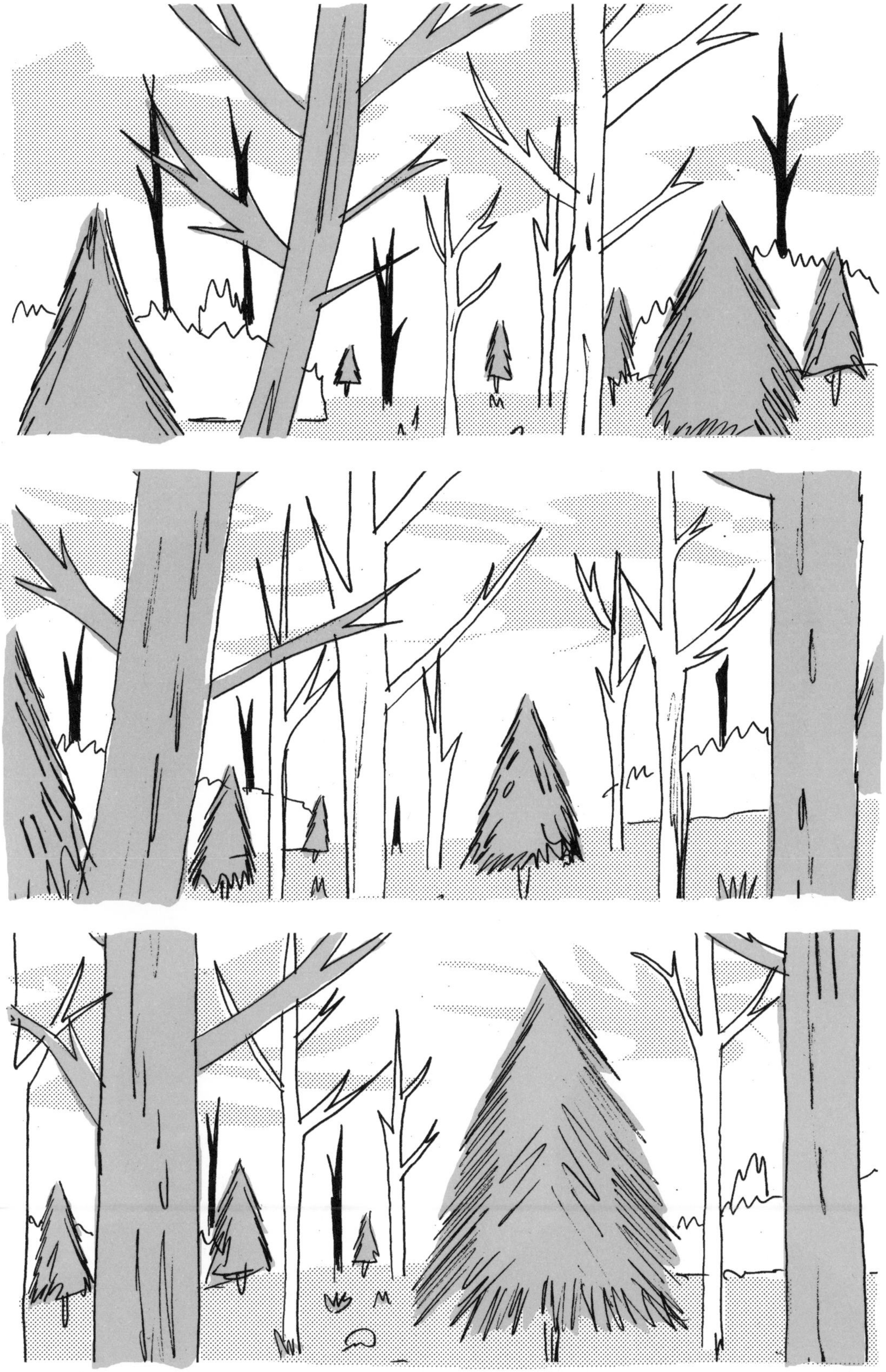

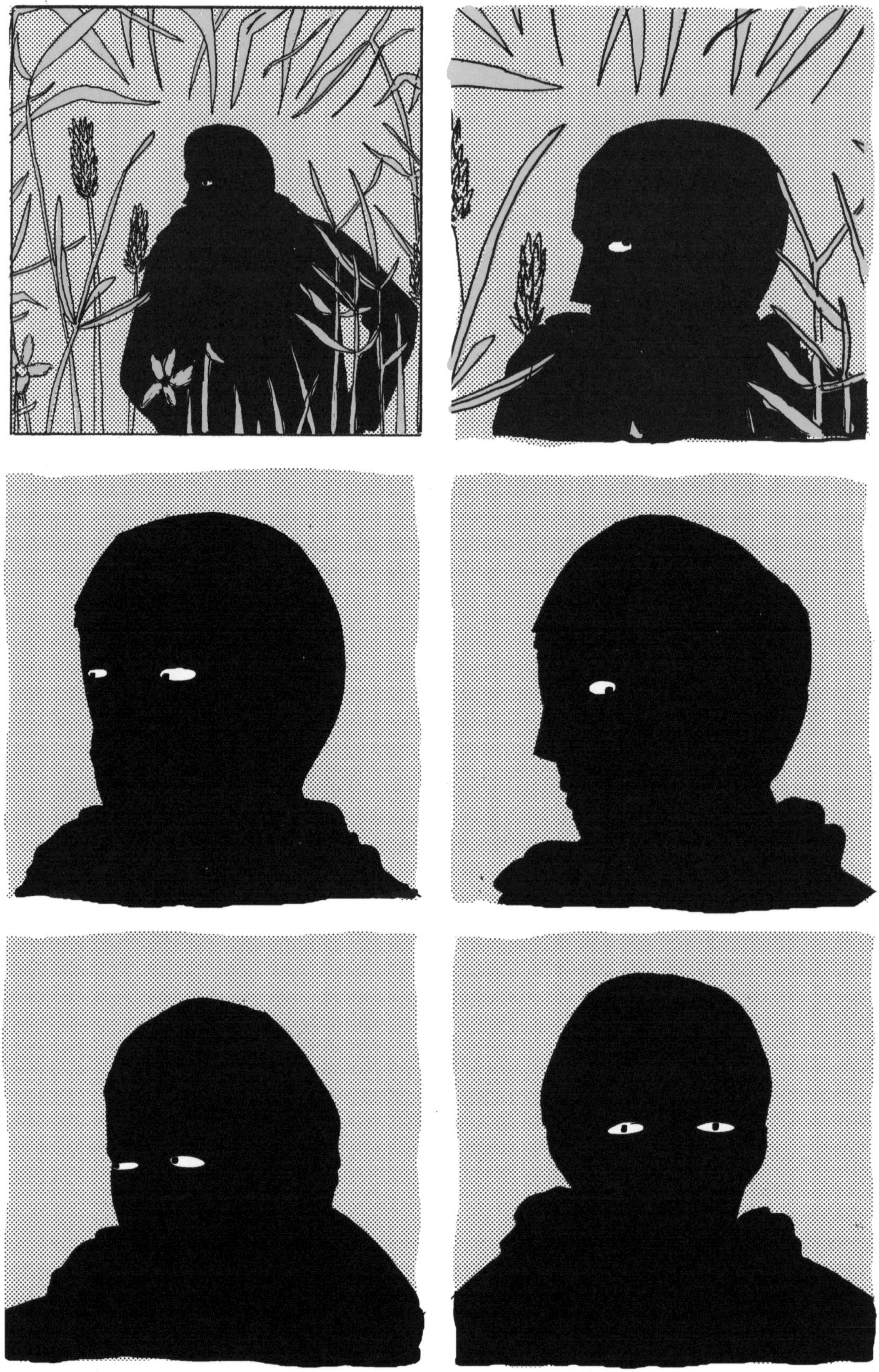

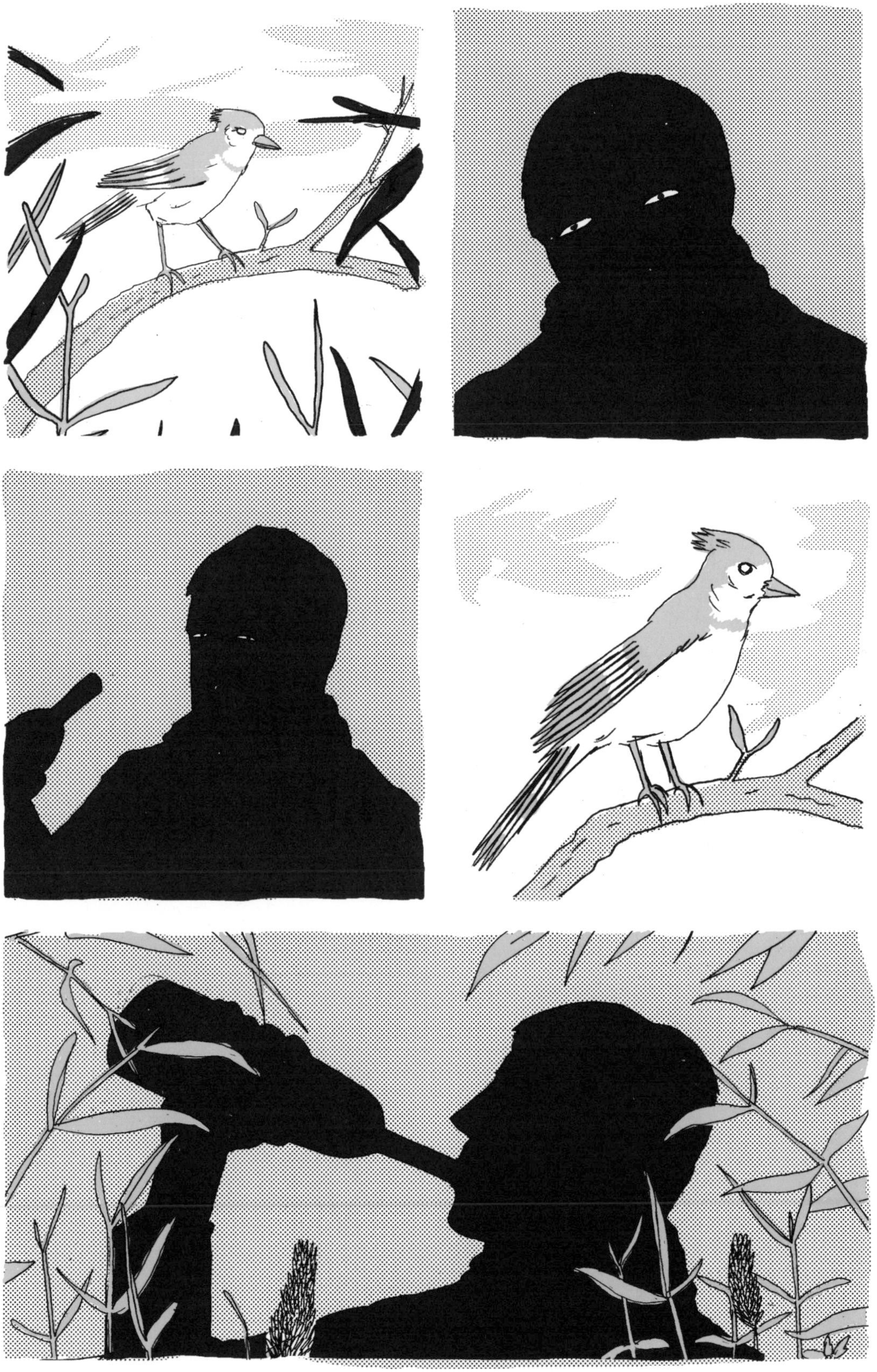

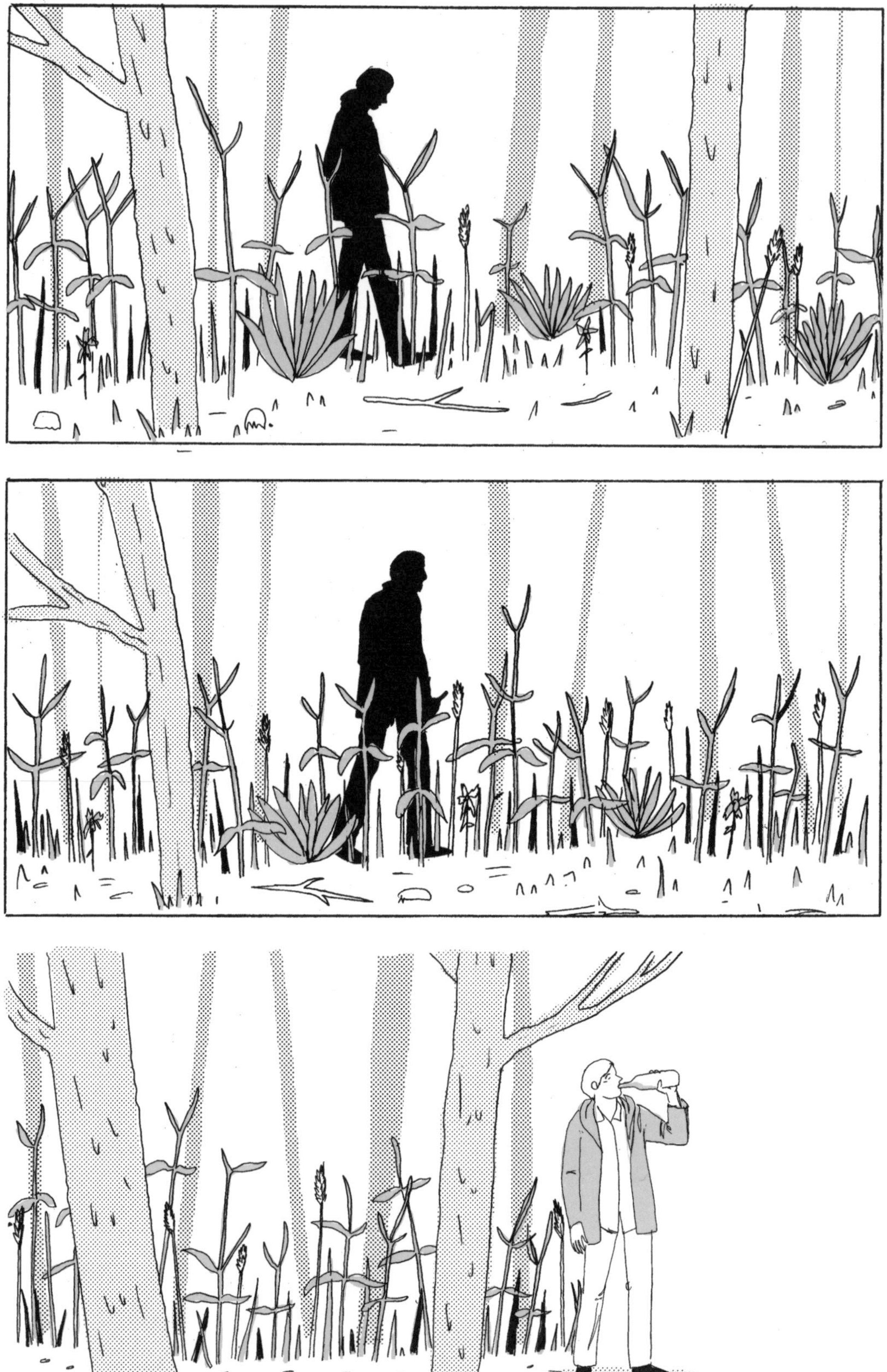

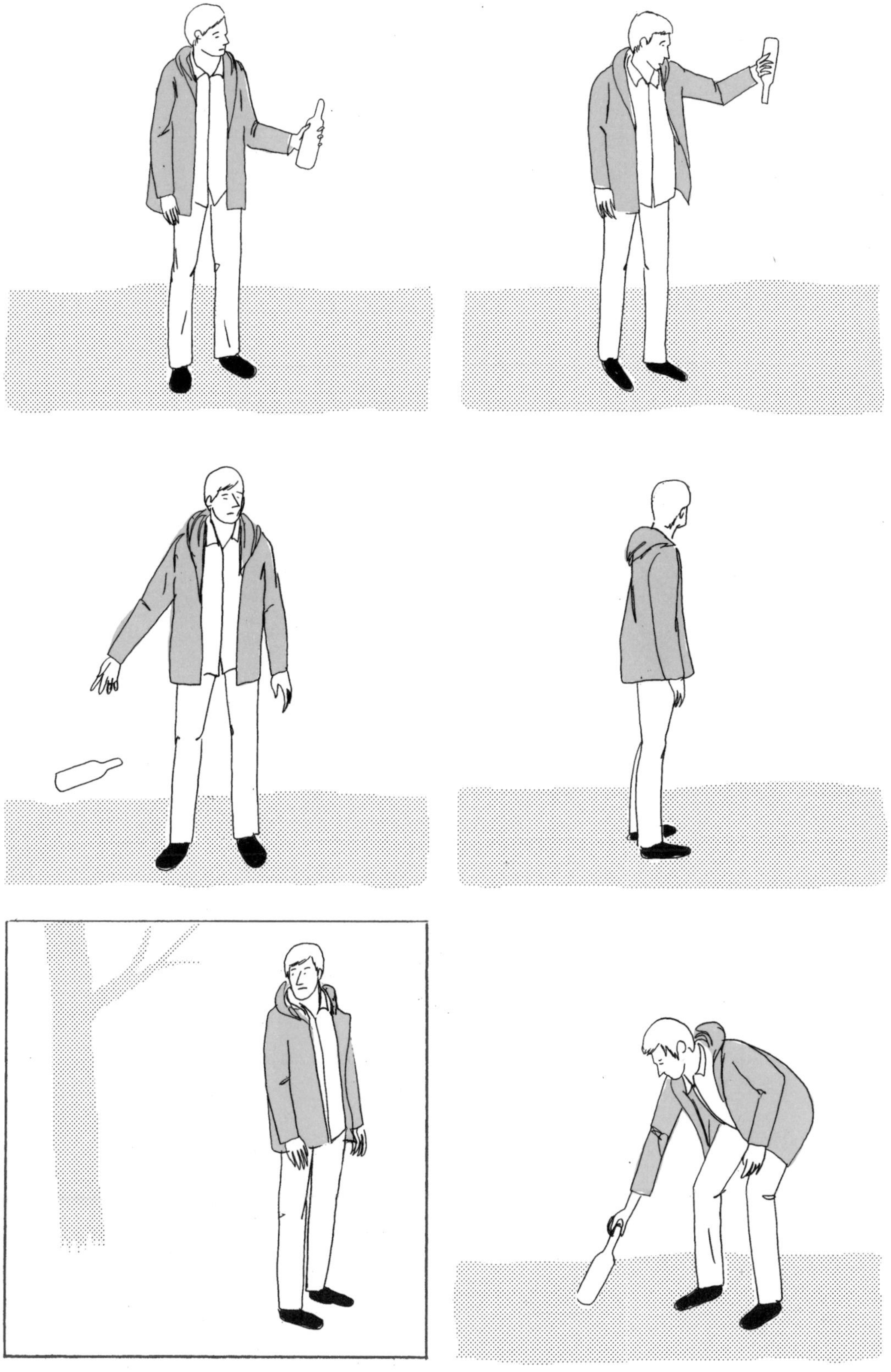

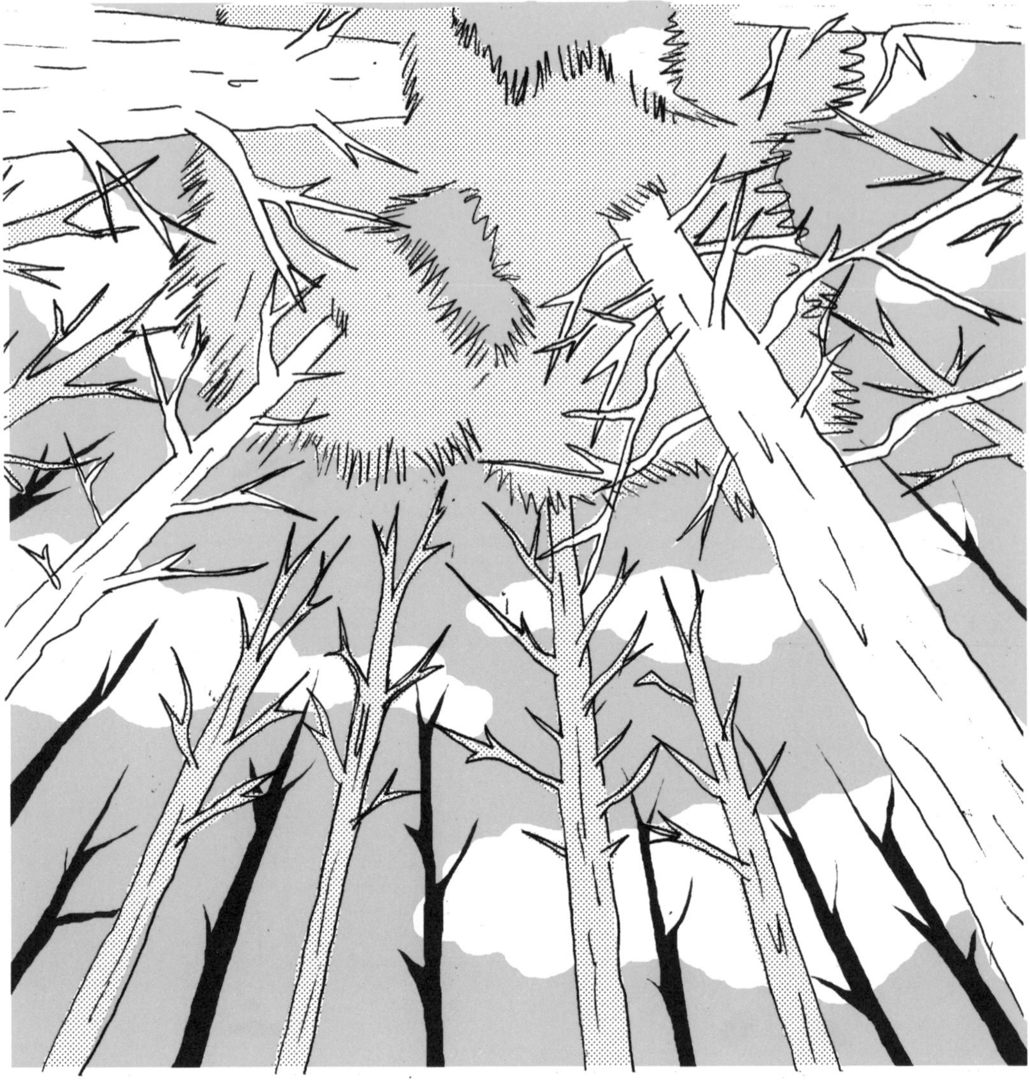
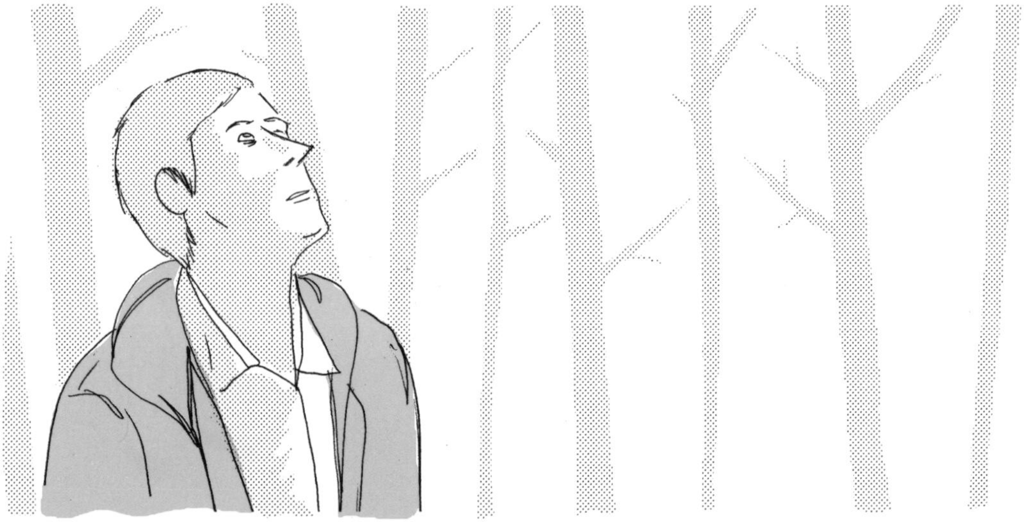

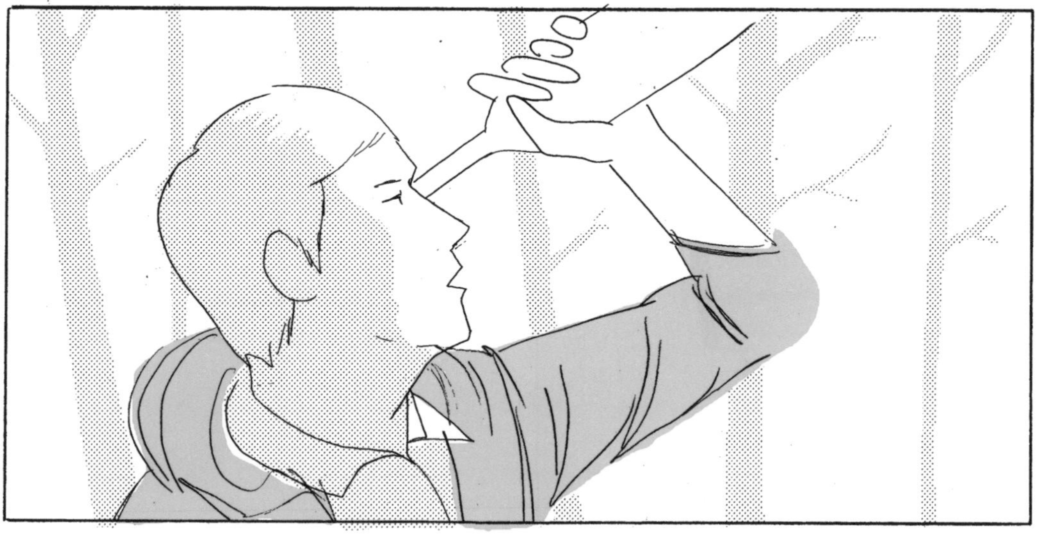

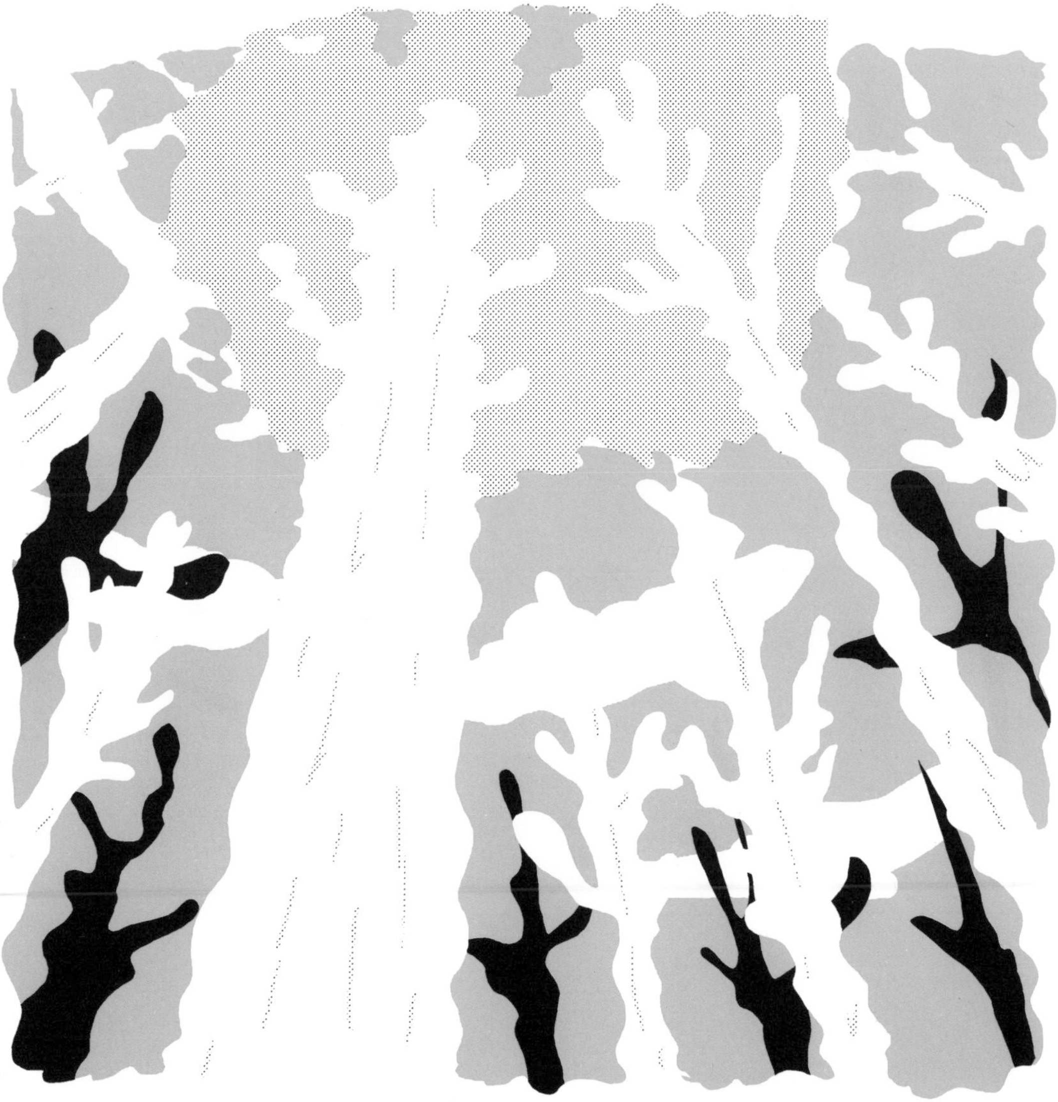

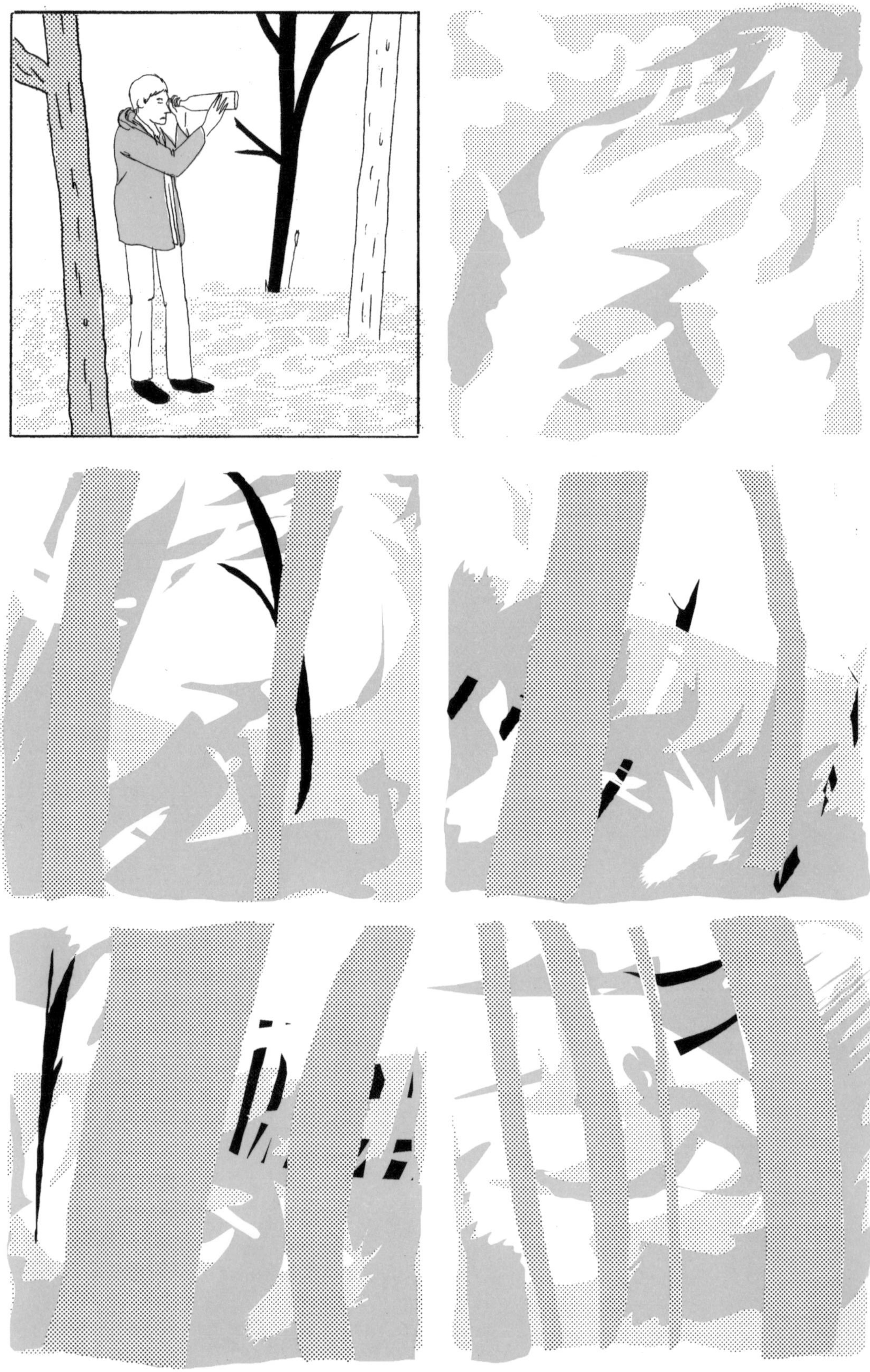

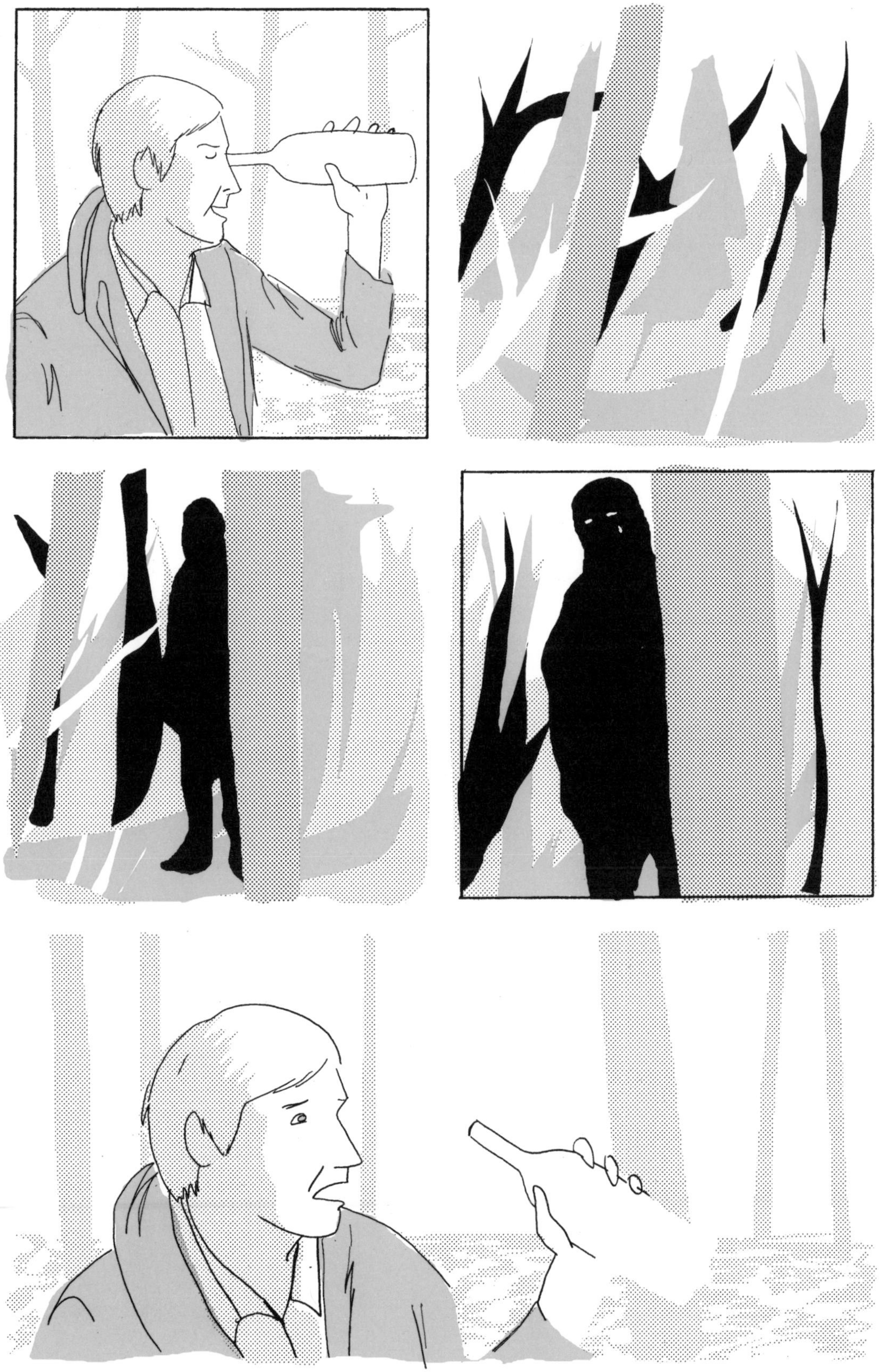

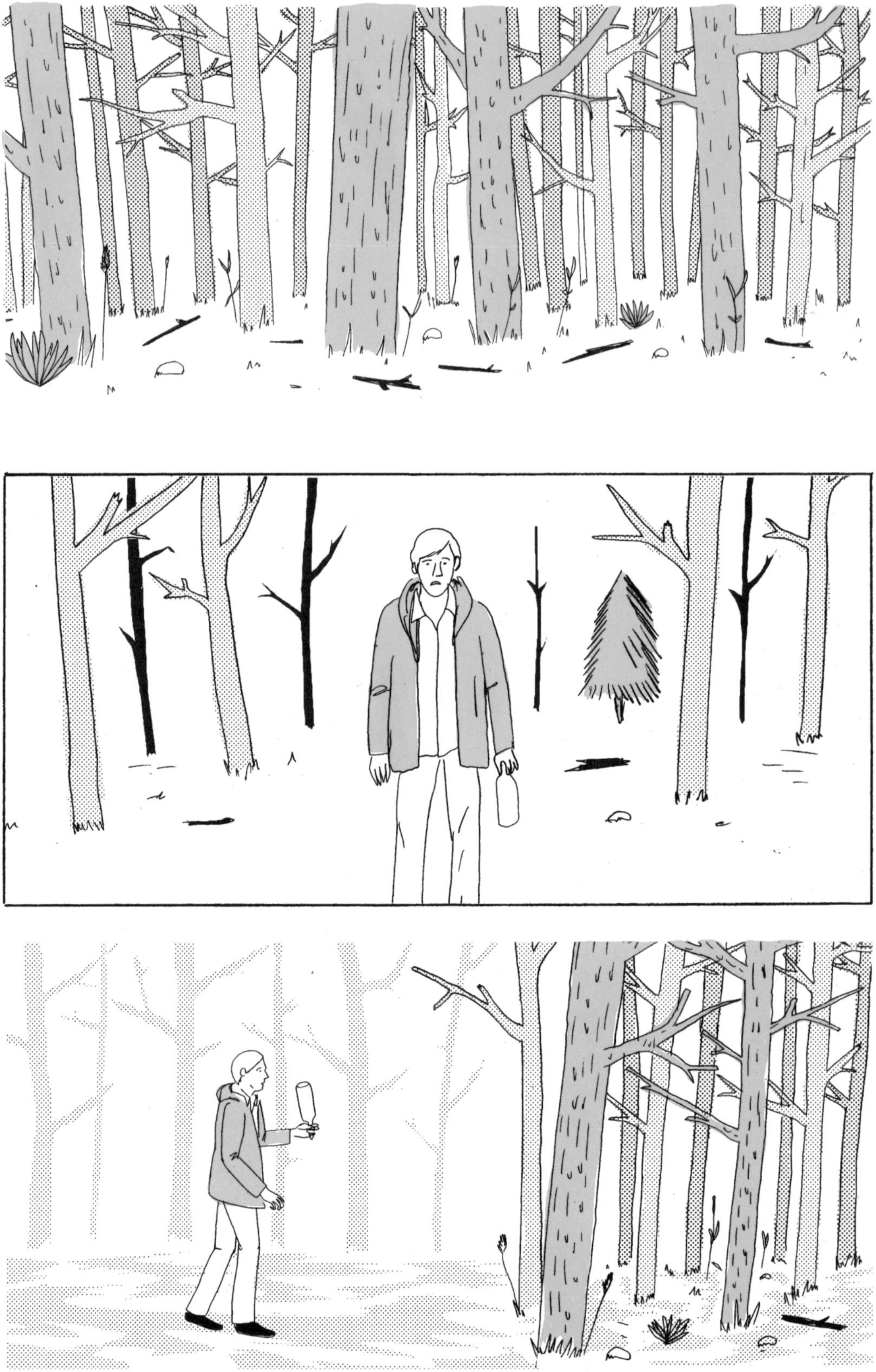

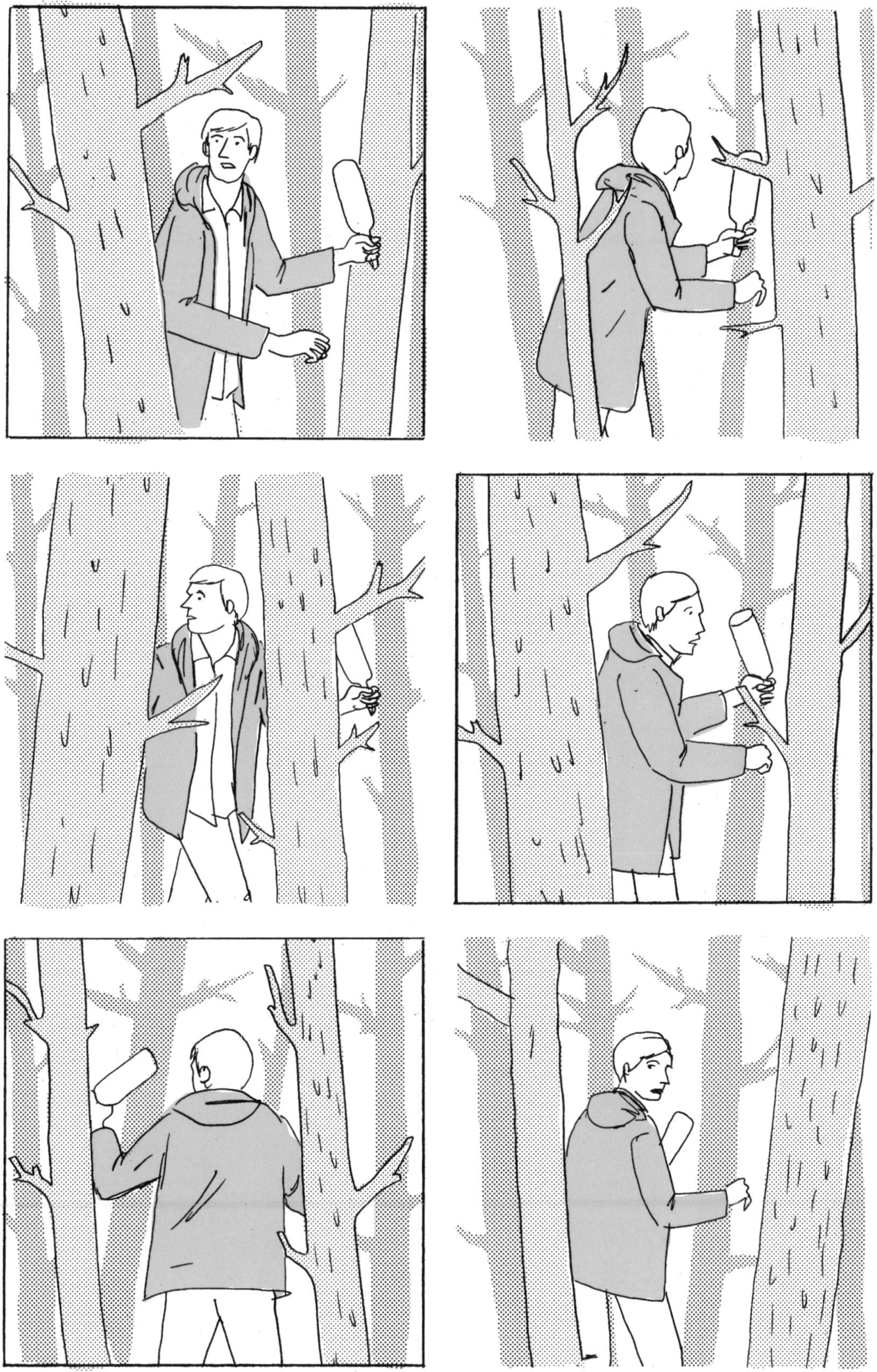

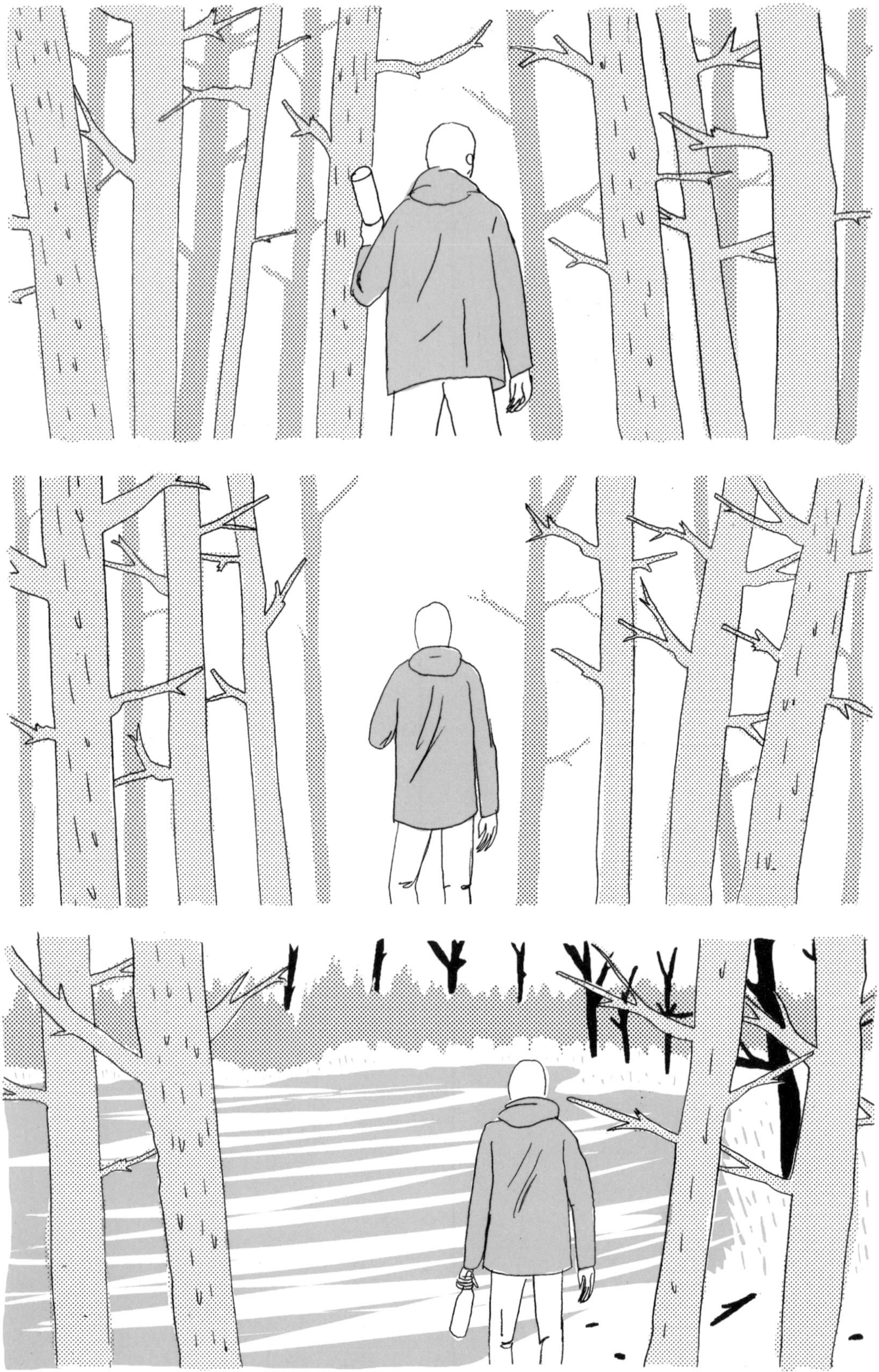

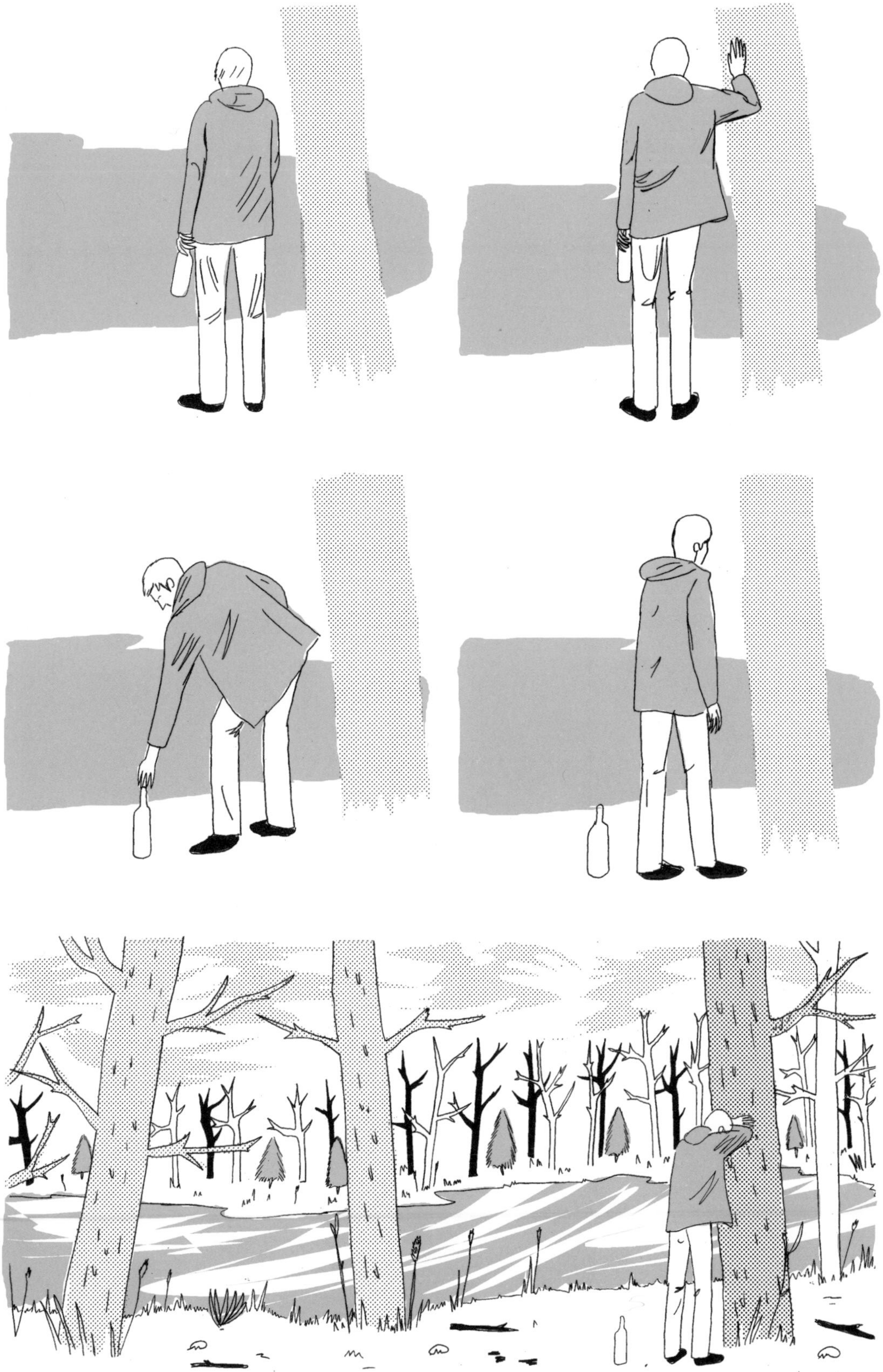

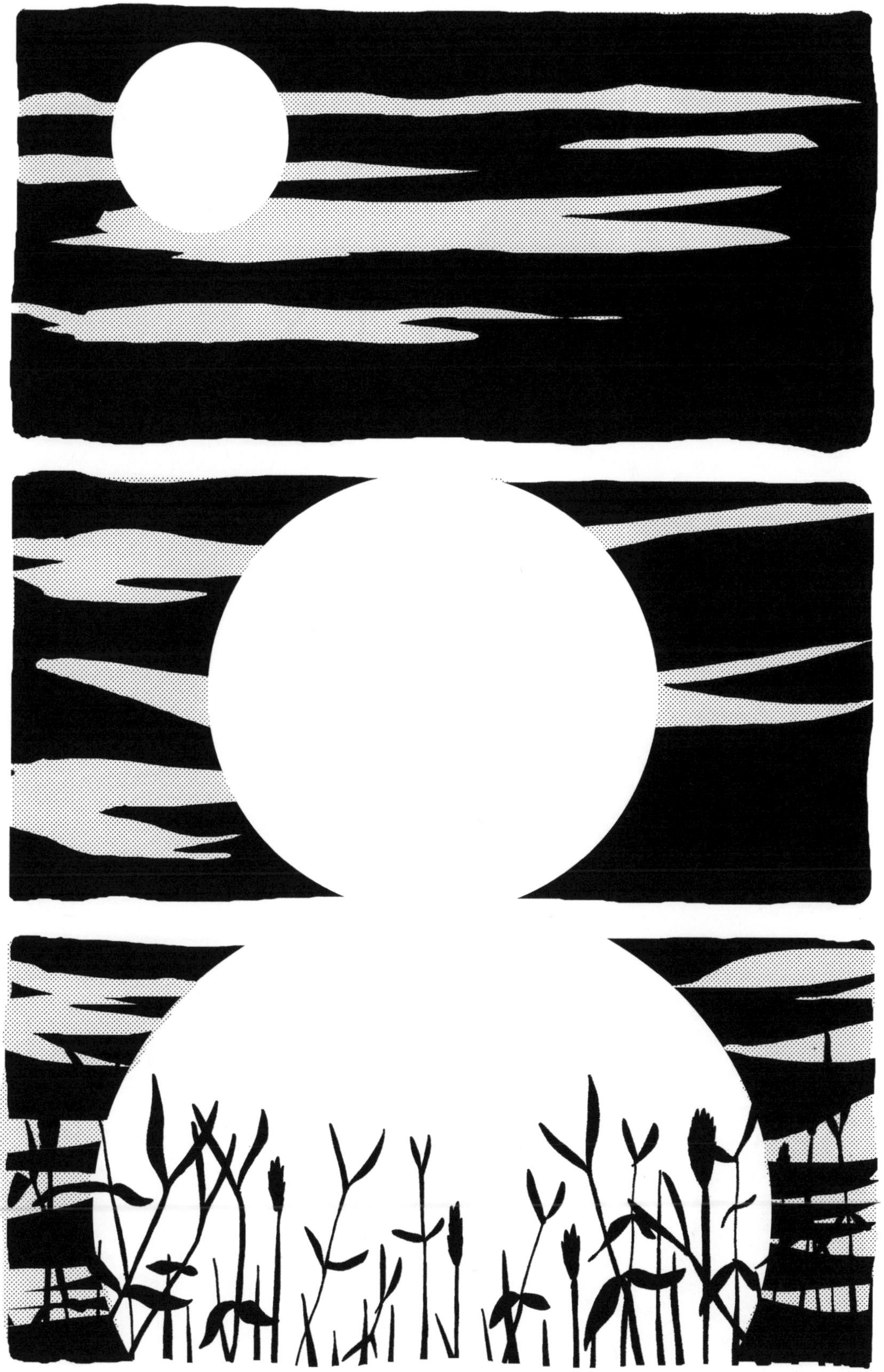

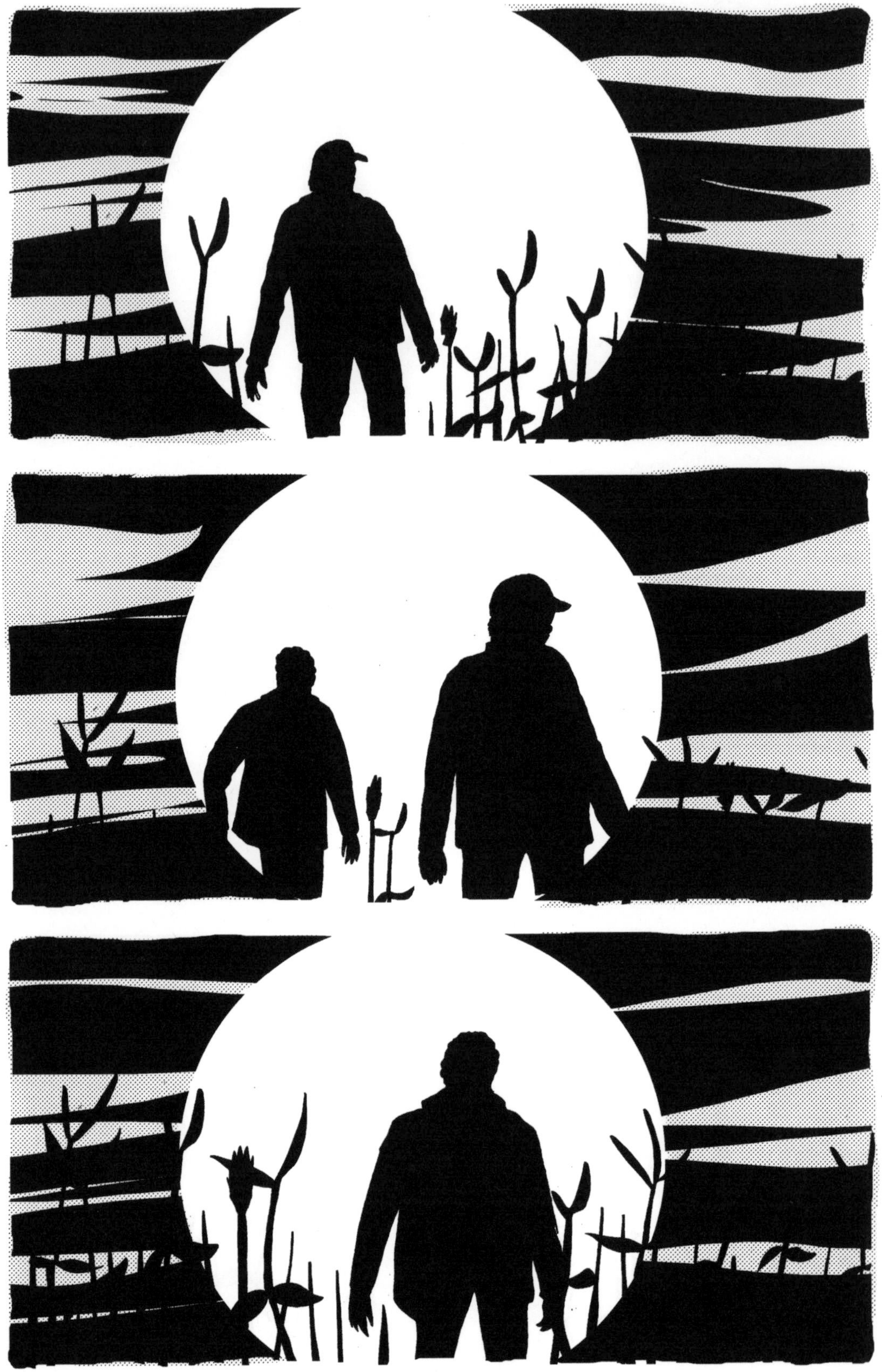

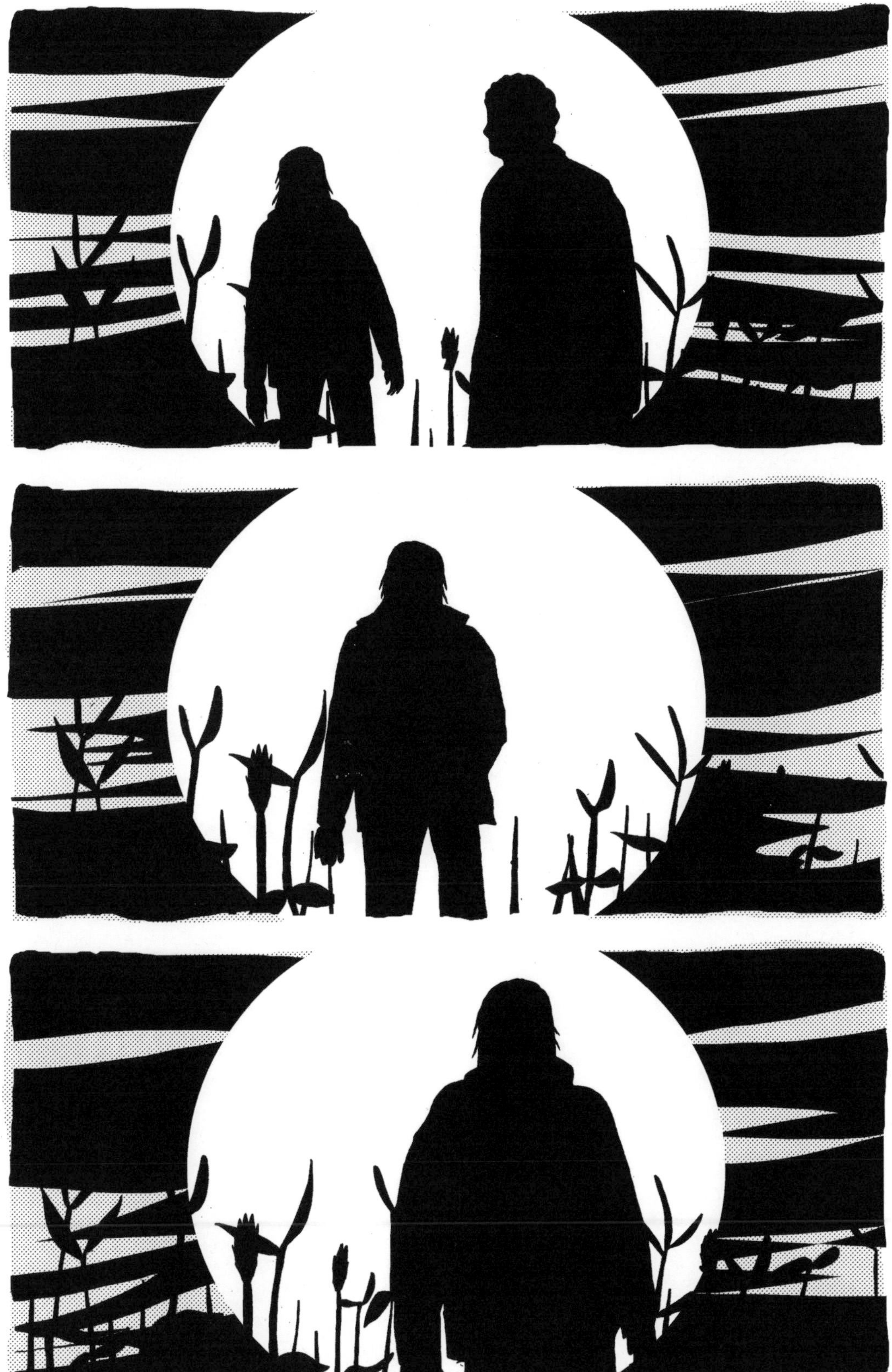

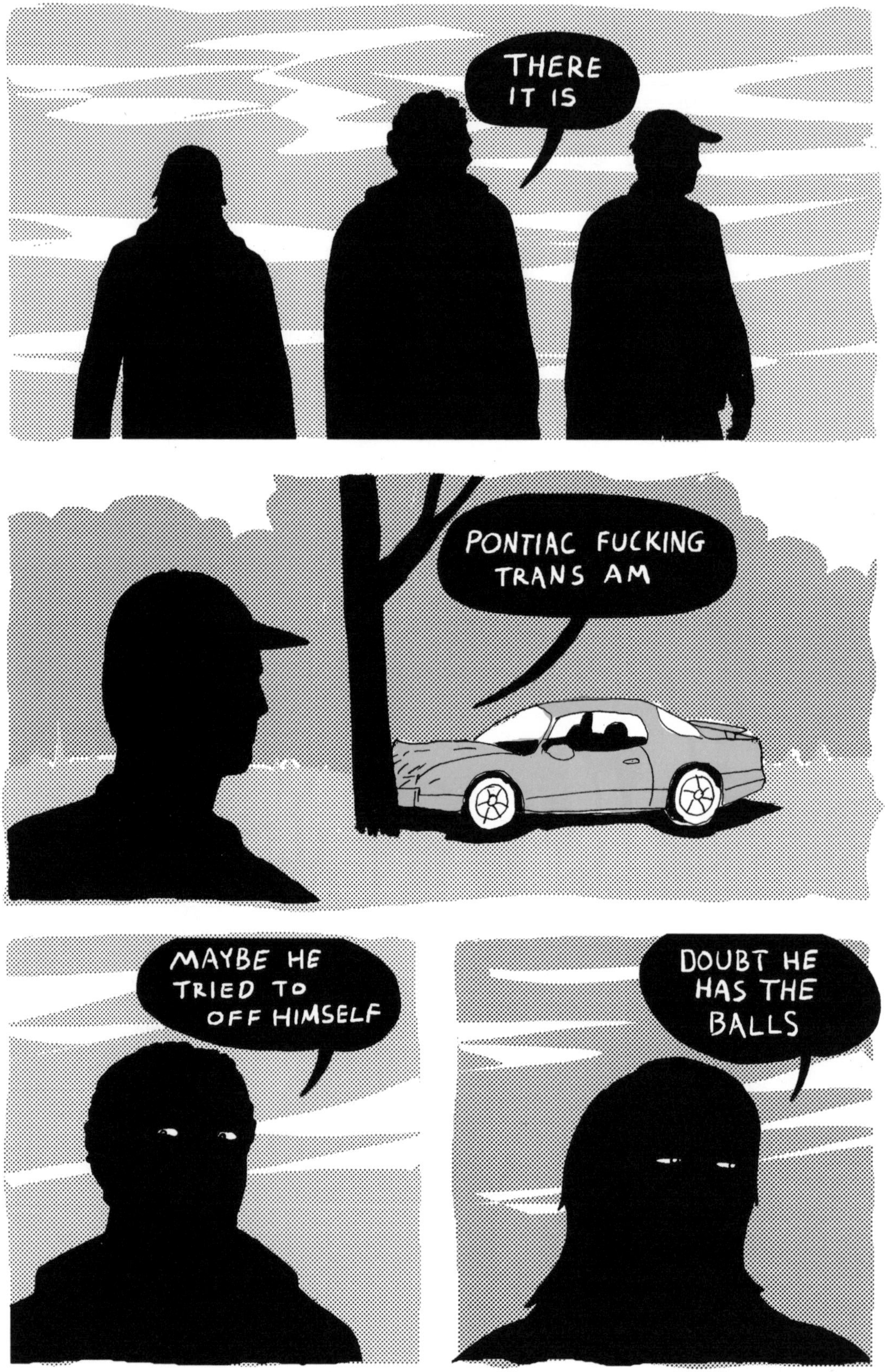
THERE IT IS
PONTIAC FUCKING TRANS AM
MAYBE HE TRIED TO OFF HIMSELF
DOUBT HE HAS THE BALLS

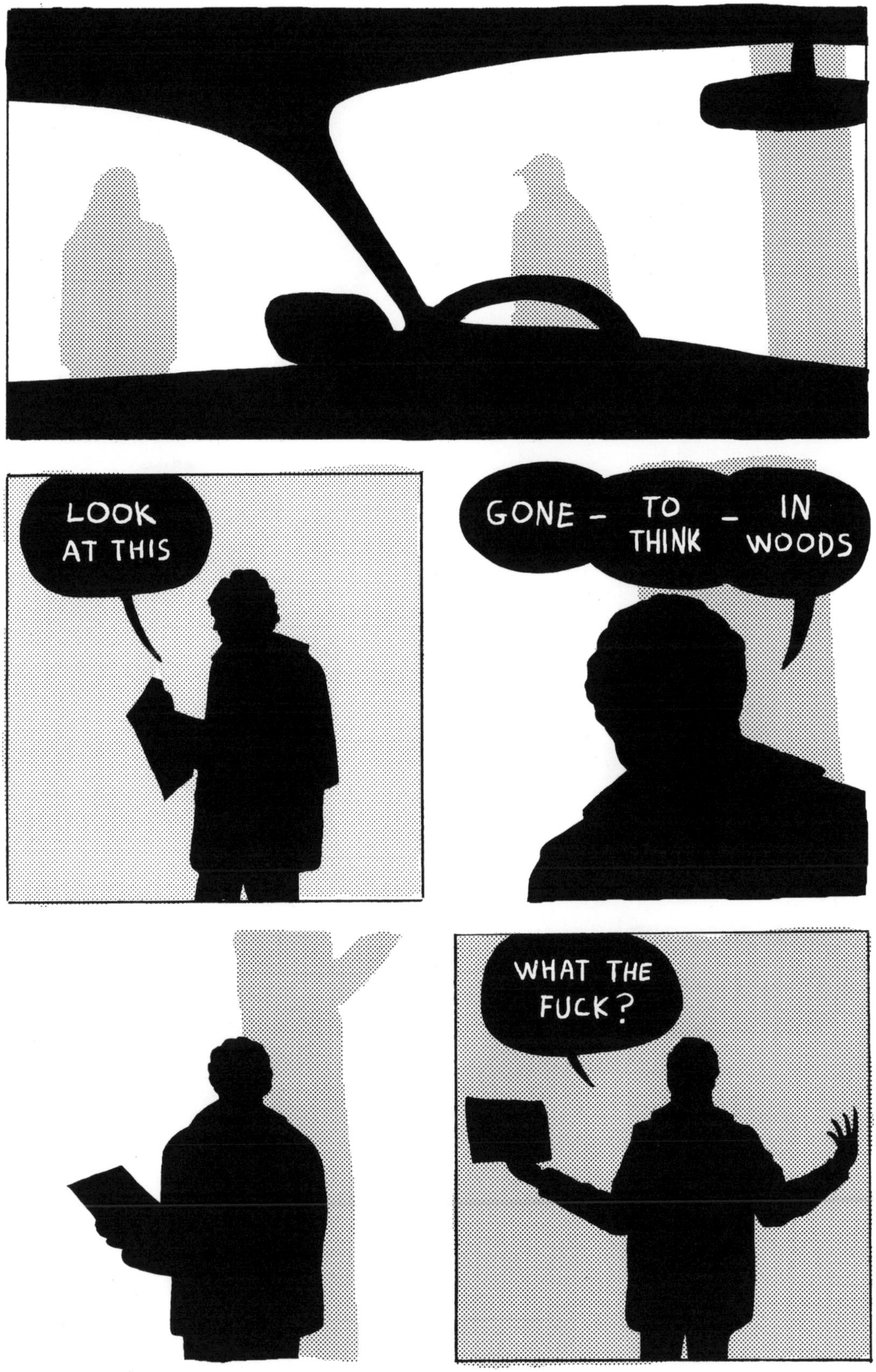
LOOK AT THIS
GONE - TO THINK - IN WOODS
WHAT THE FUCK?

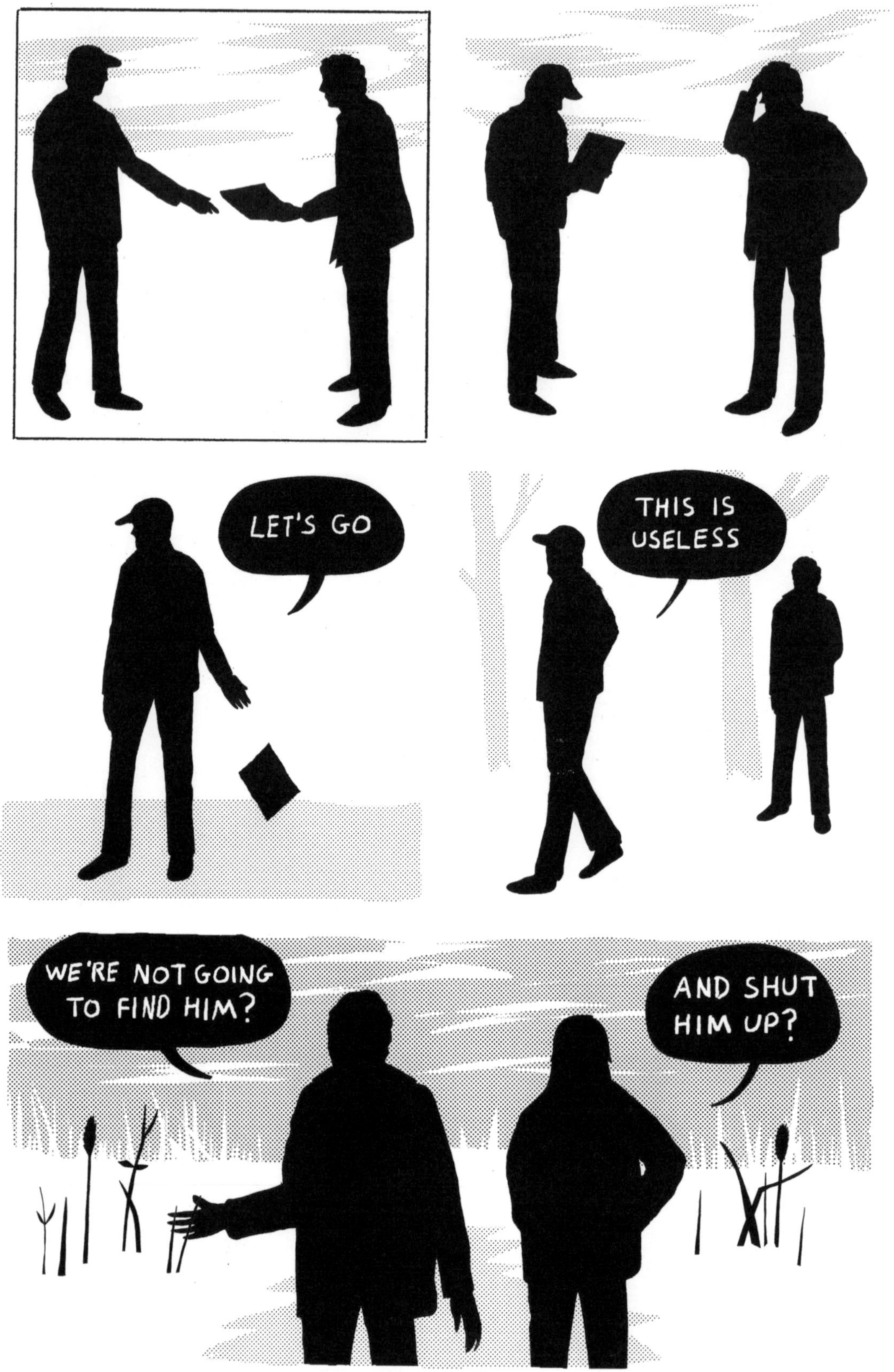
LET'S GO
THIS IS USELESS
WE'RE NOT GOING TO FIND HIM?
AND SHUT HIM UP?

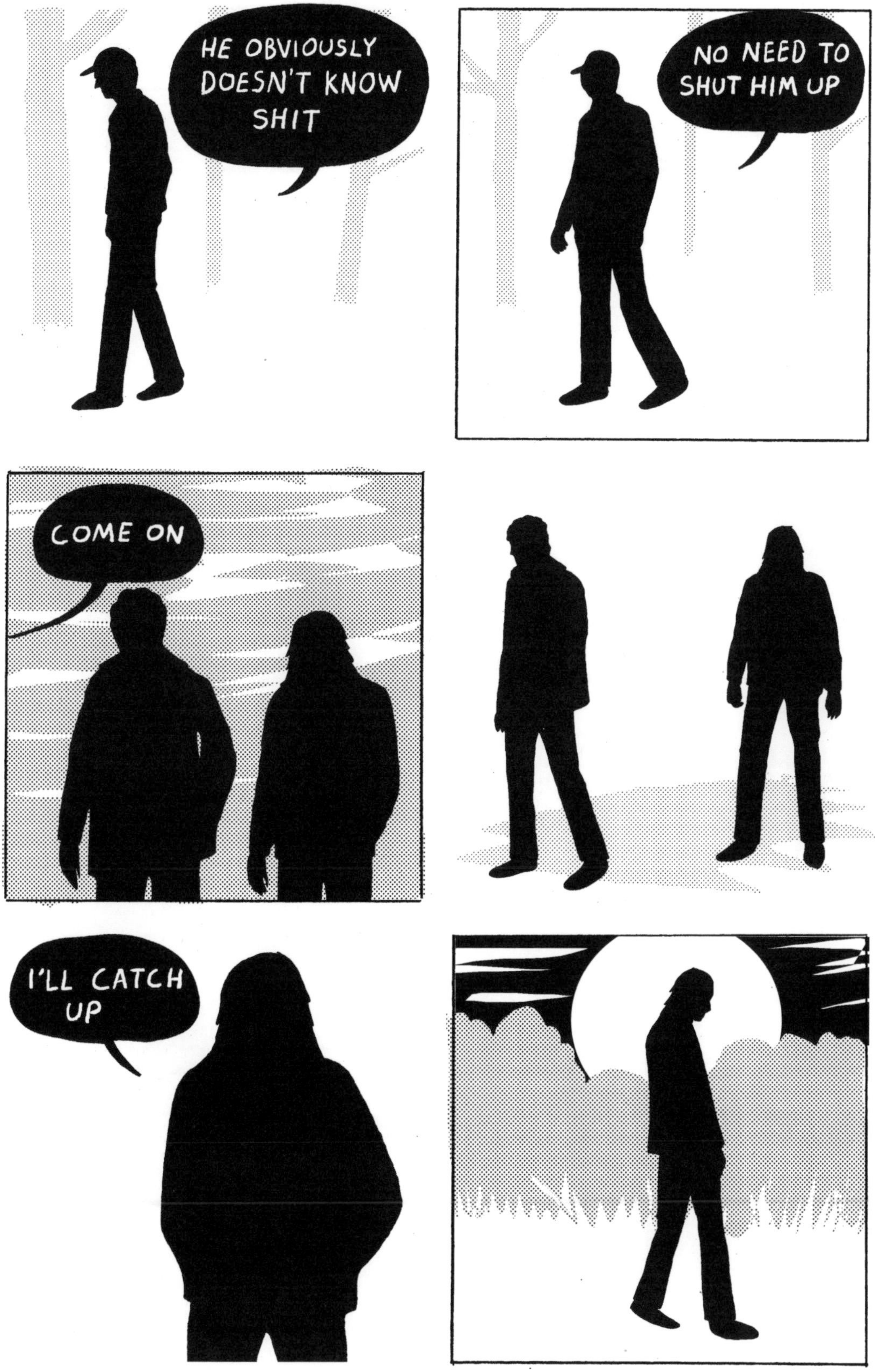
HE OBVIOUSLY DOESN'T KNOW SHIT
NO NEED TO SHUT HIM UP
COME ON
I'LL CATCH UP

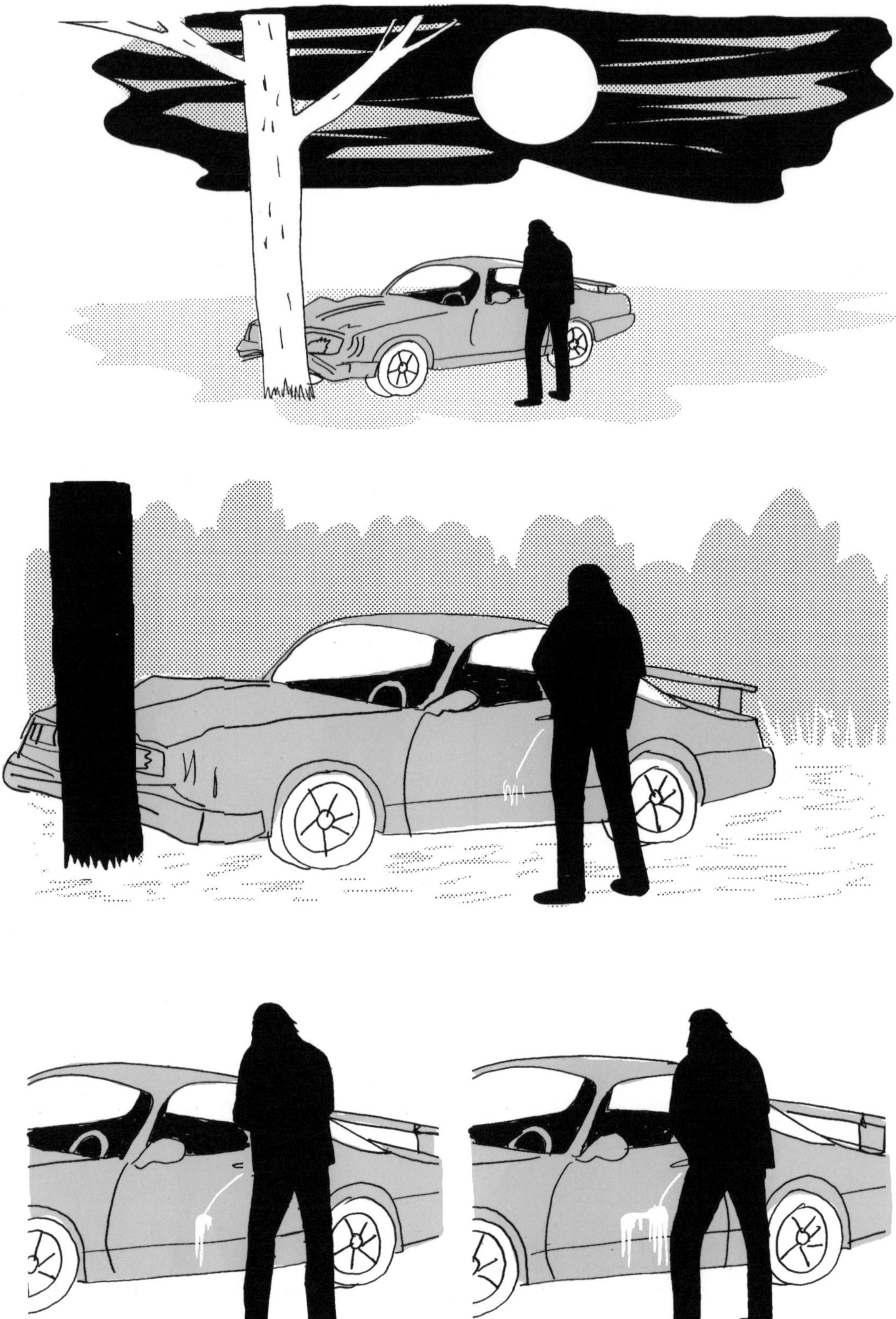

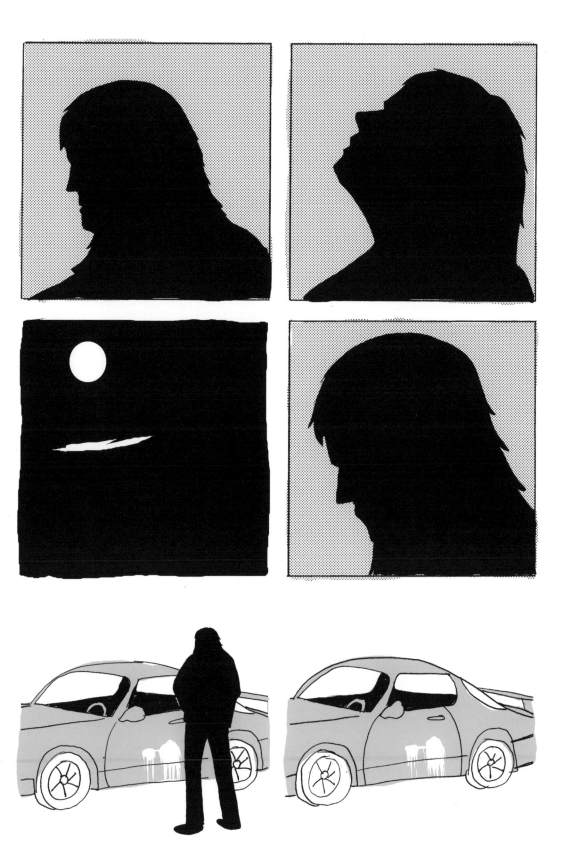

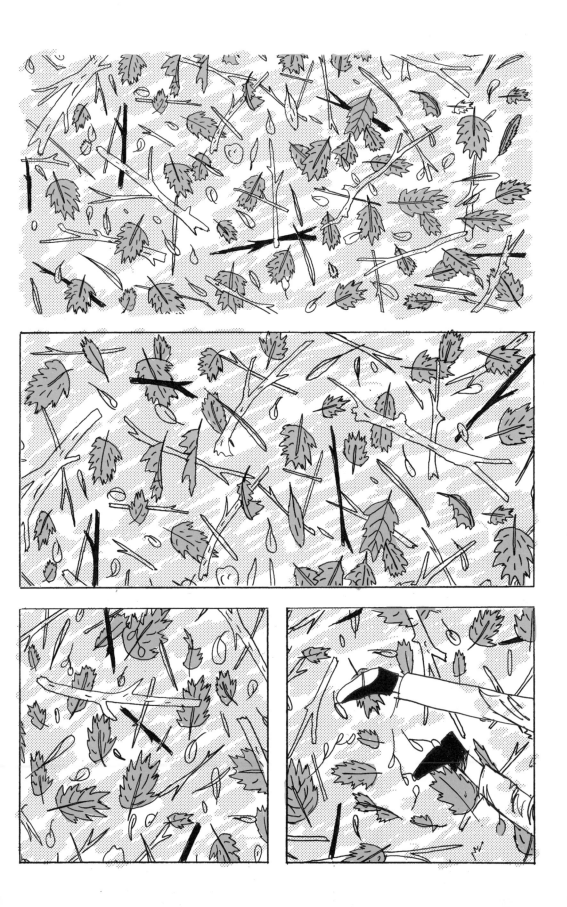

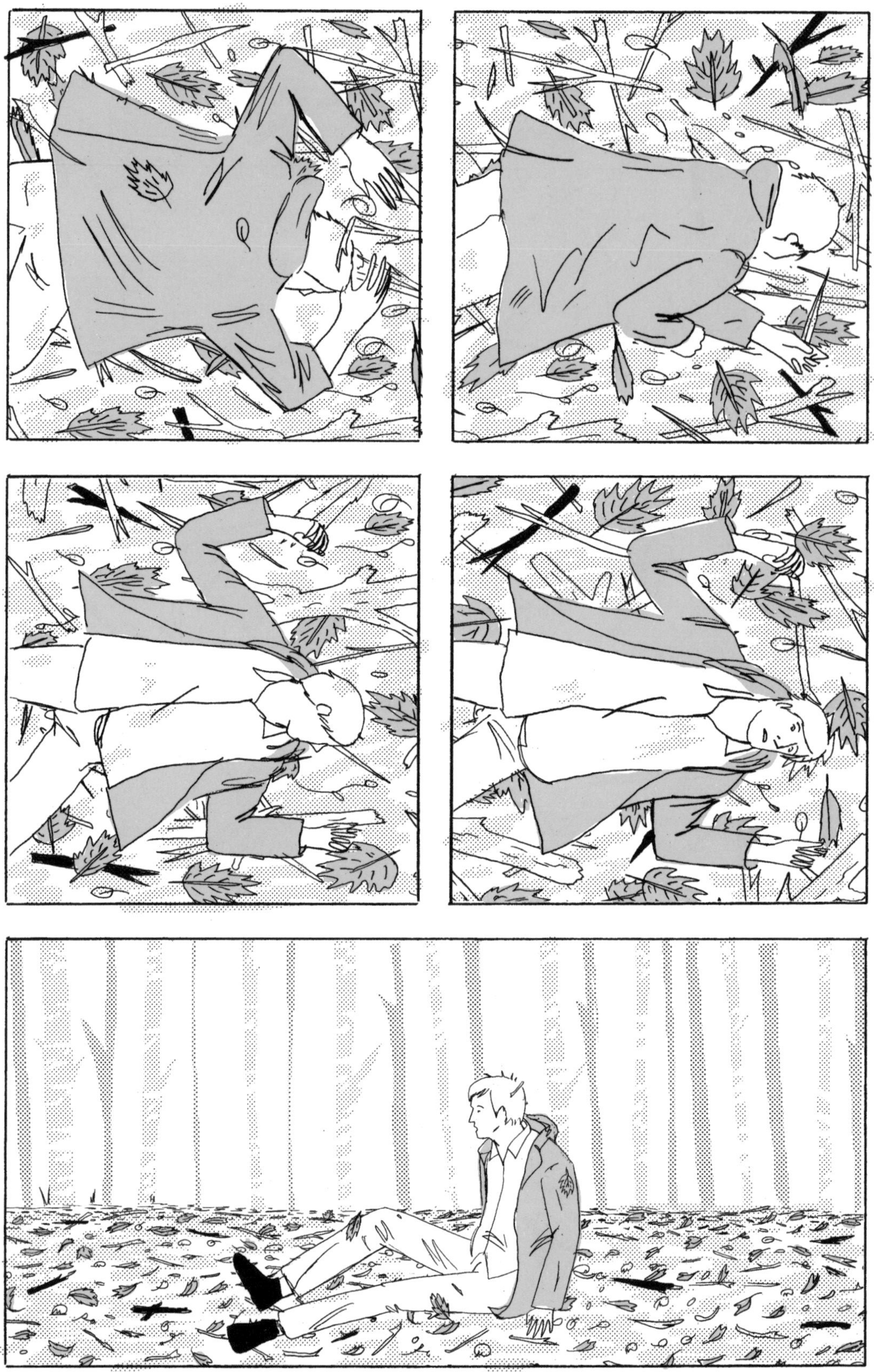

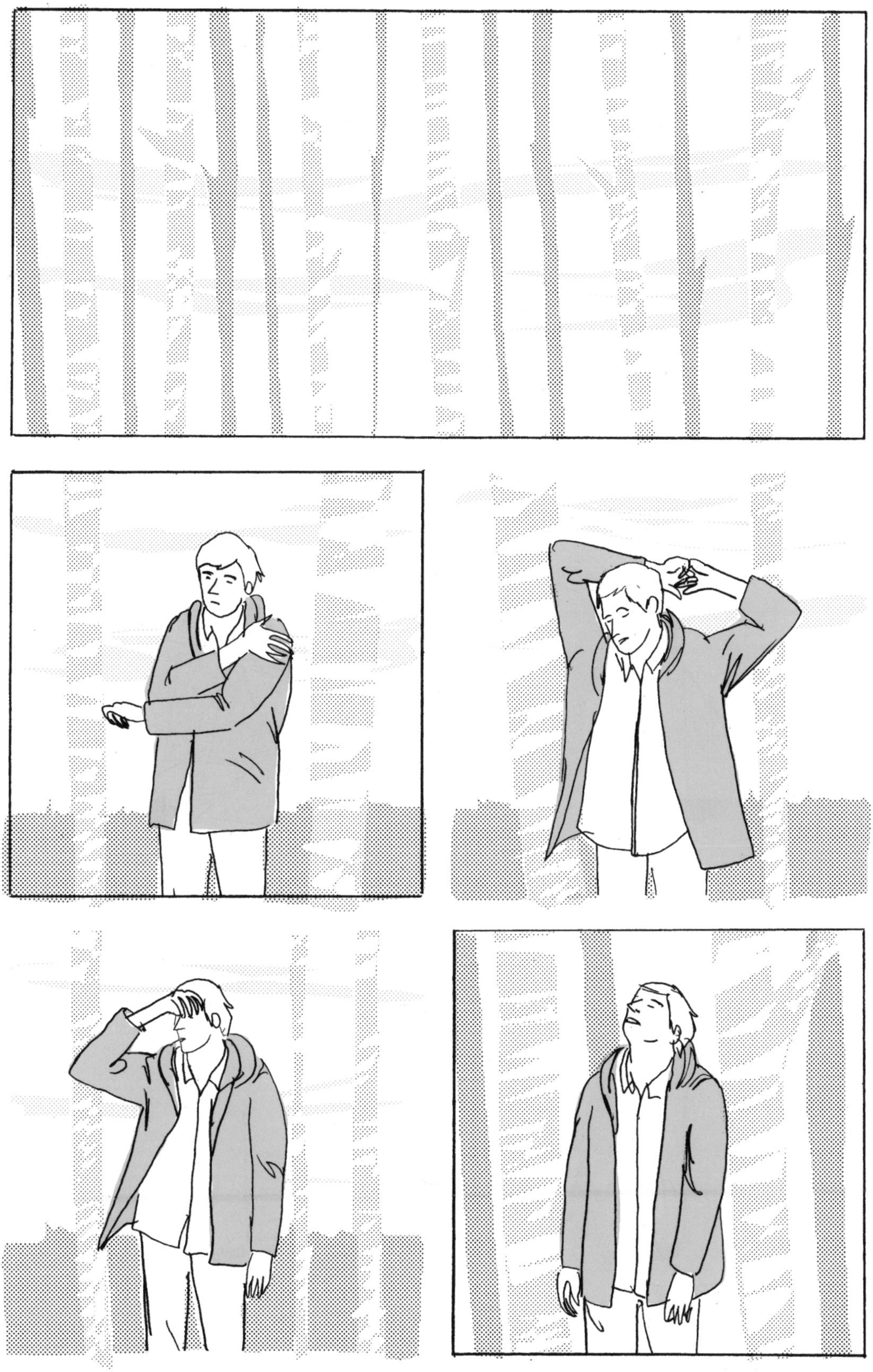

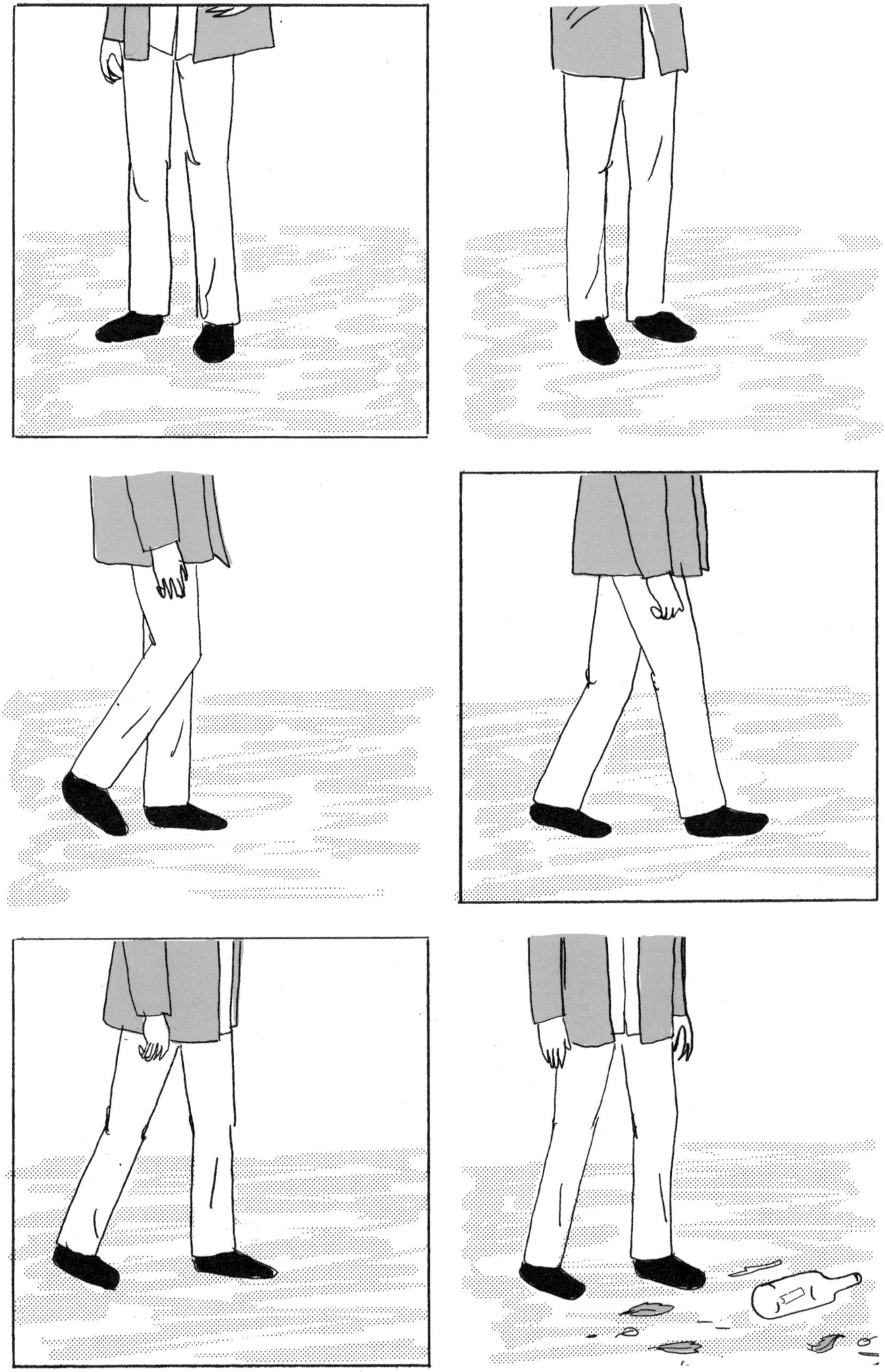

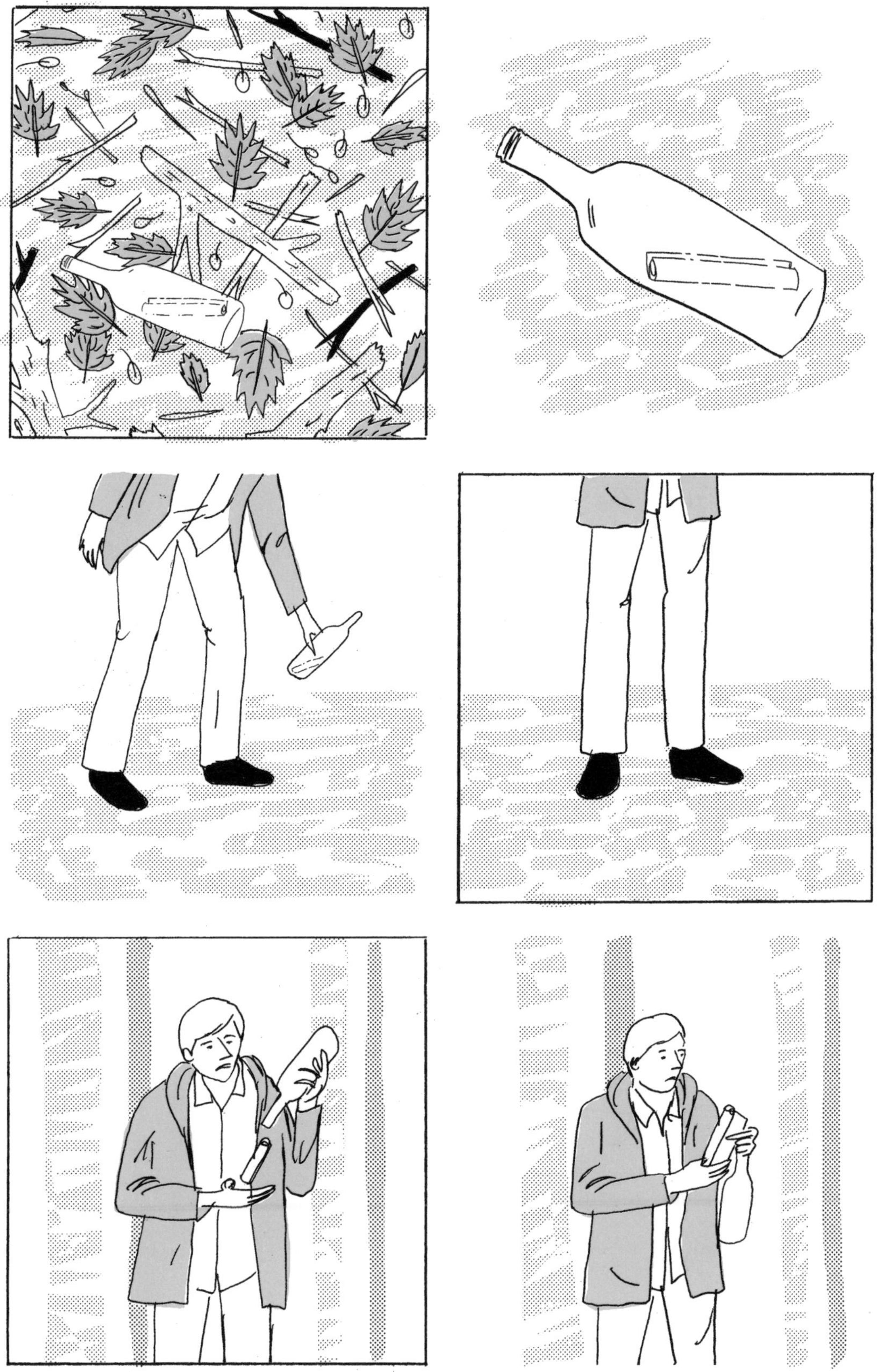

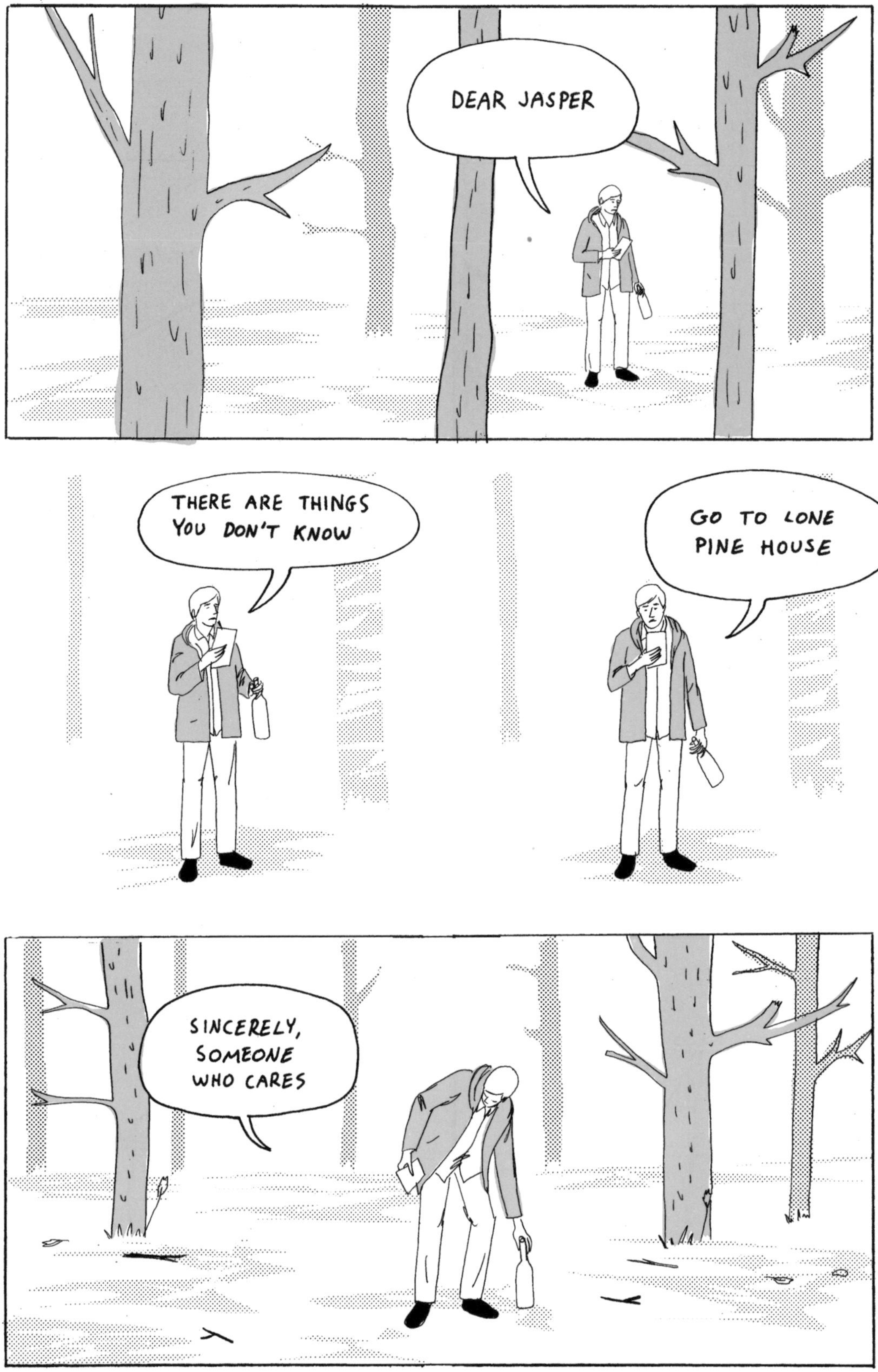
DEAR JASPER
THERE ARE THINGS YOU DON'T KNOW
GO TO LONE PINE HOUSE
SINCERELY, SOMEONE WHO CARES

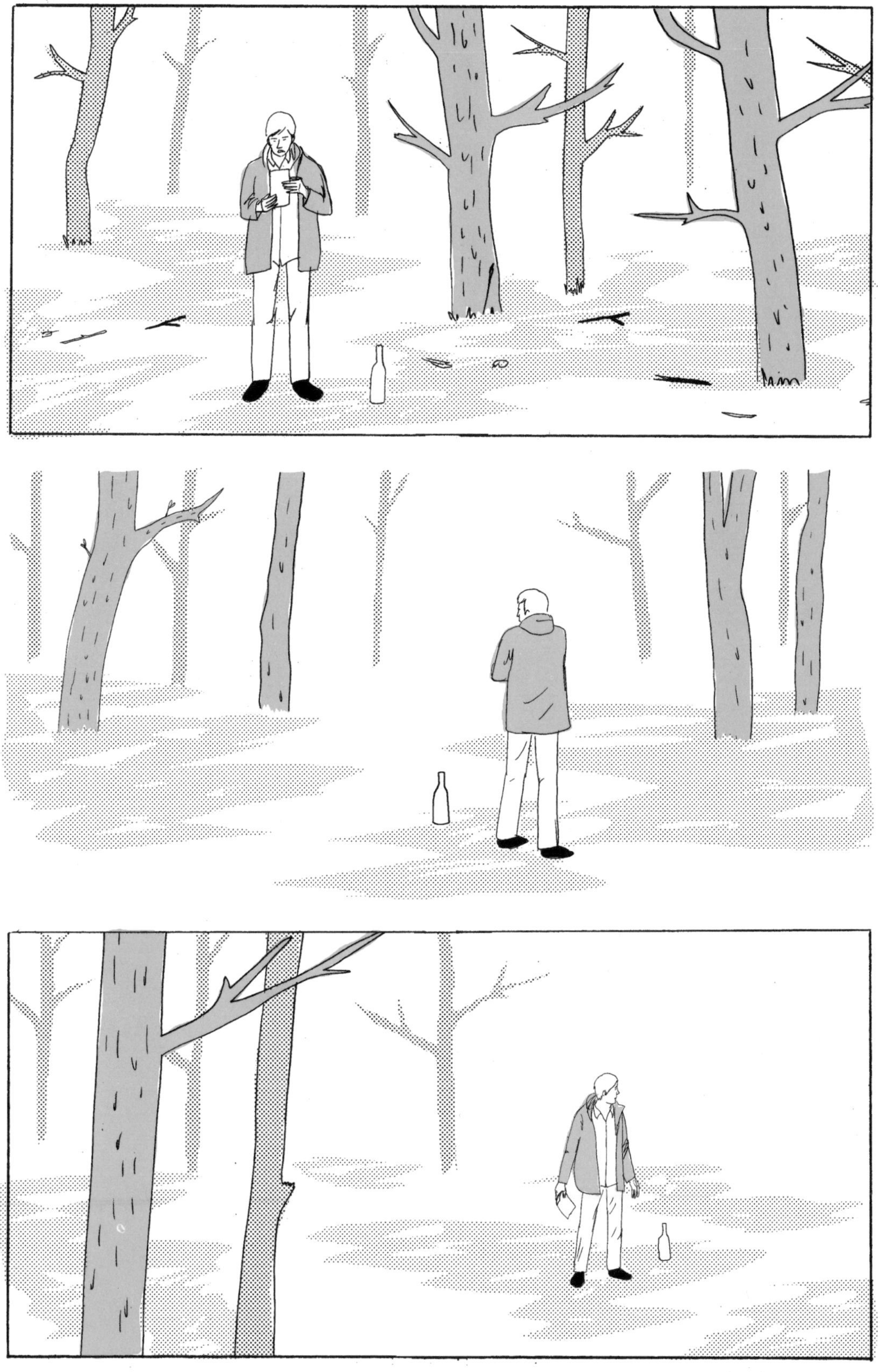

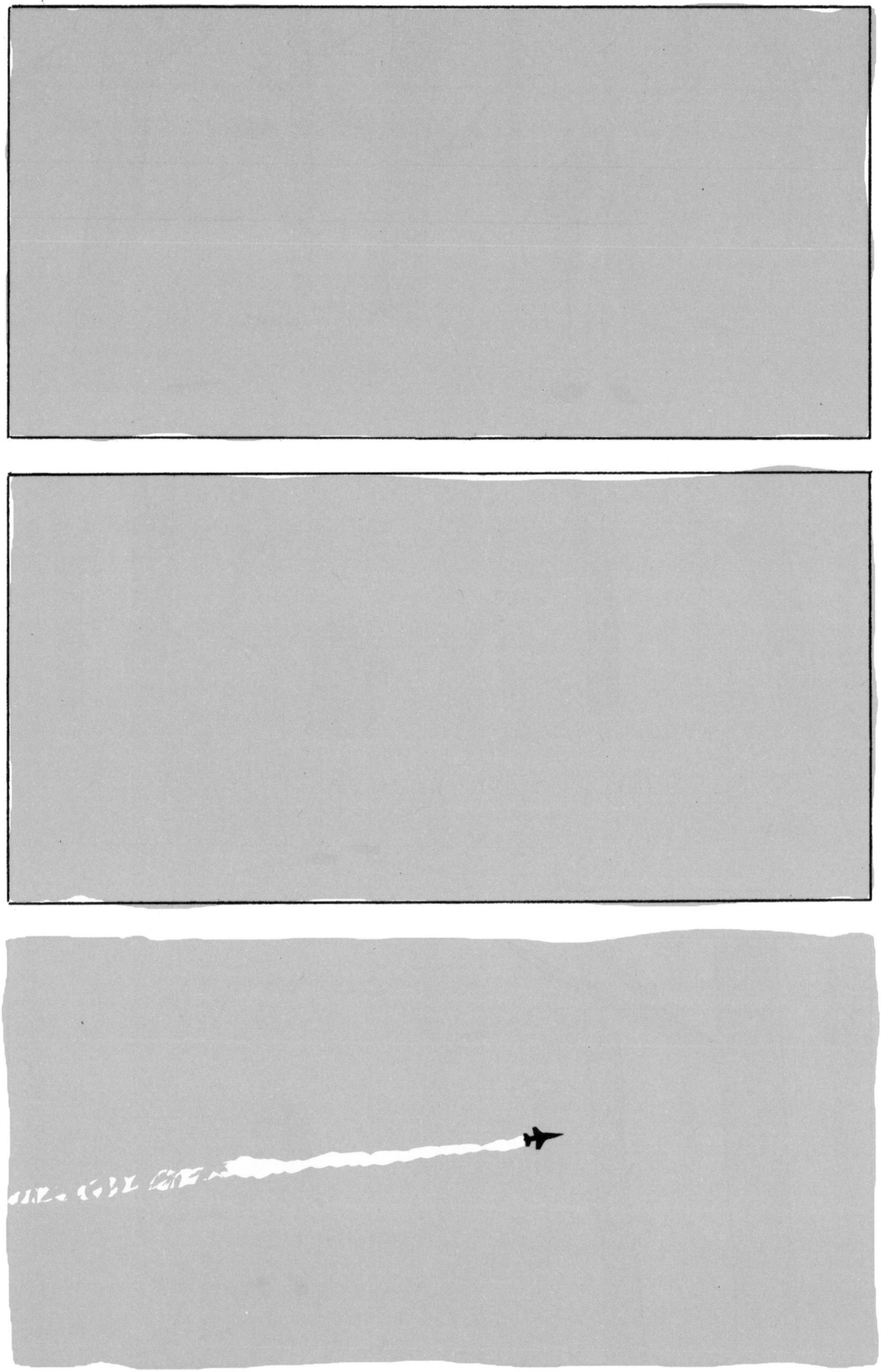

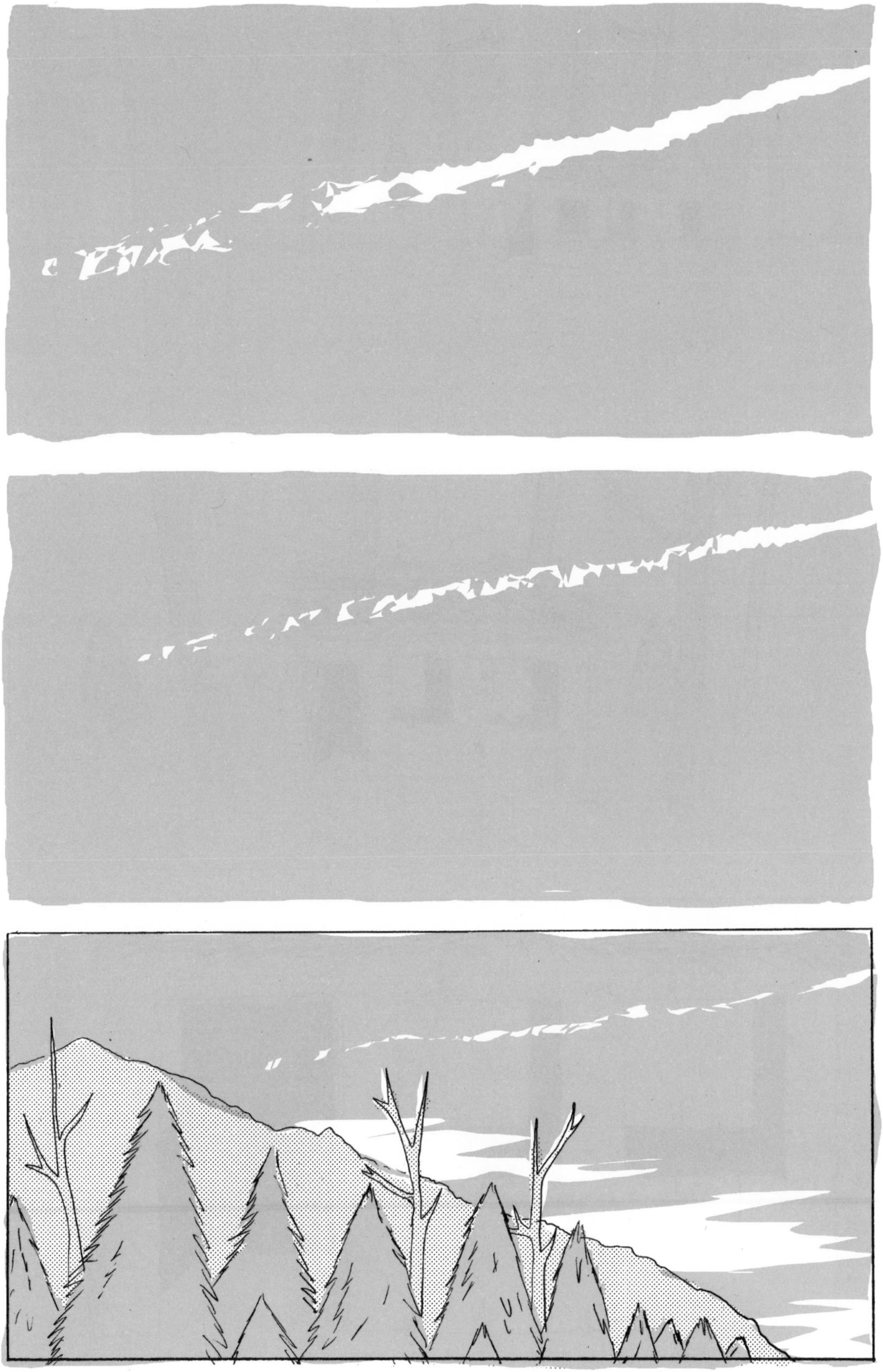

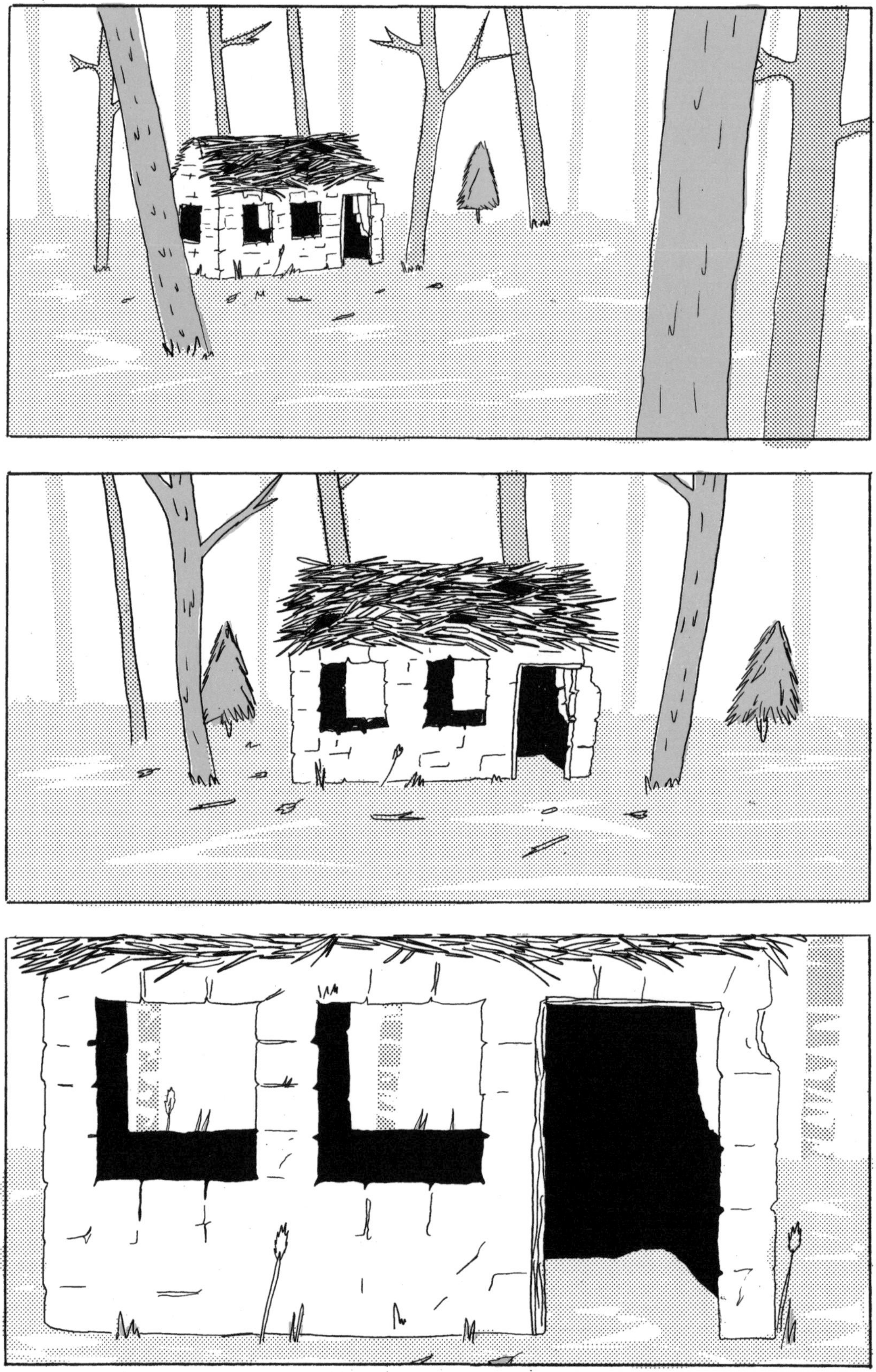

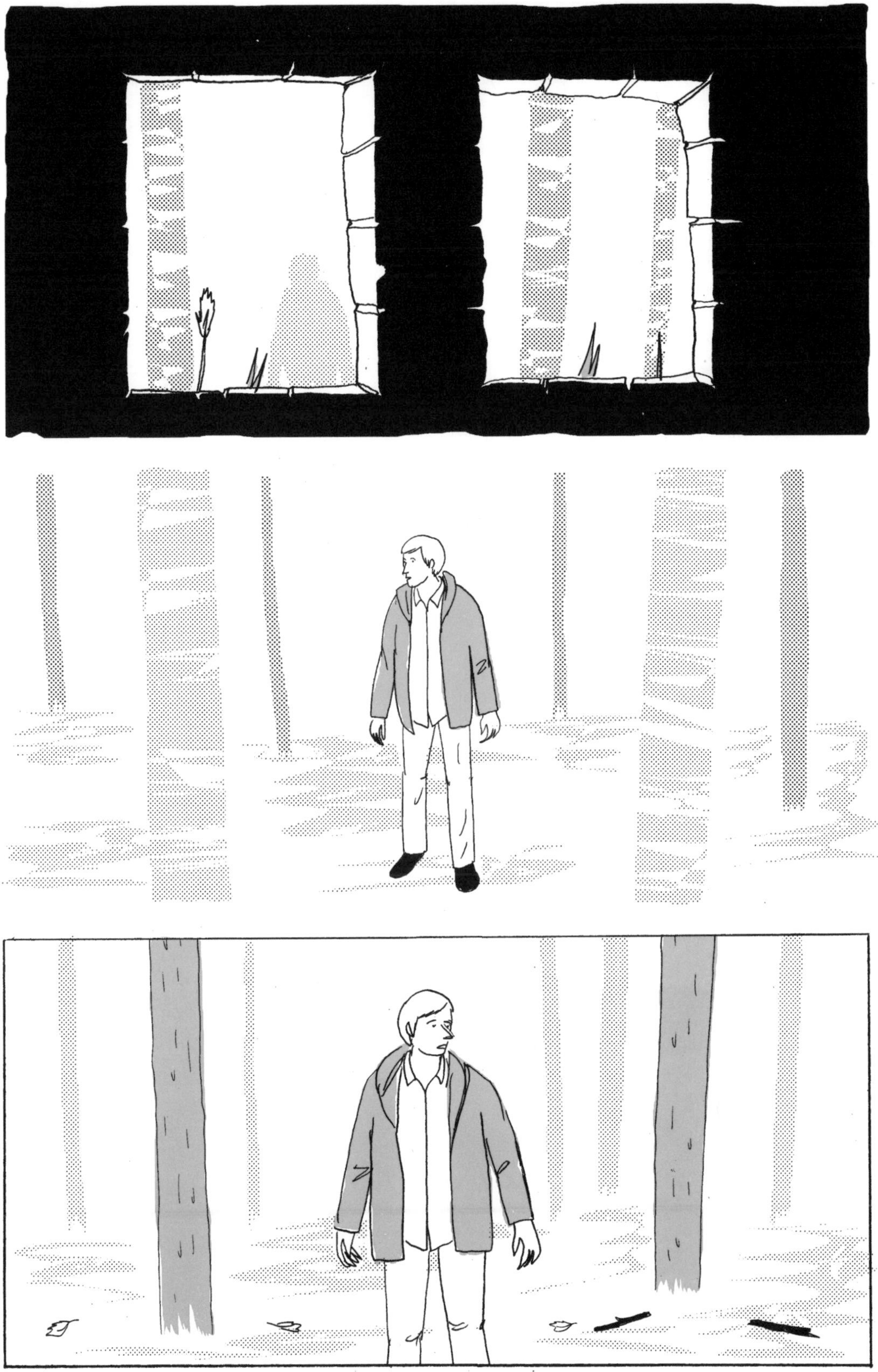

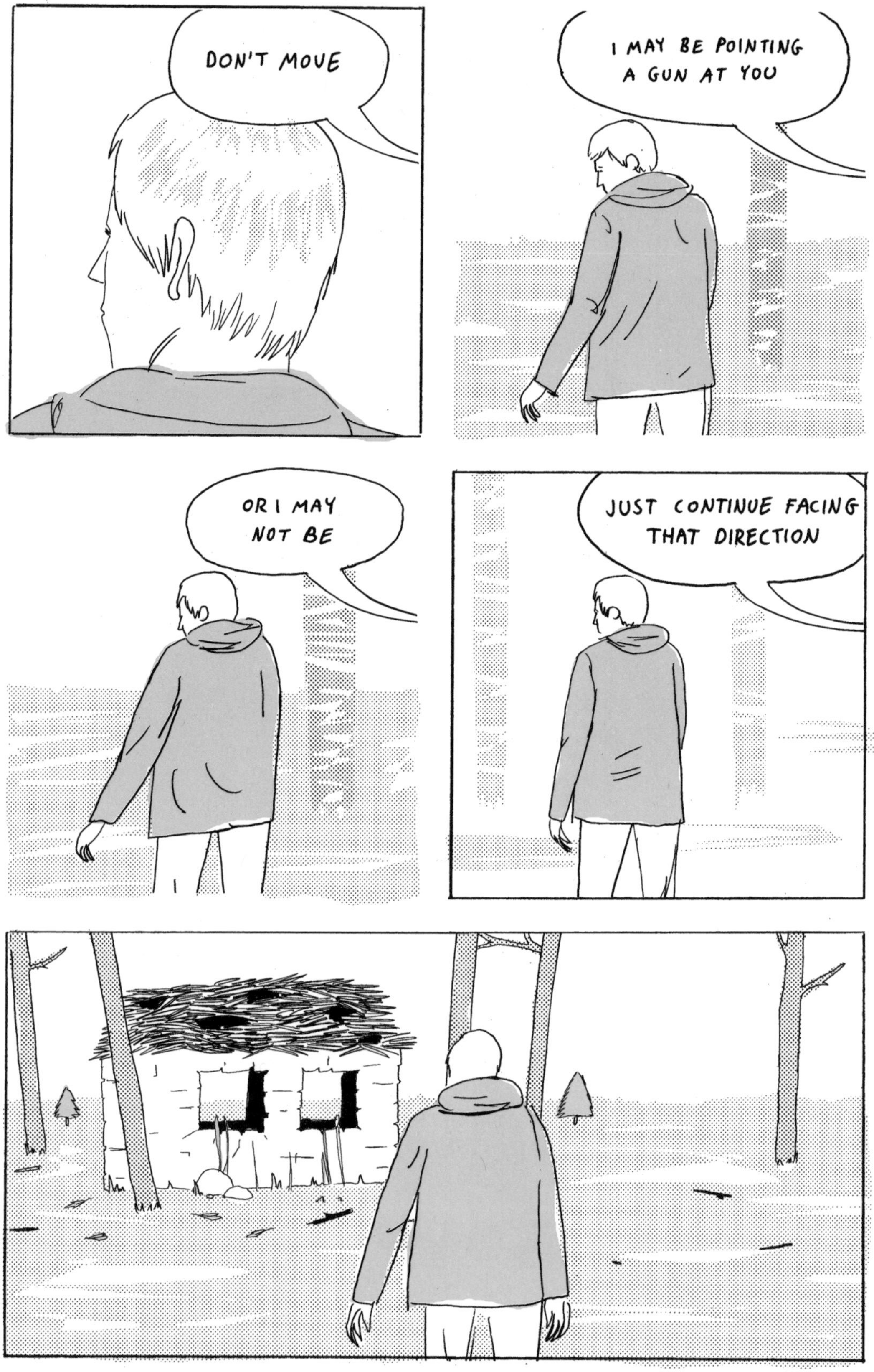
DON'T MOVE
I MAY BE POINTING A GUN AT YOU
OR I MAY NOT BE
JUST CONTINUE FACING THAT DIRECTION

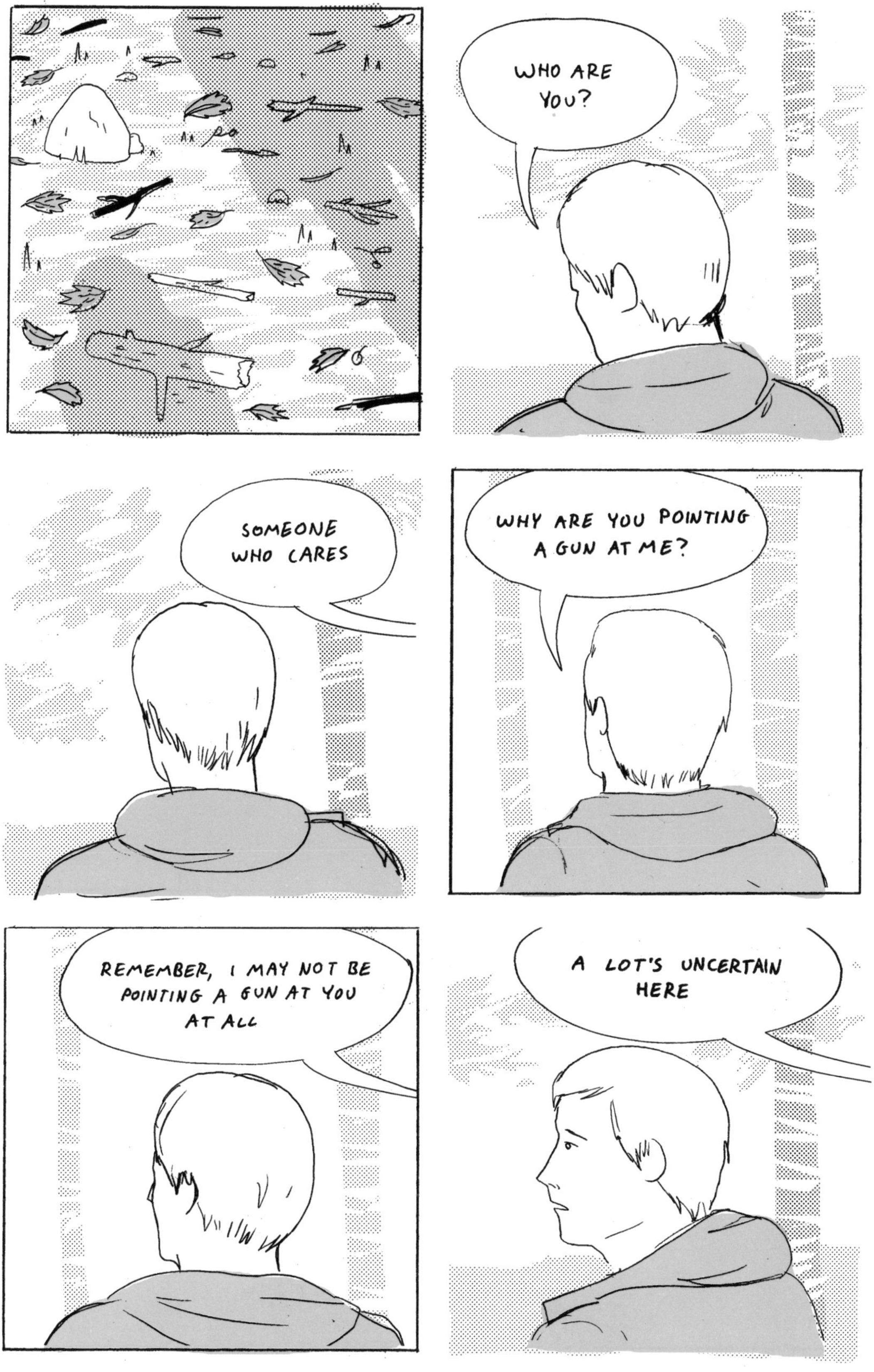
WHO ARE YOU?
SOMEONE WHO CARES
WHY ARE YOU POINTING A GUN AT ME?
REMEMBER, I MAY NOT BE POINTING A GUN AT YOU AT ALL
A LOT'S UNCERTAIN HERE

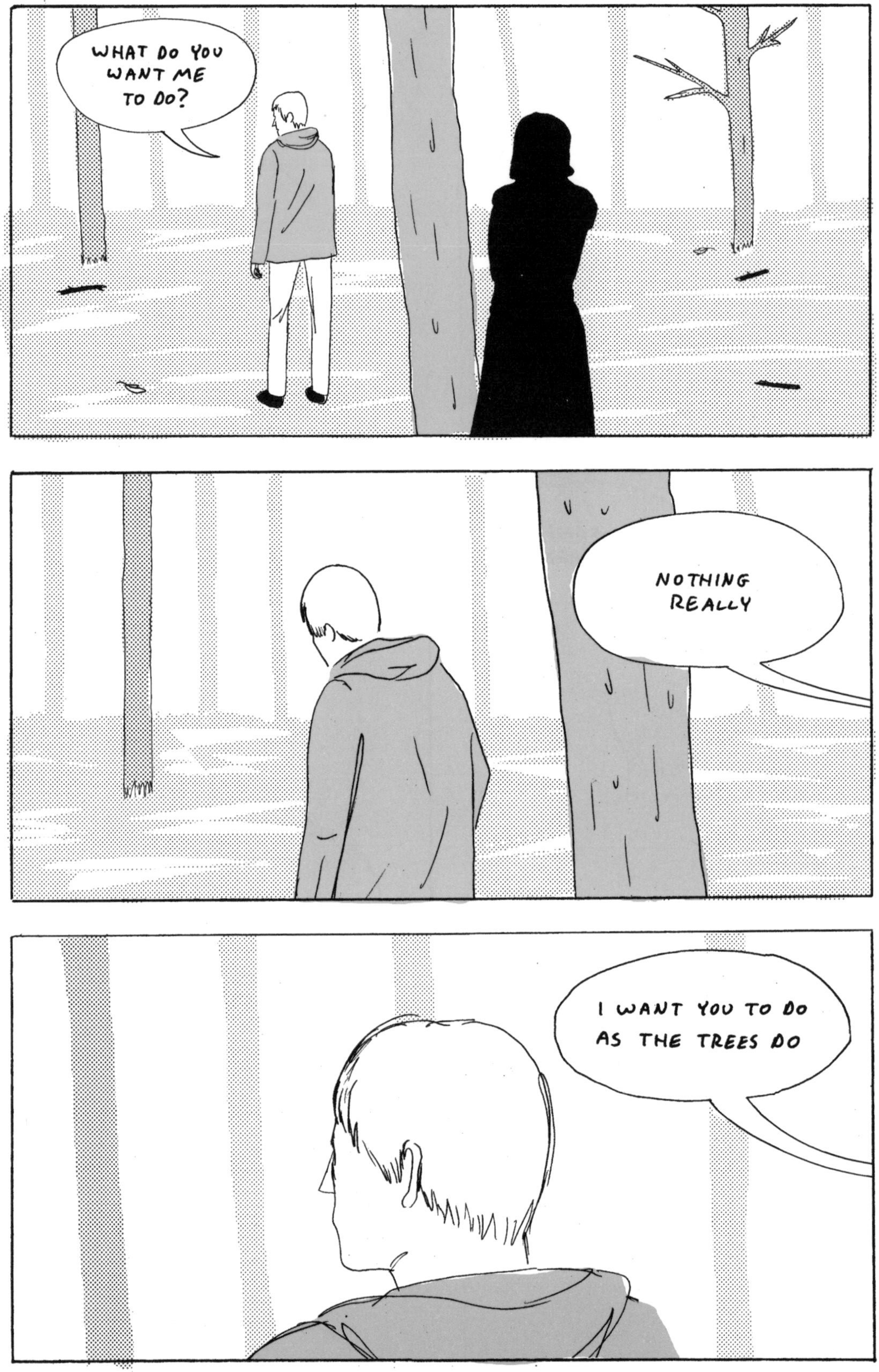
WHAT DO YOU WANT ME TO DO?
NOTHING REALLY
I WANT YOU TO DO AS THE TREES DO

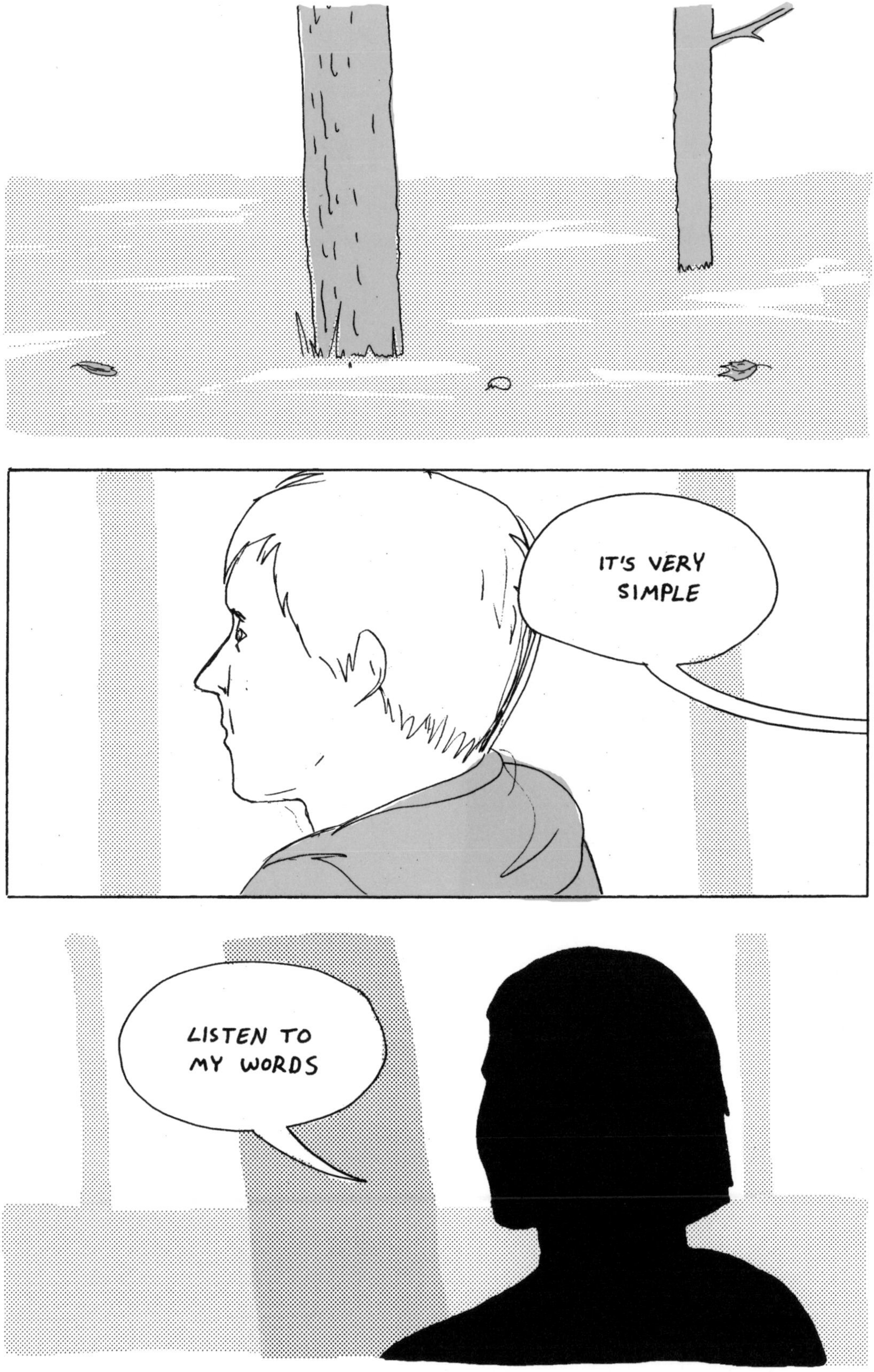
IT'S VERY SIMPLE
LISTEN TO MY WORDS

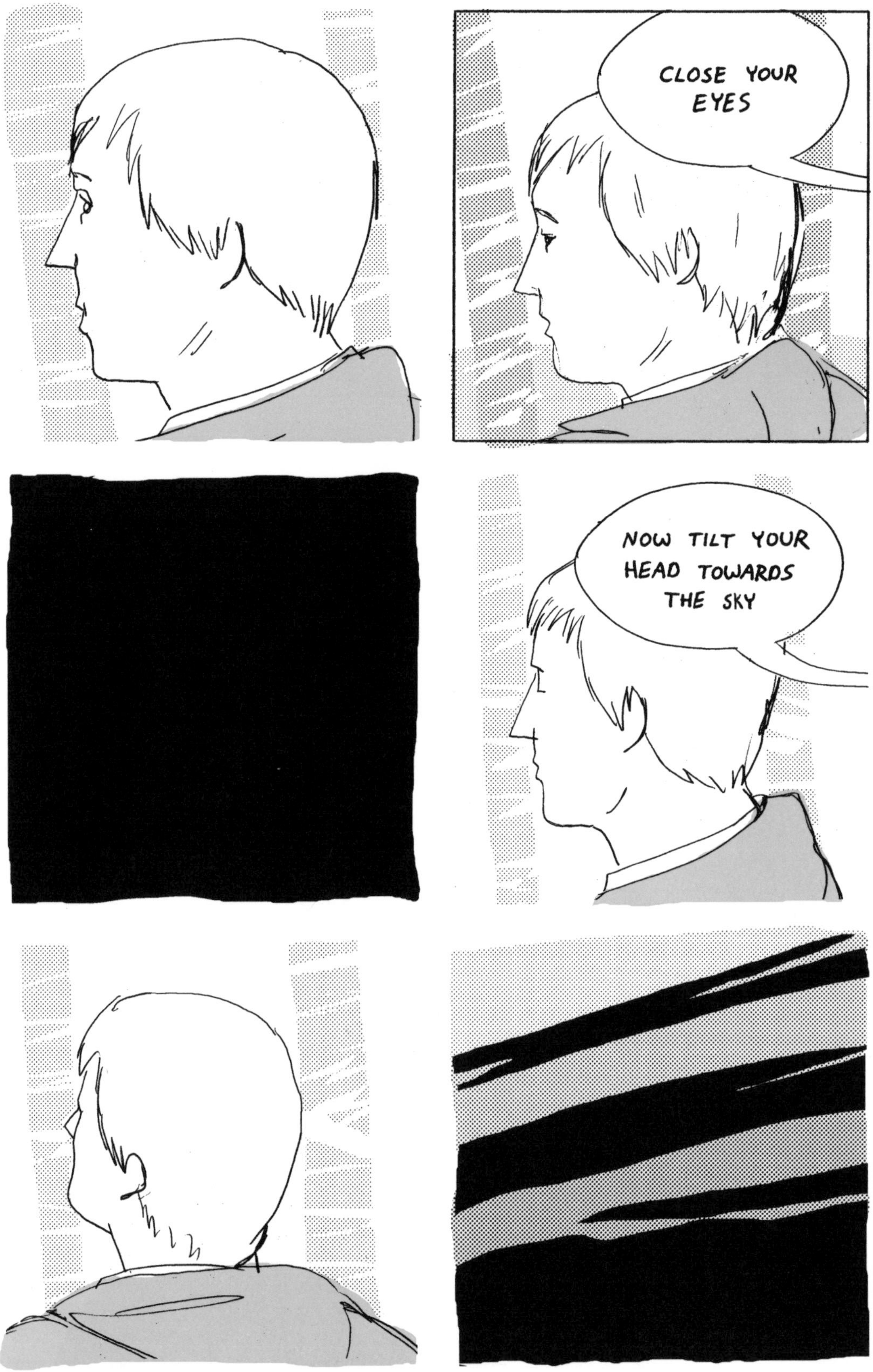
CLOSE YOUR EYES
NOW TILT YOUR HEAD TOWARDS THE SKY

SEE THE LIGHT
SHINE THROUGH
YOUR VEINS

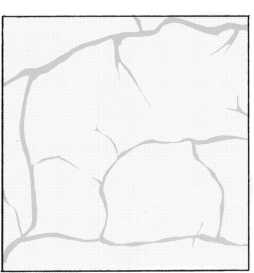
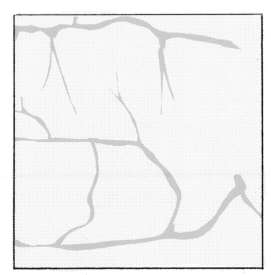

YOUR VEINS ARE
THE VEINS OF
TREE LEAVES

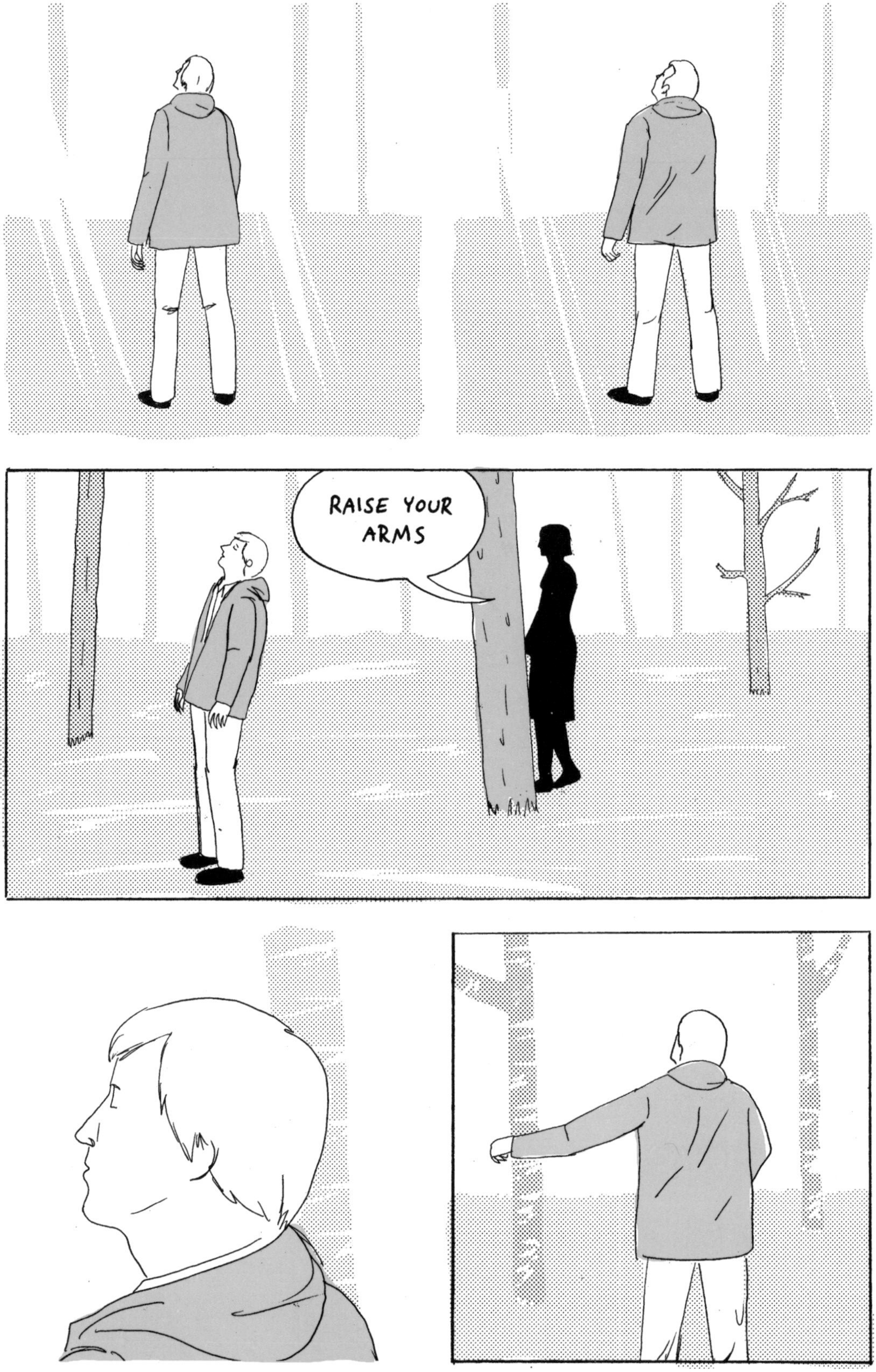
RAISE YOUR ARMS

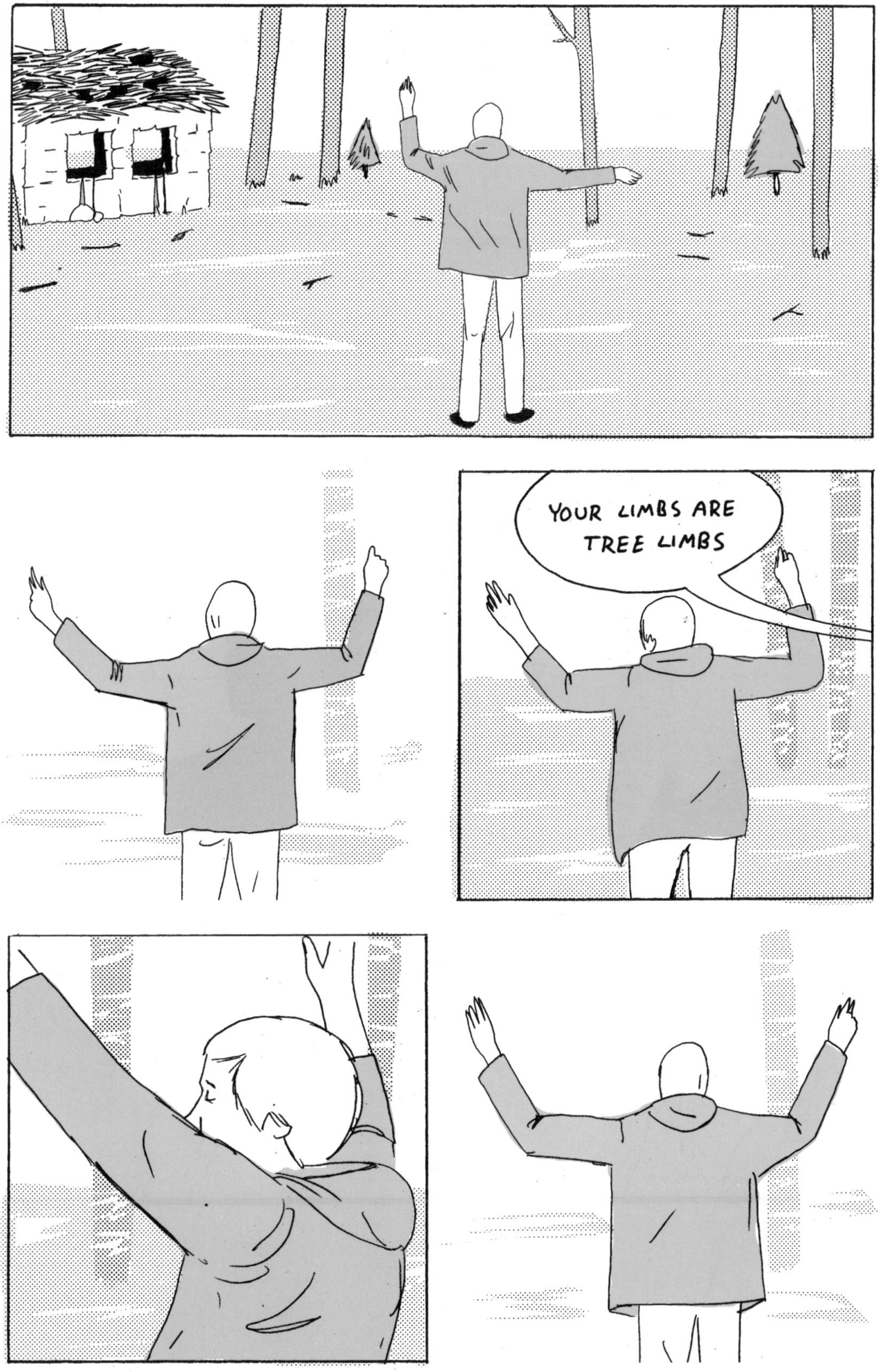
YOUR LIMBS ARE TREE LIMBS

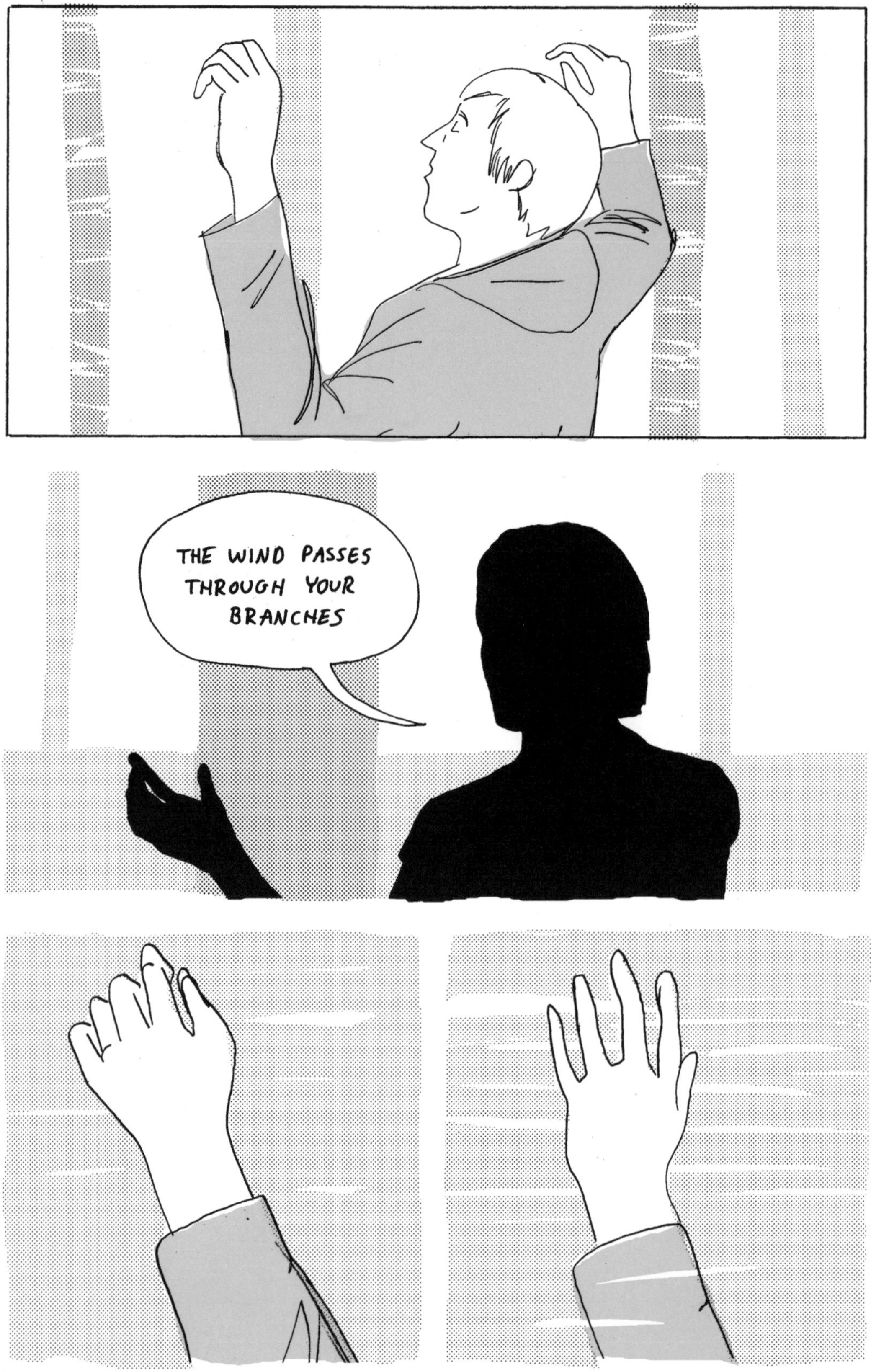
THE WIND PASSES THROUGH YOUR BRANCHES

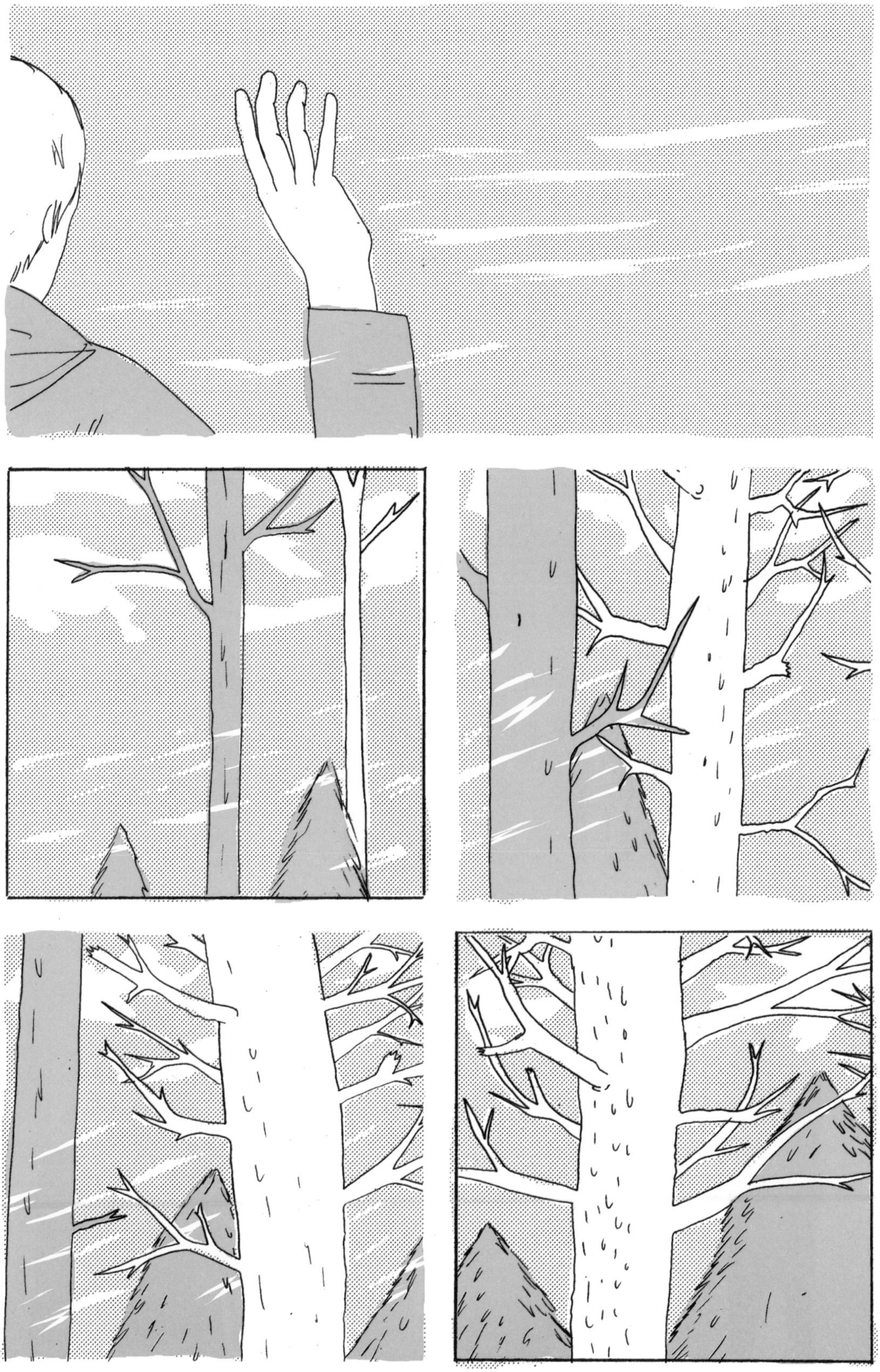

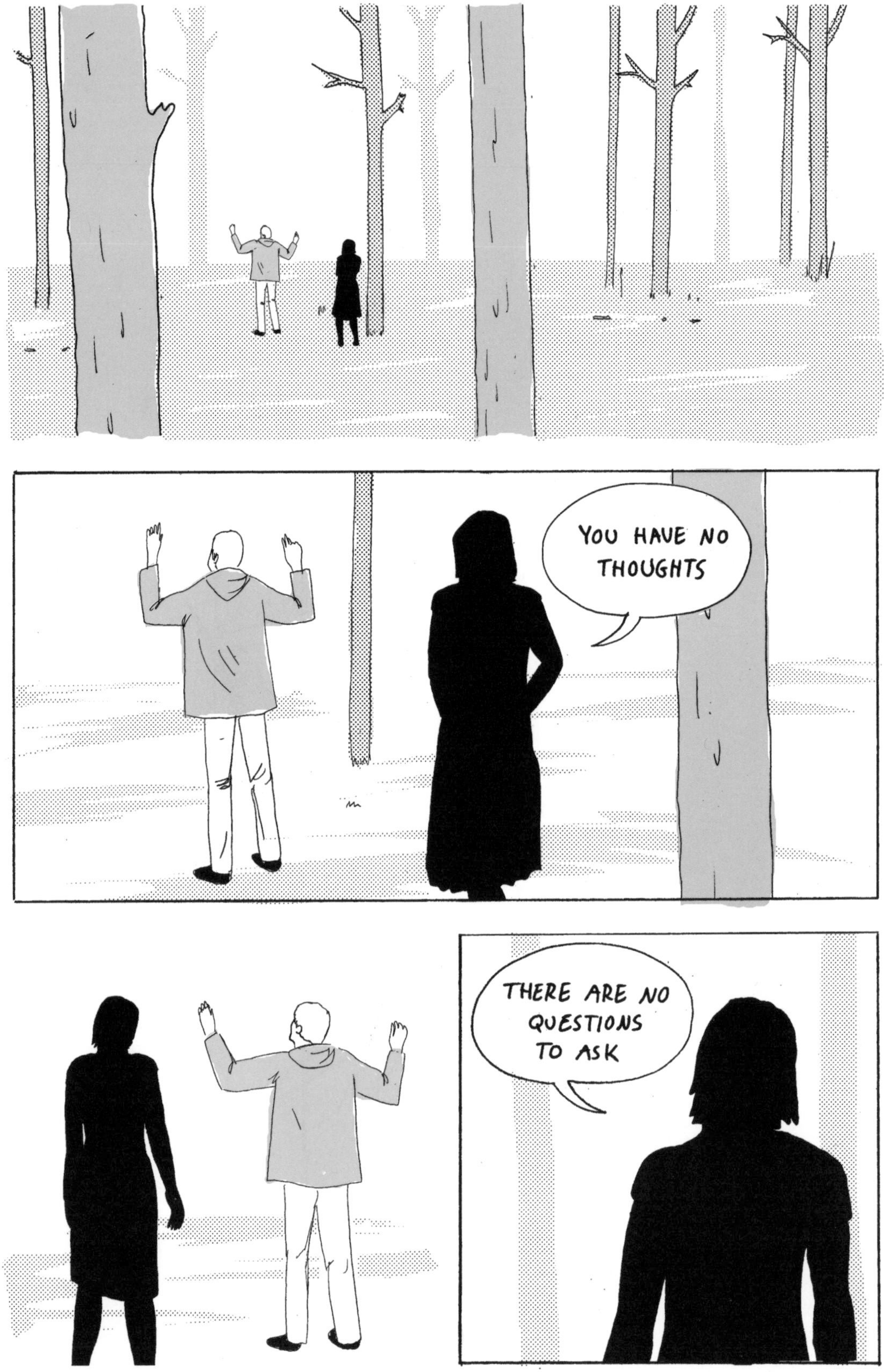
YOU HAVE NO THOUGHTS
THERE ARE NO QUESTIONS TO ASK

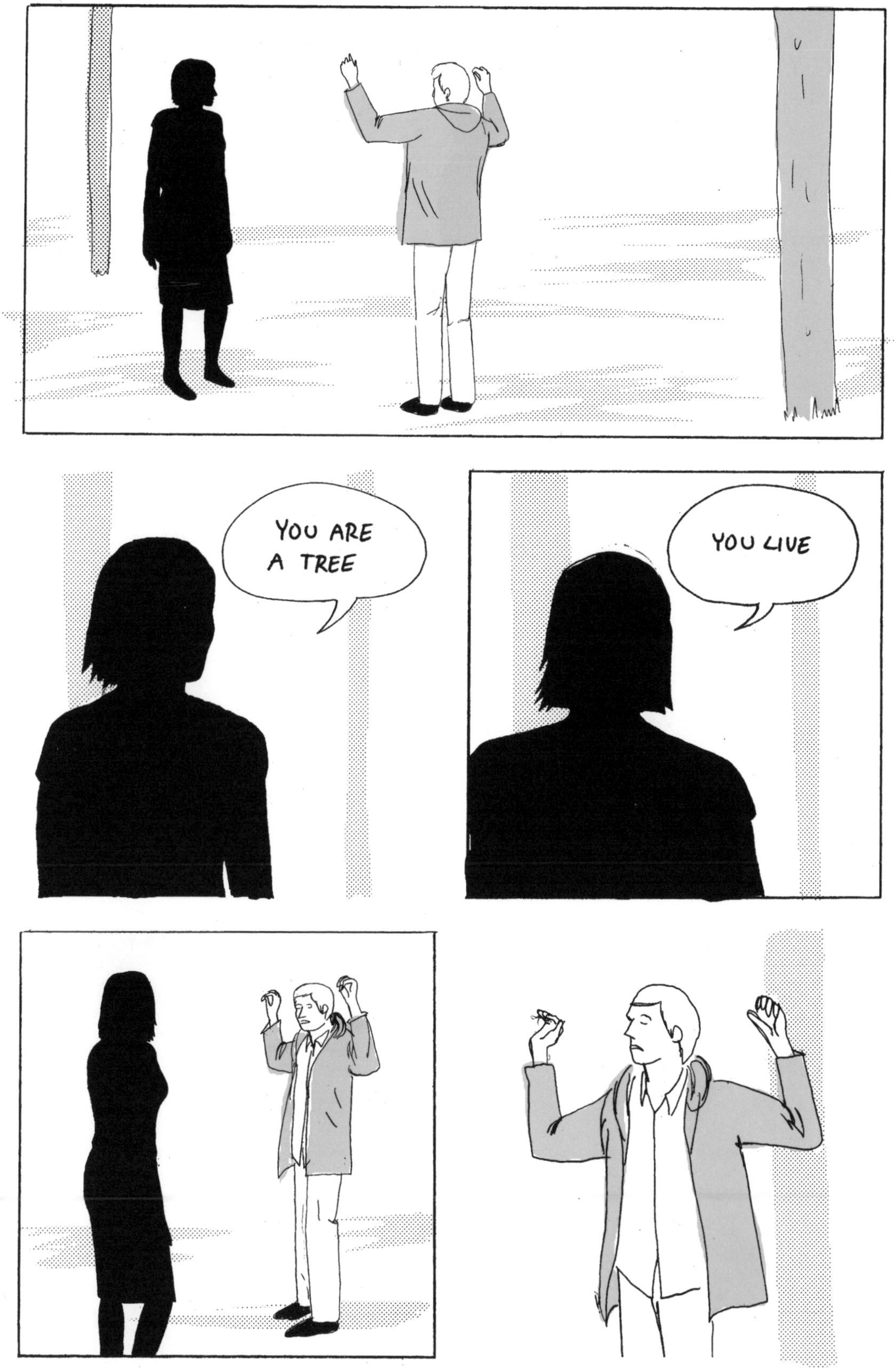
YOU ARE A TREE
YOU LIVE

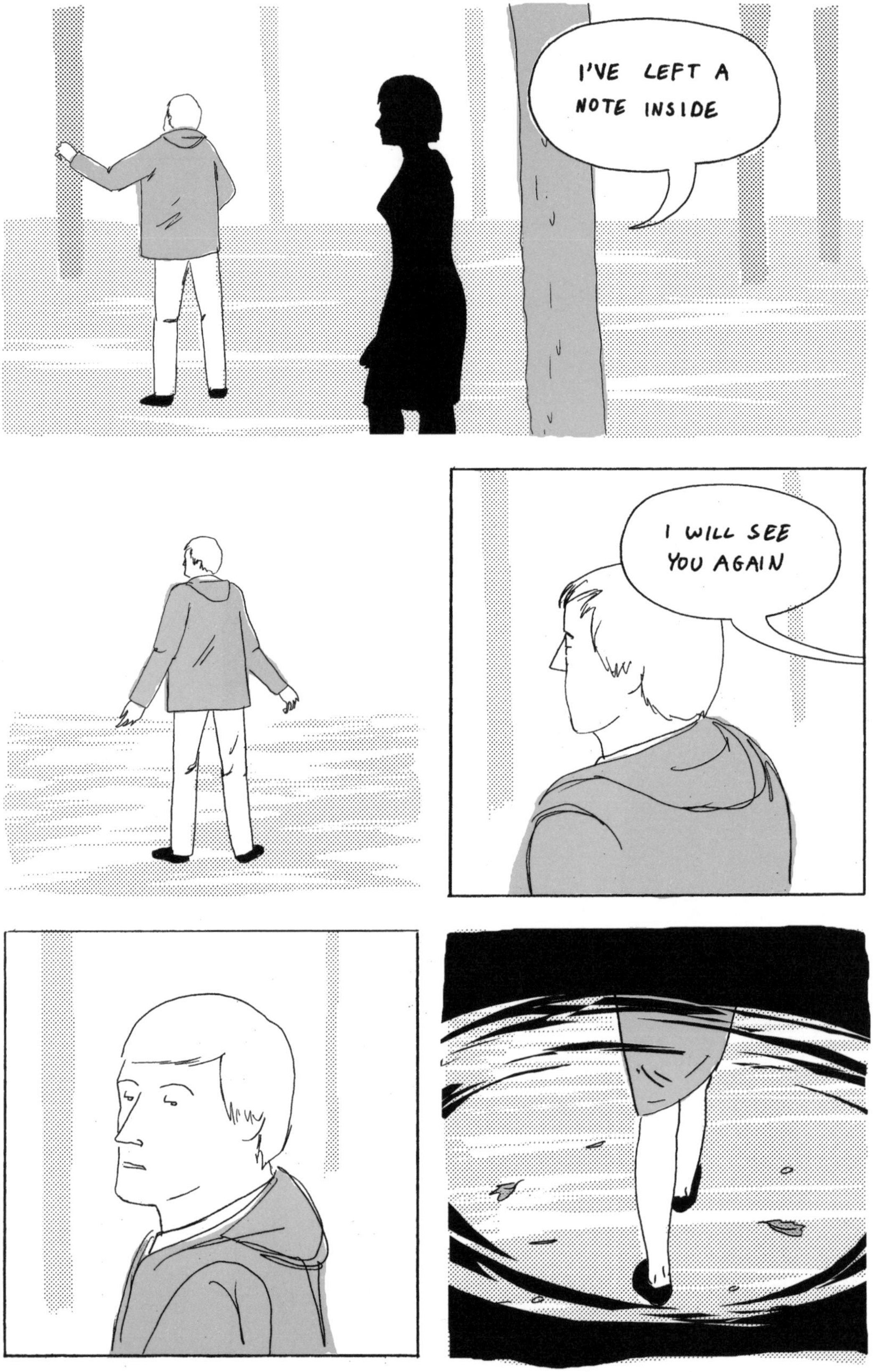
I'VE LEFT A NOTE INSIDE
I WILL SEE YOU AGAIN

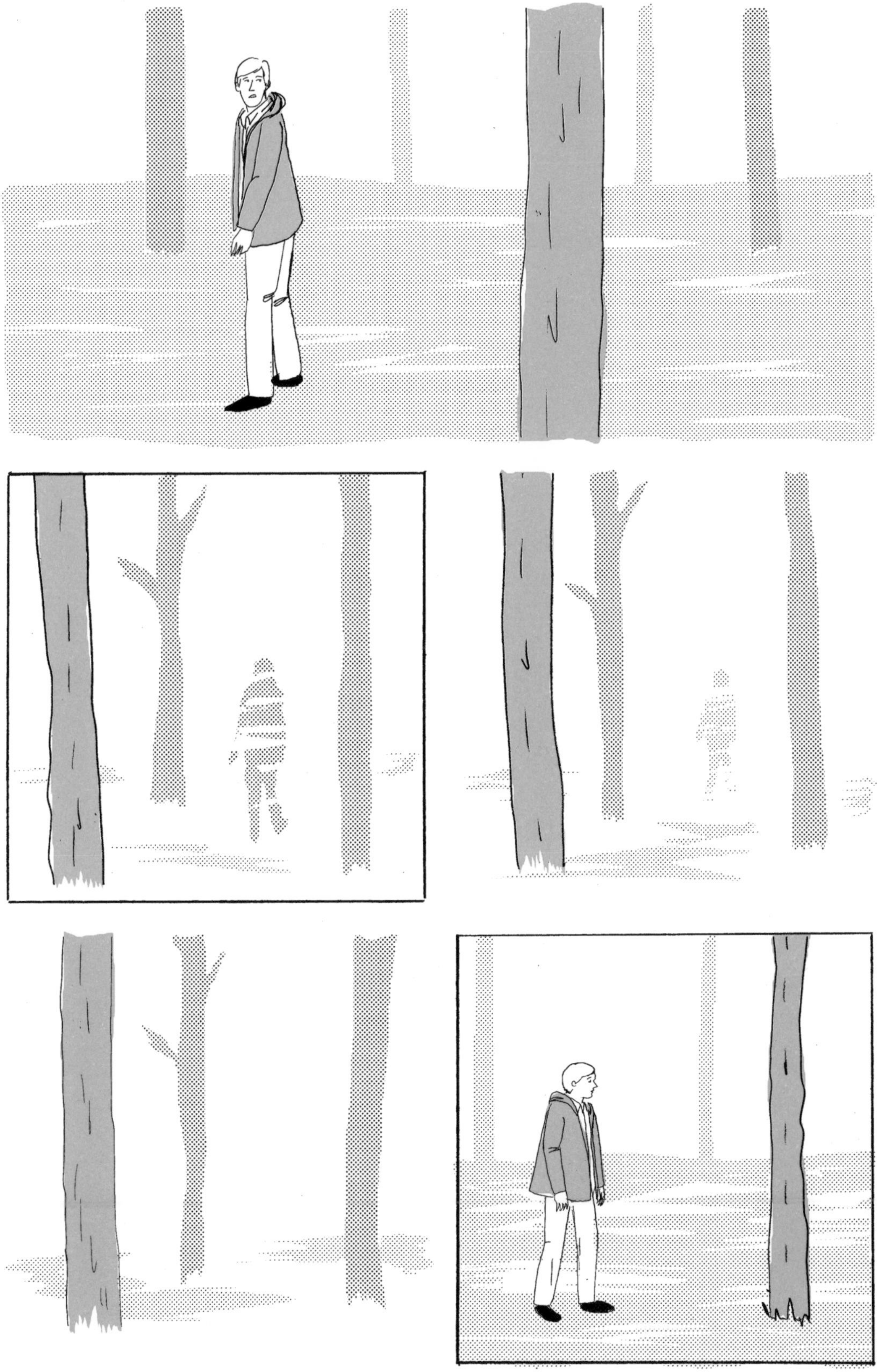

She did not

leave you

ken f

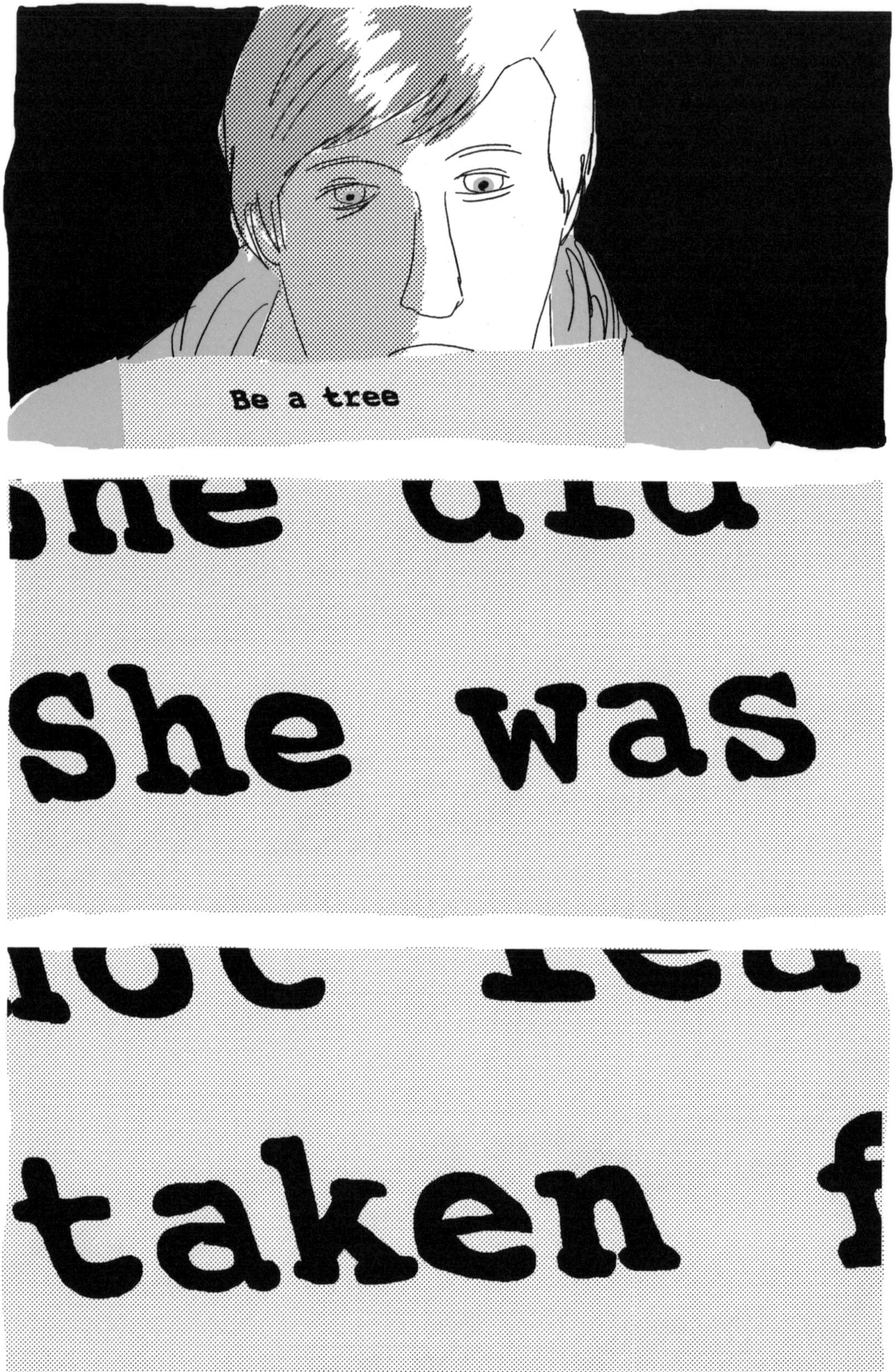
Be a tree
She was
taken

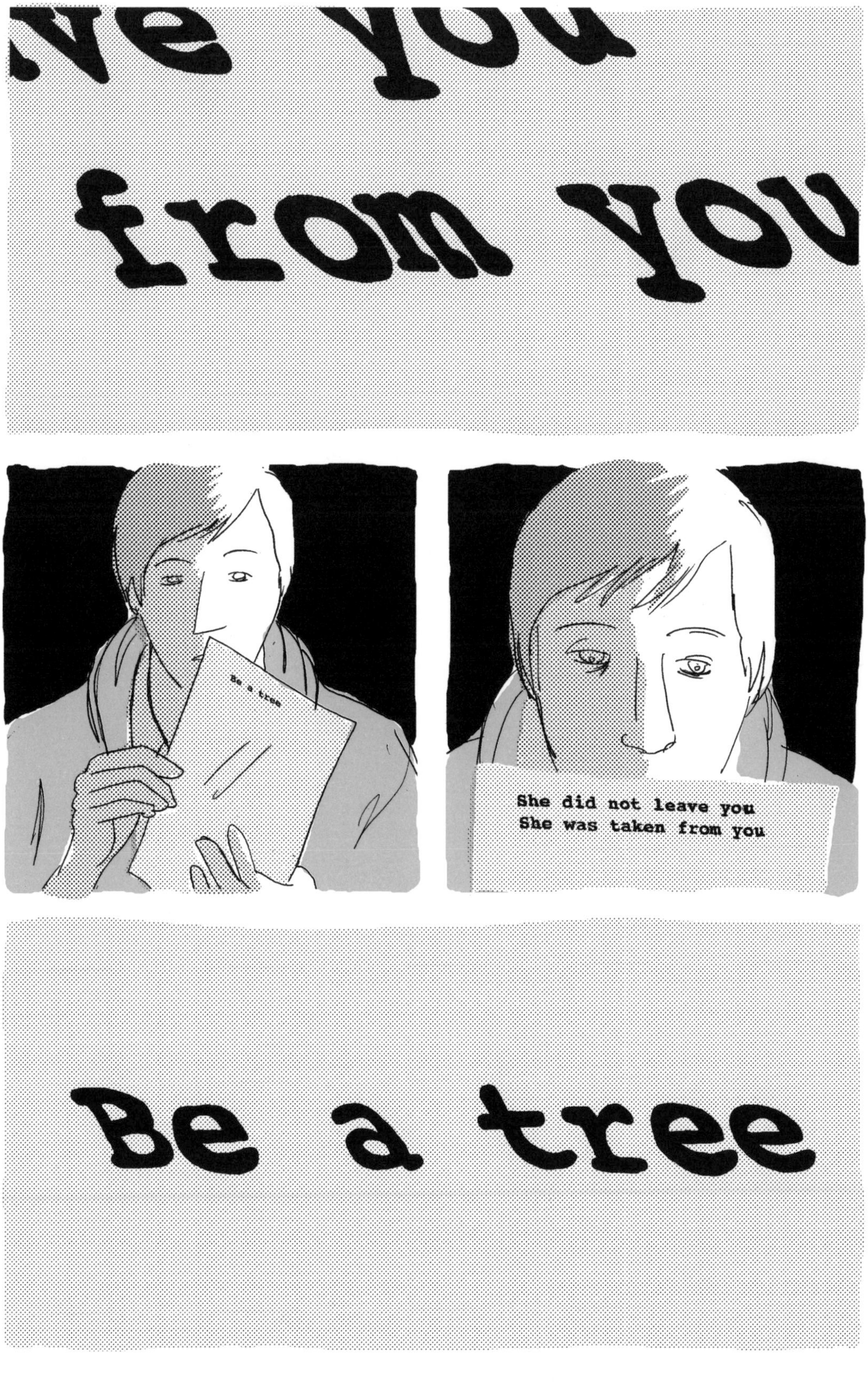
from you
Be a tree
She did not leave you
She was taken from you
Be a tree

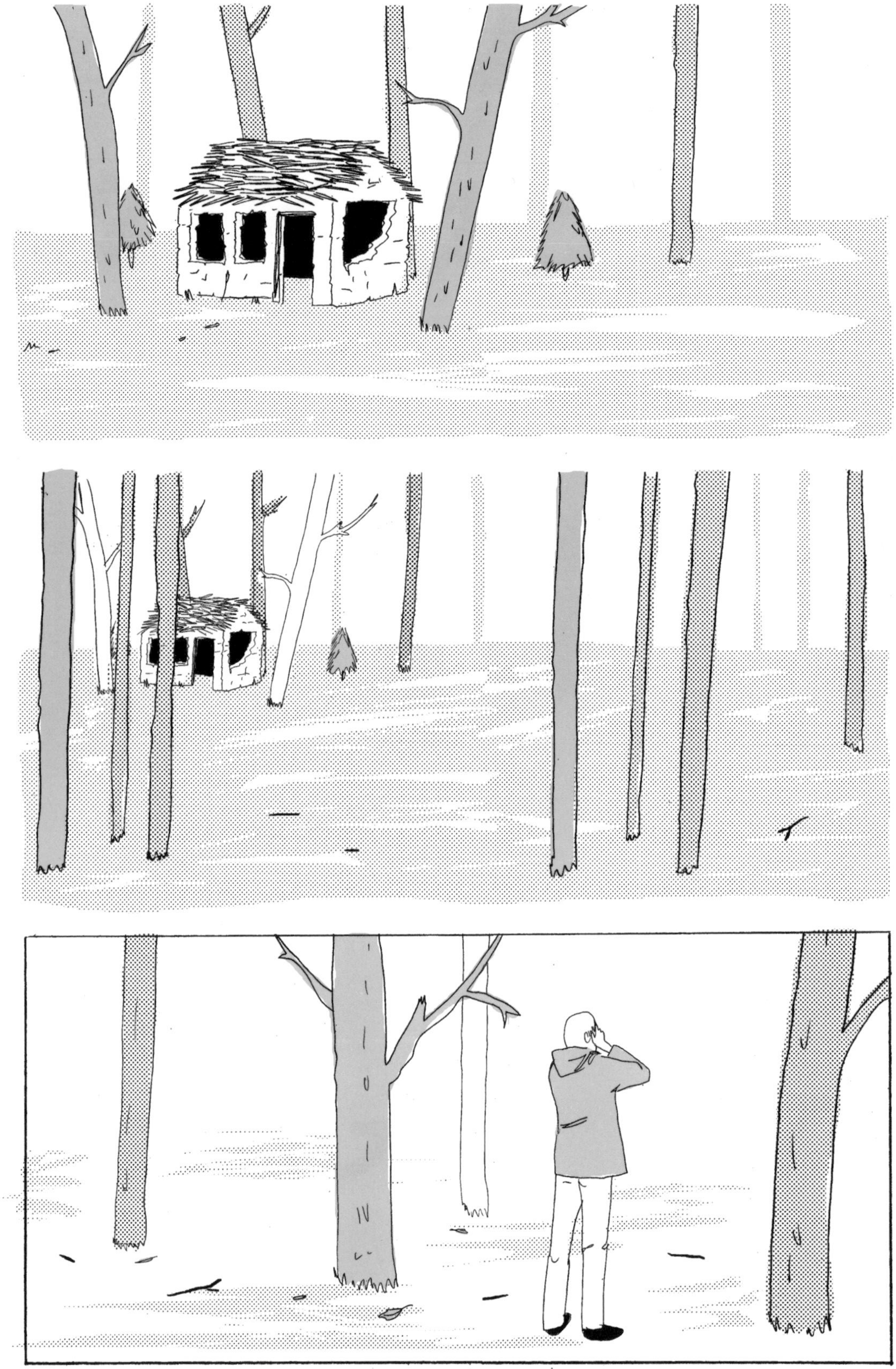

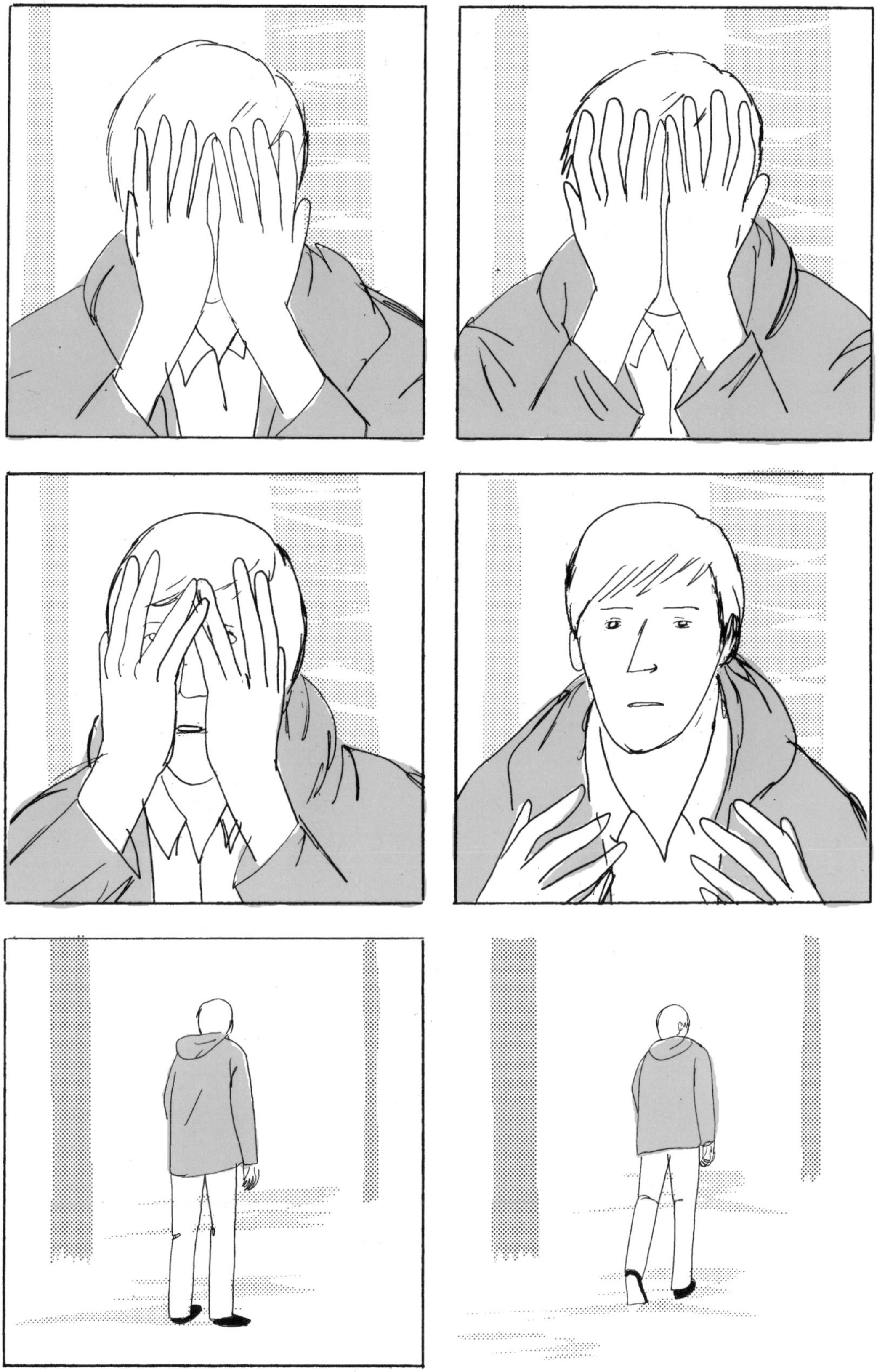

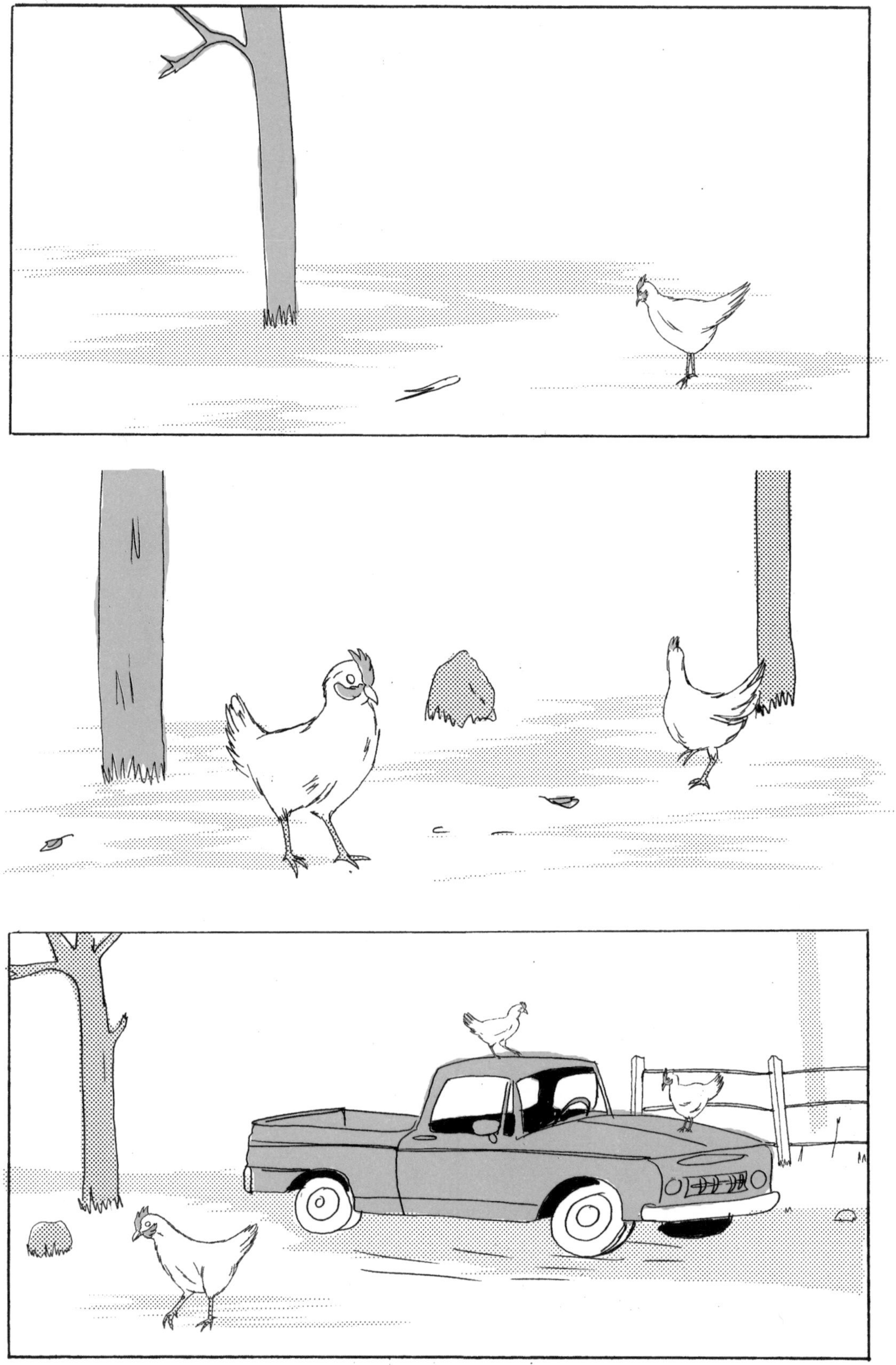

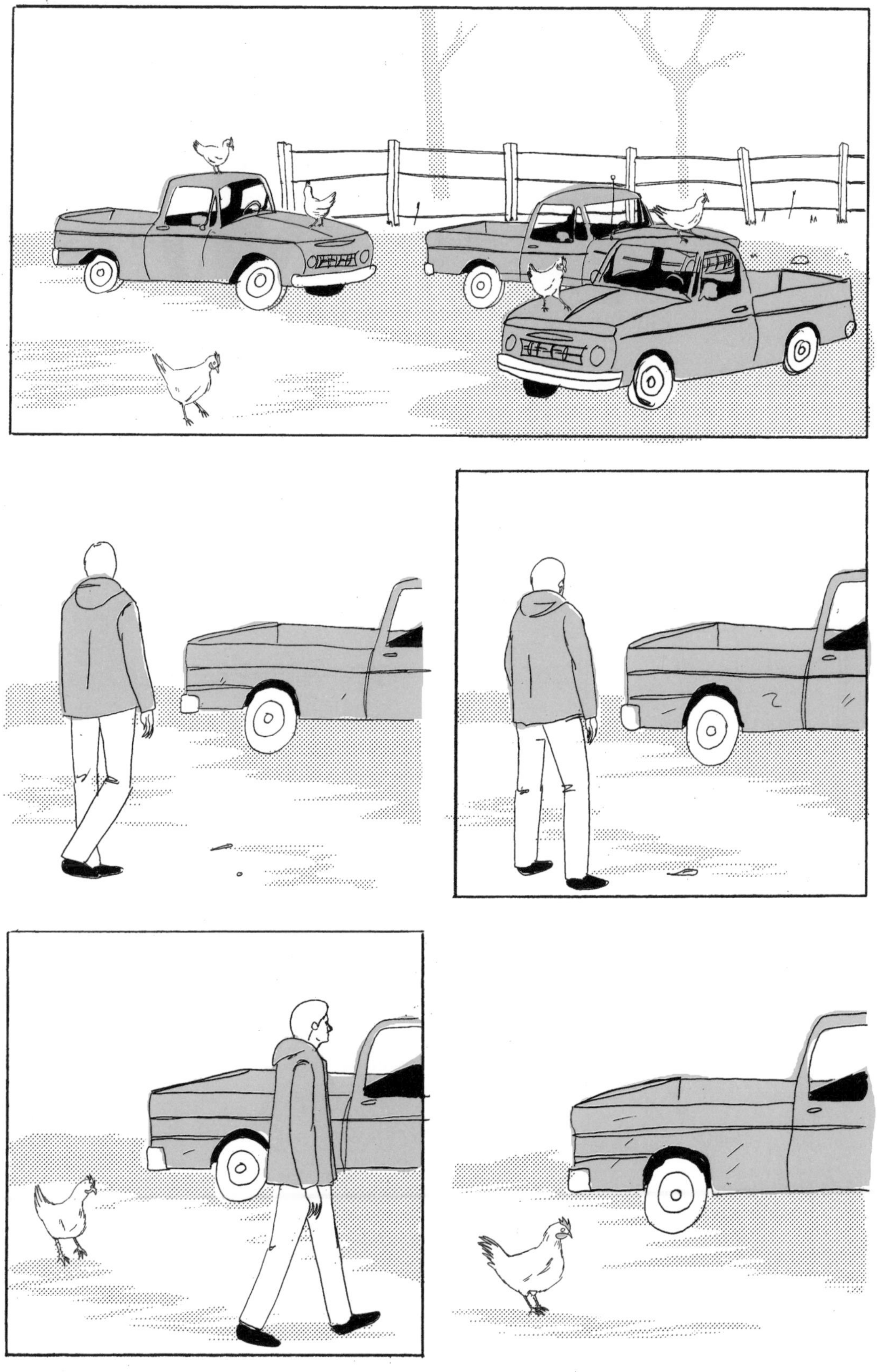

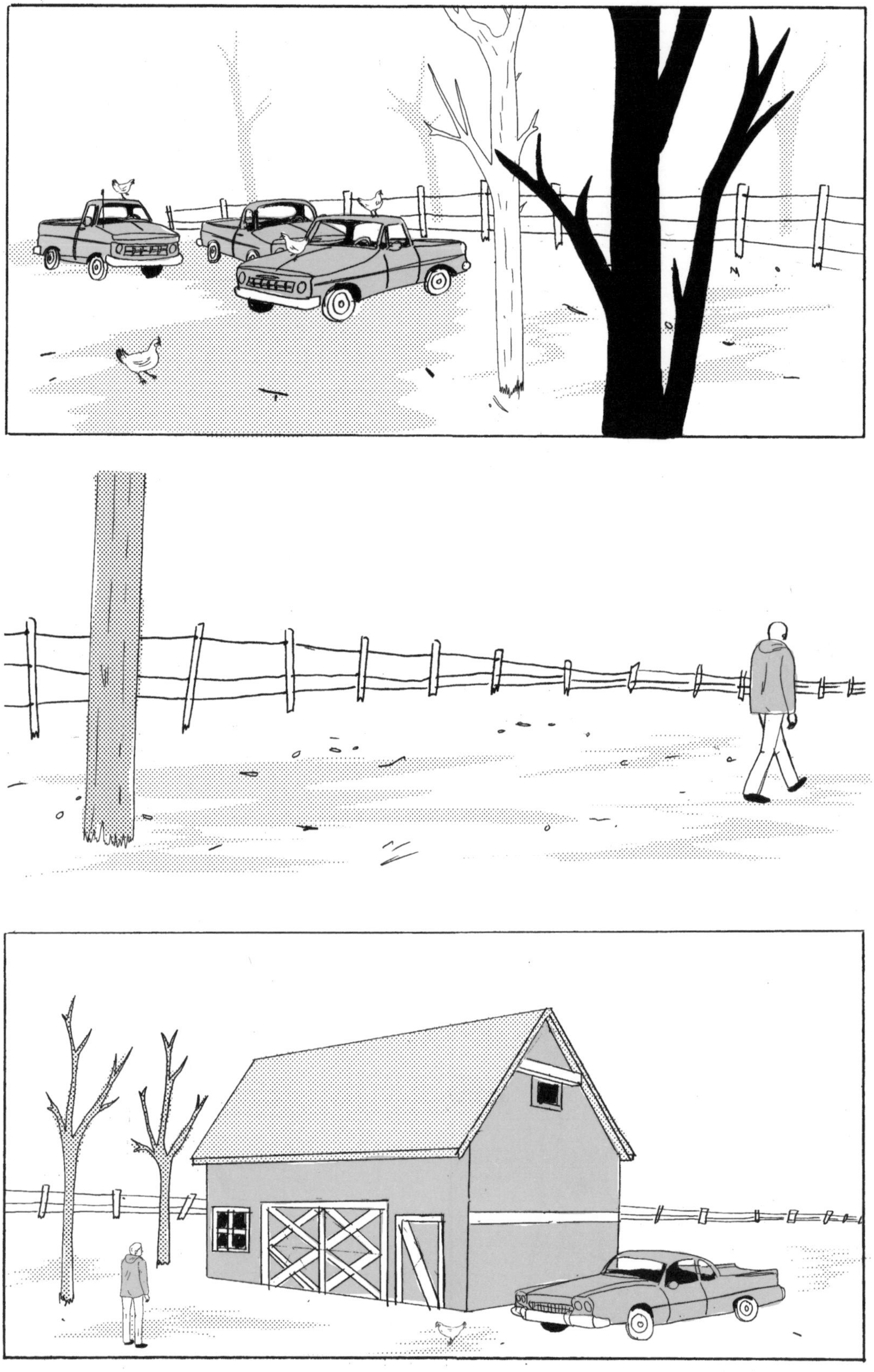

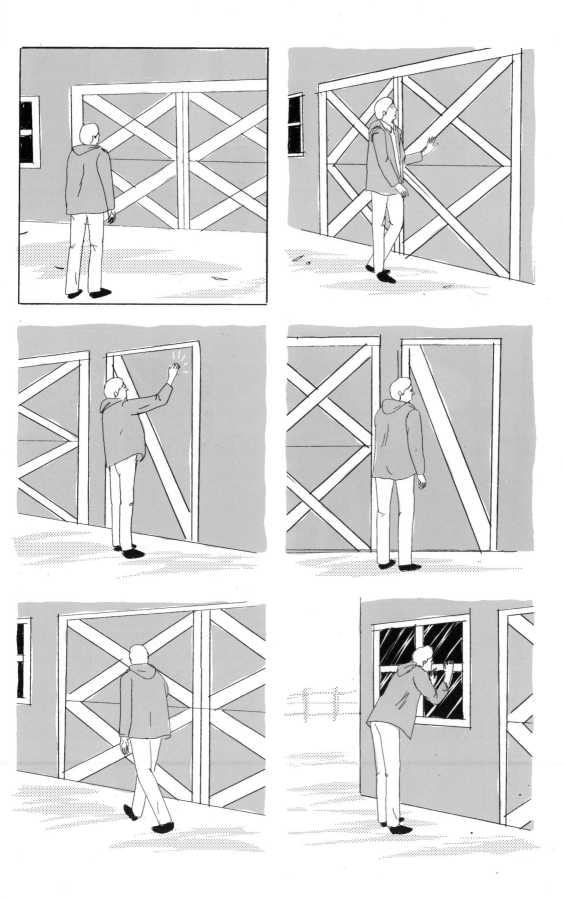

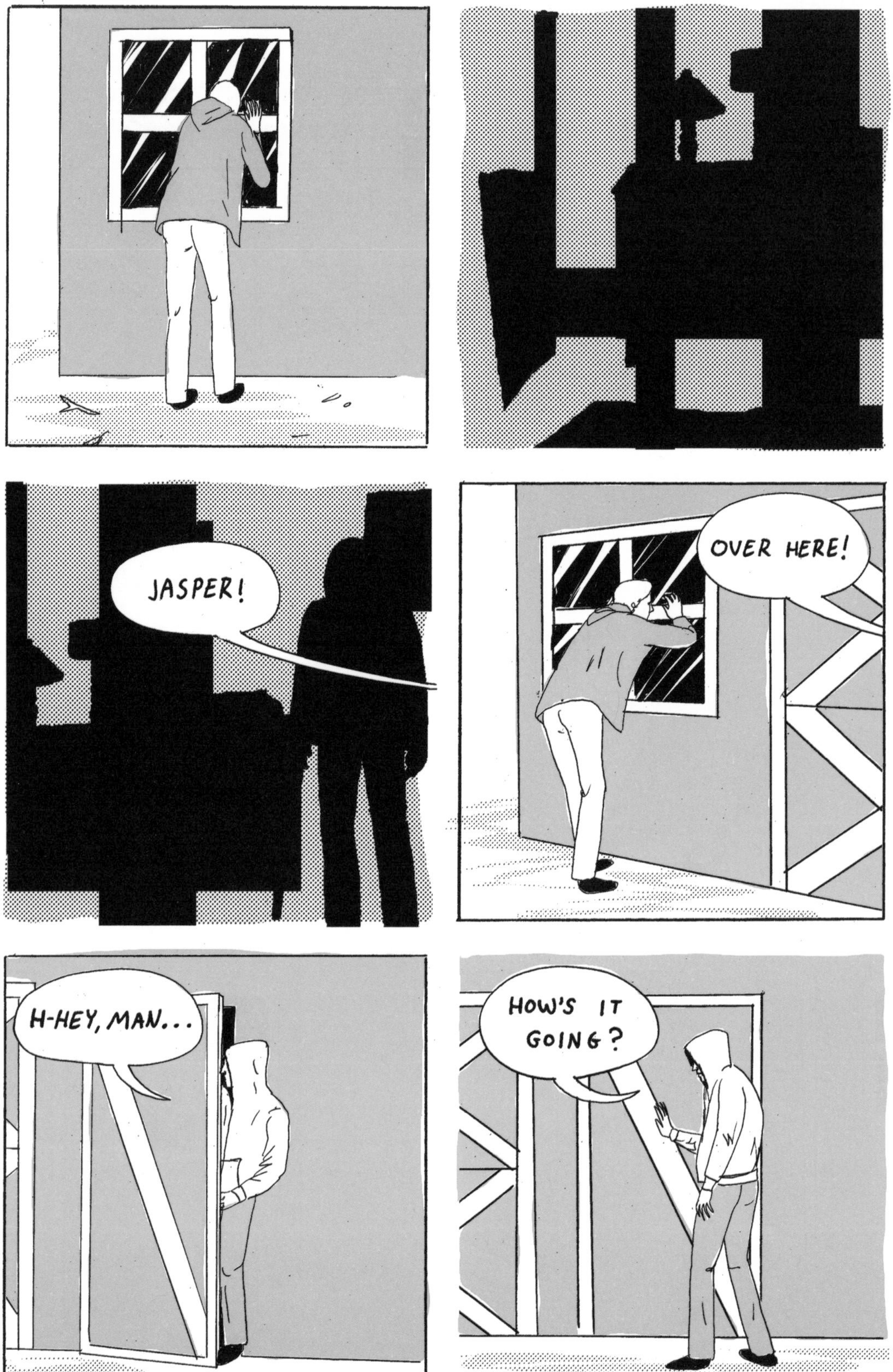
JASPER!
OVER HERE!
H-HEY, MAN...
HOW'S IT GOING?

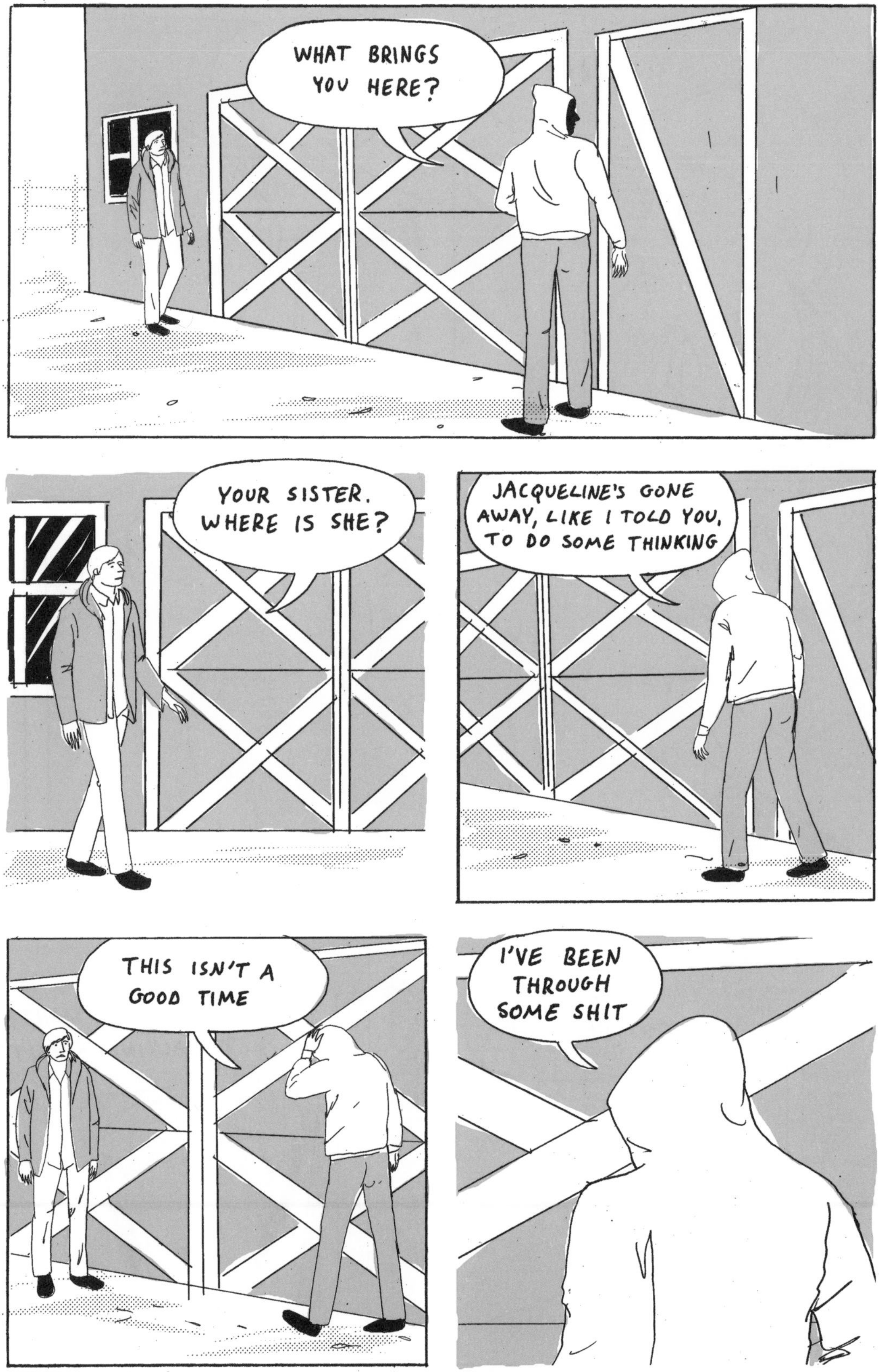
WHAT BRINGS YOU HERE?
YOUR SISTER. WHERE IS SHE?
JACQUELINE'S GONE AWAY, LIKE I TOLD YOU, TO DO SOME THINKING
THIS ISN'T A GOOD TIME
I'VE BEEN THROUGH SOME SHIT

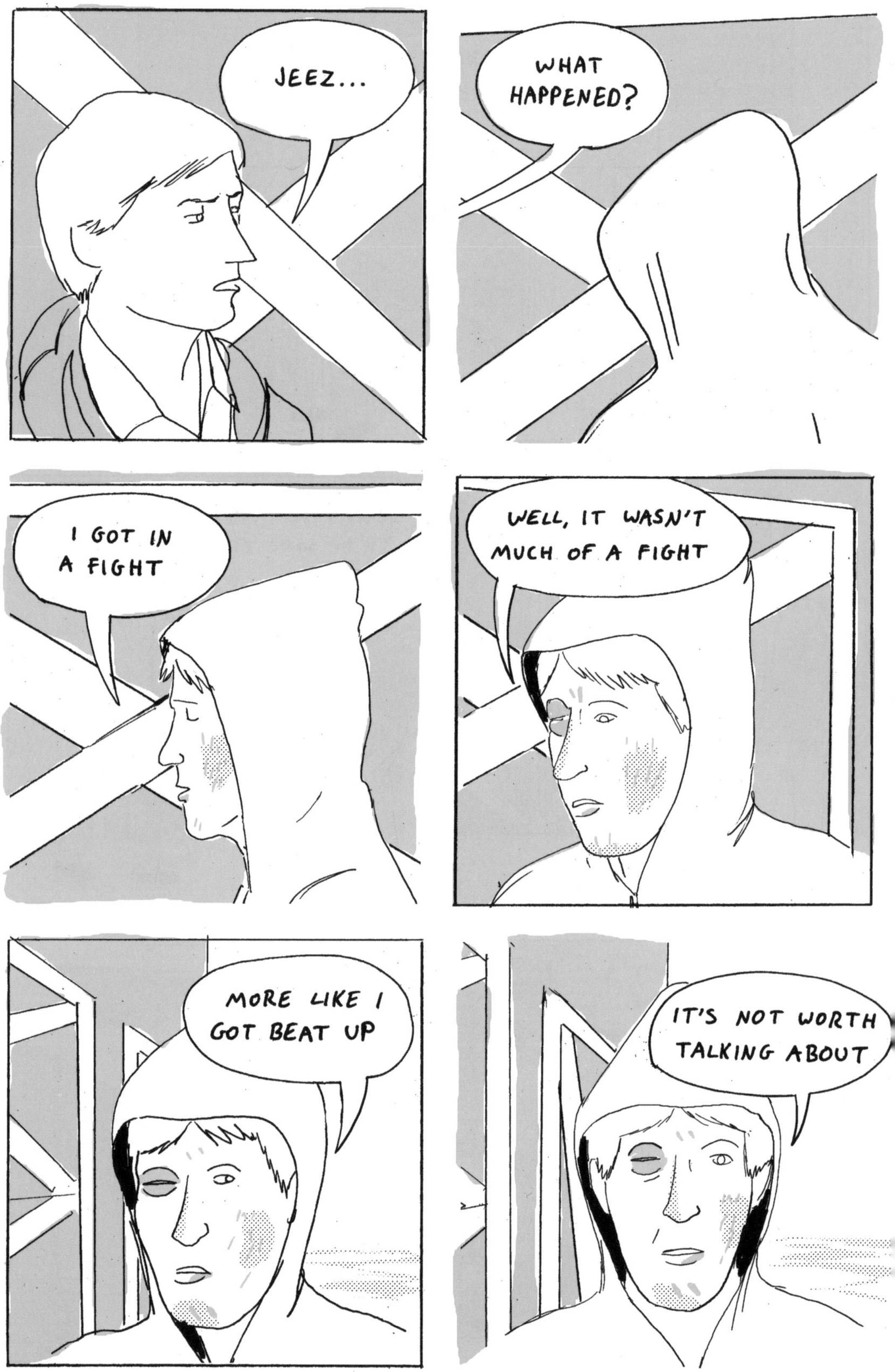
JEEZ...
WHAT HAPPENED?
I GOT IN A FIGHT
WELL, IT WASN'T MUCH OF A FIGHT
MORE LIKE I GOT BEAT UP
IT'S NOT WORTH TALKING ABOUT

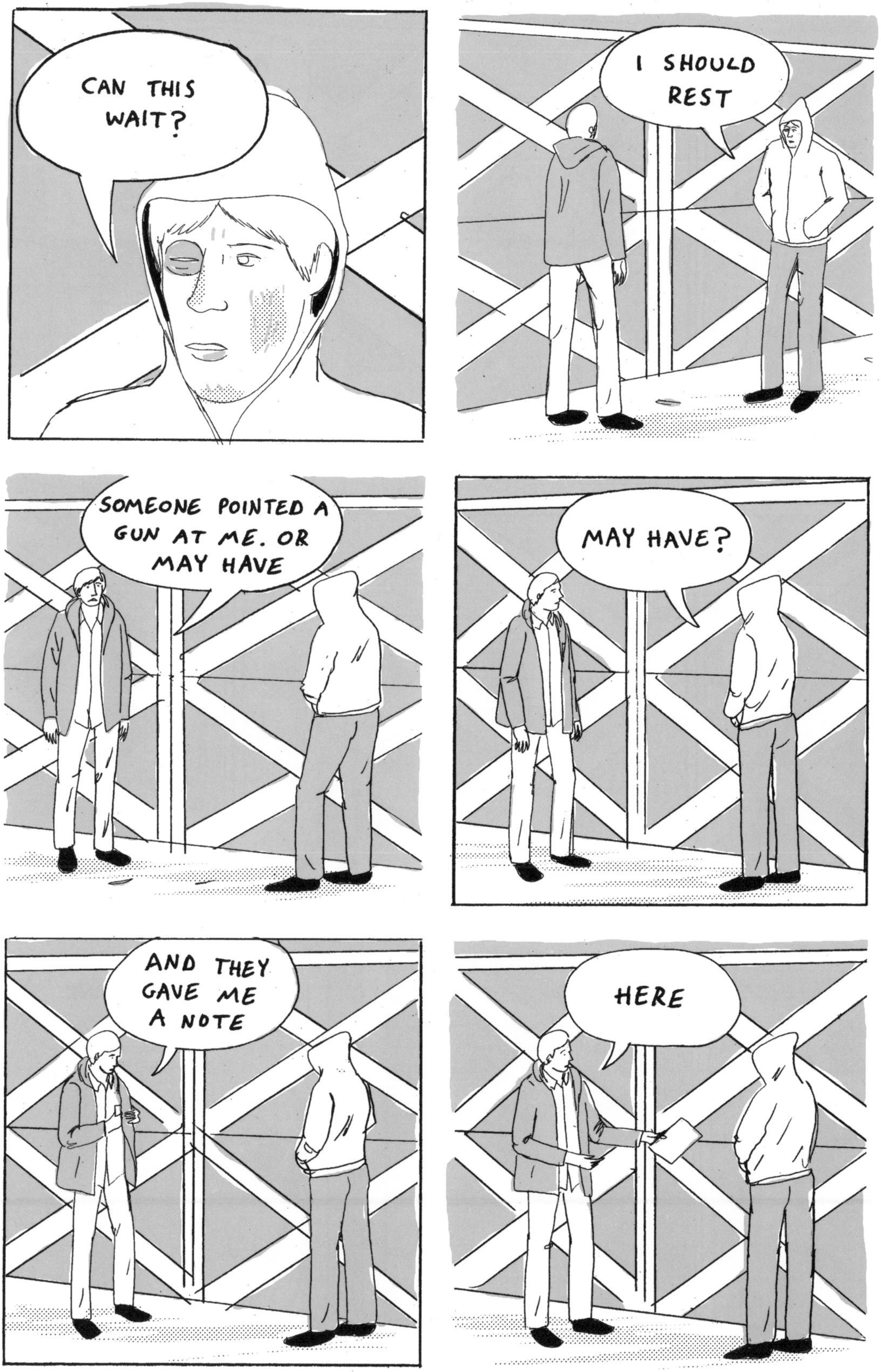
CAN THIS WAIT?
I SHOULD REST
SOMEONE POINTED A GUN AT ME. OR MAY HAVE
MAY HAVE?
AND THEY GAVE ME A NOTE
HERE

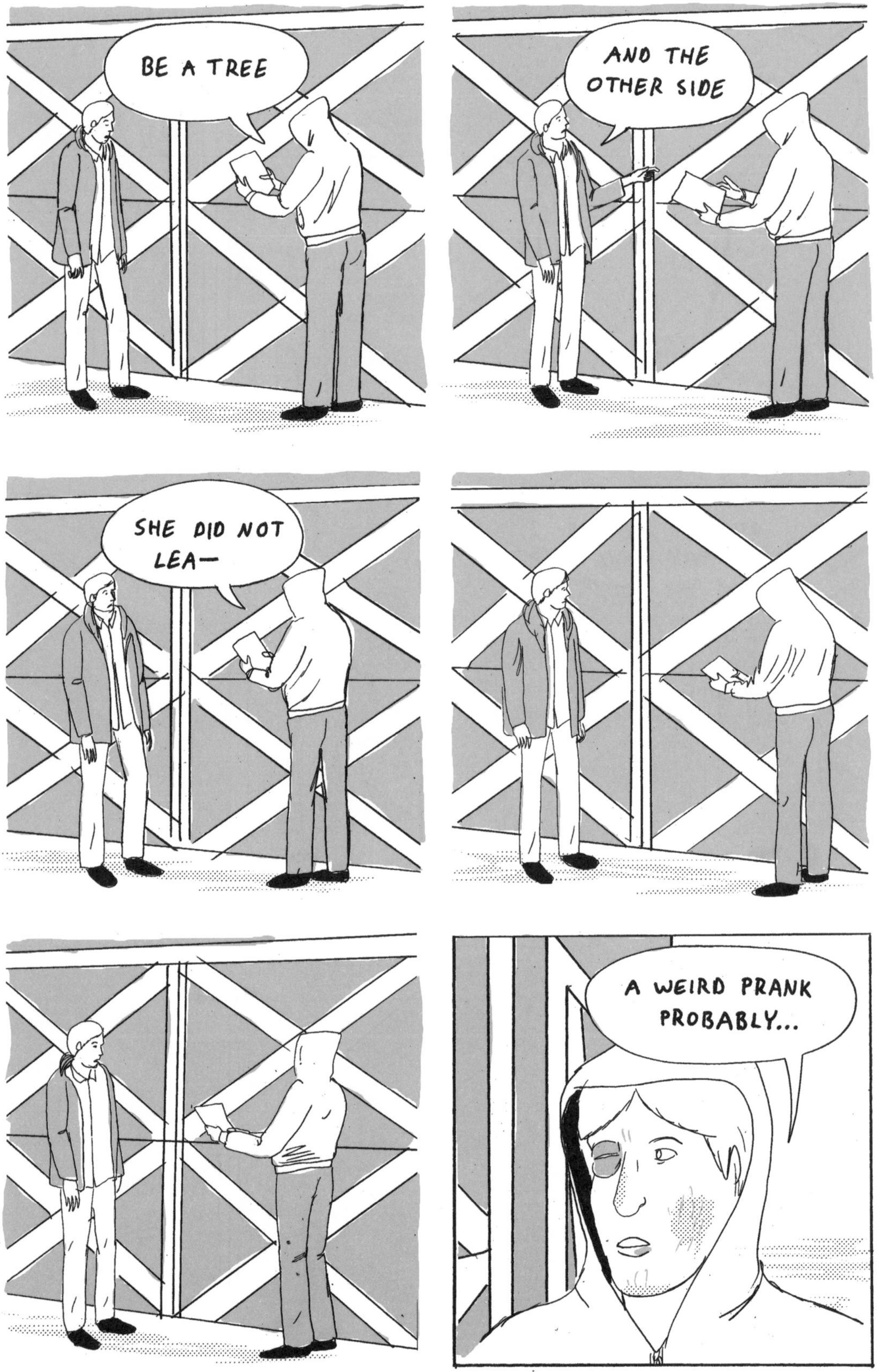

BE A TREE
AND THE OTHER SIDE
SHE DID NOT LEA—
A WEIRD PRANK PROBABLY...

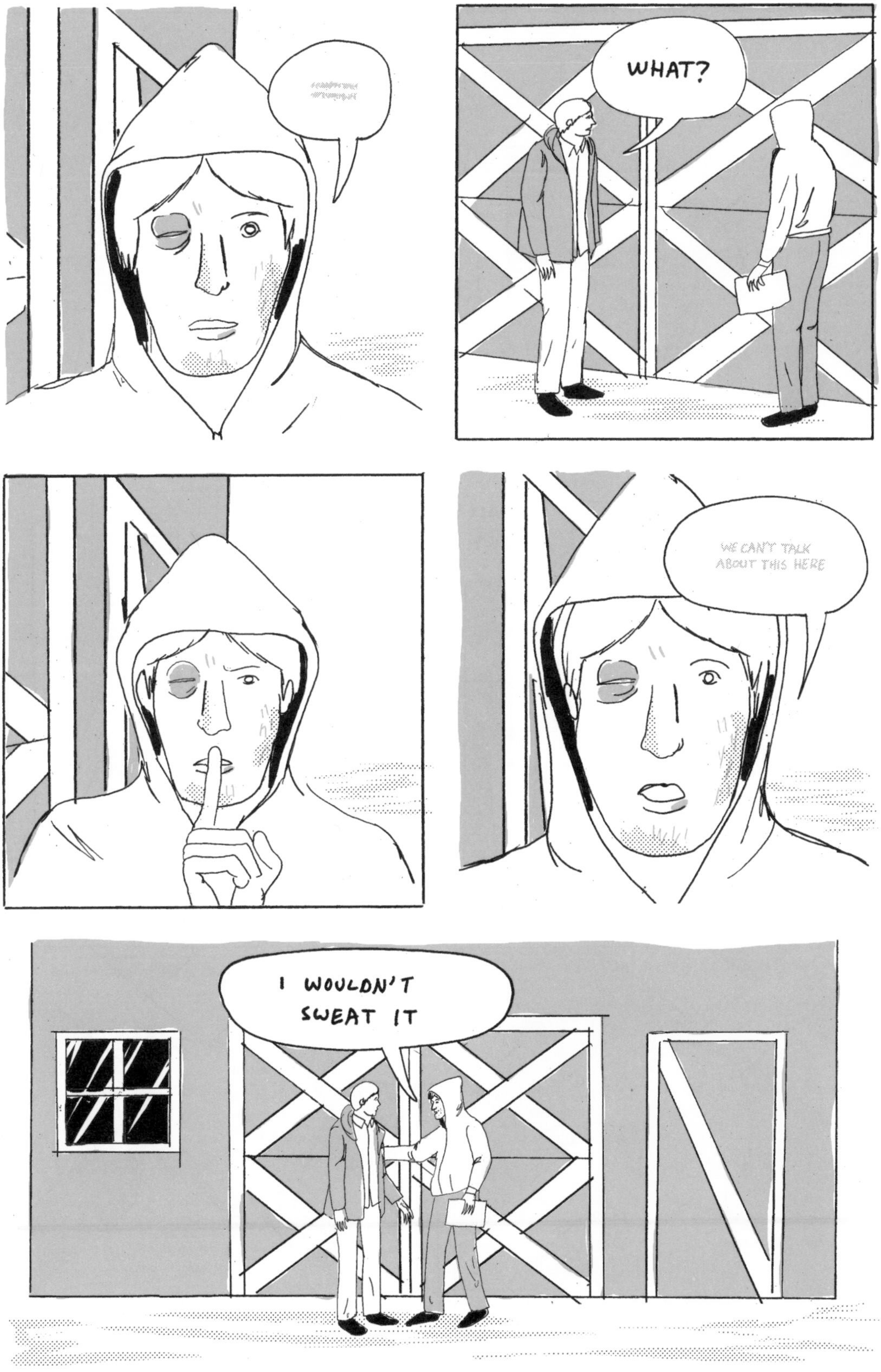
WHAT?
WE CAN'T TALK ABOUT THIS HERE
I WOULDN'T SWEAT IT

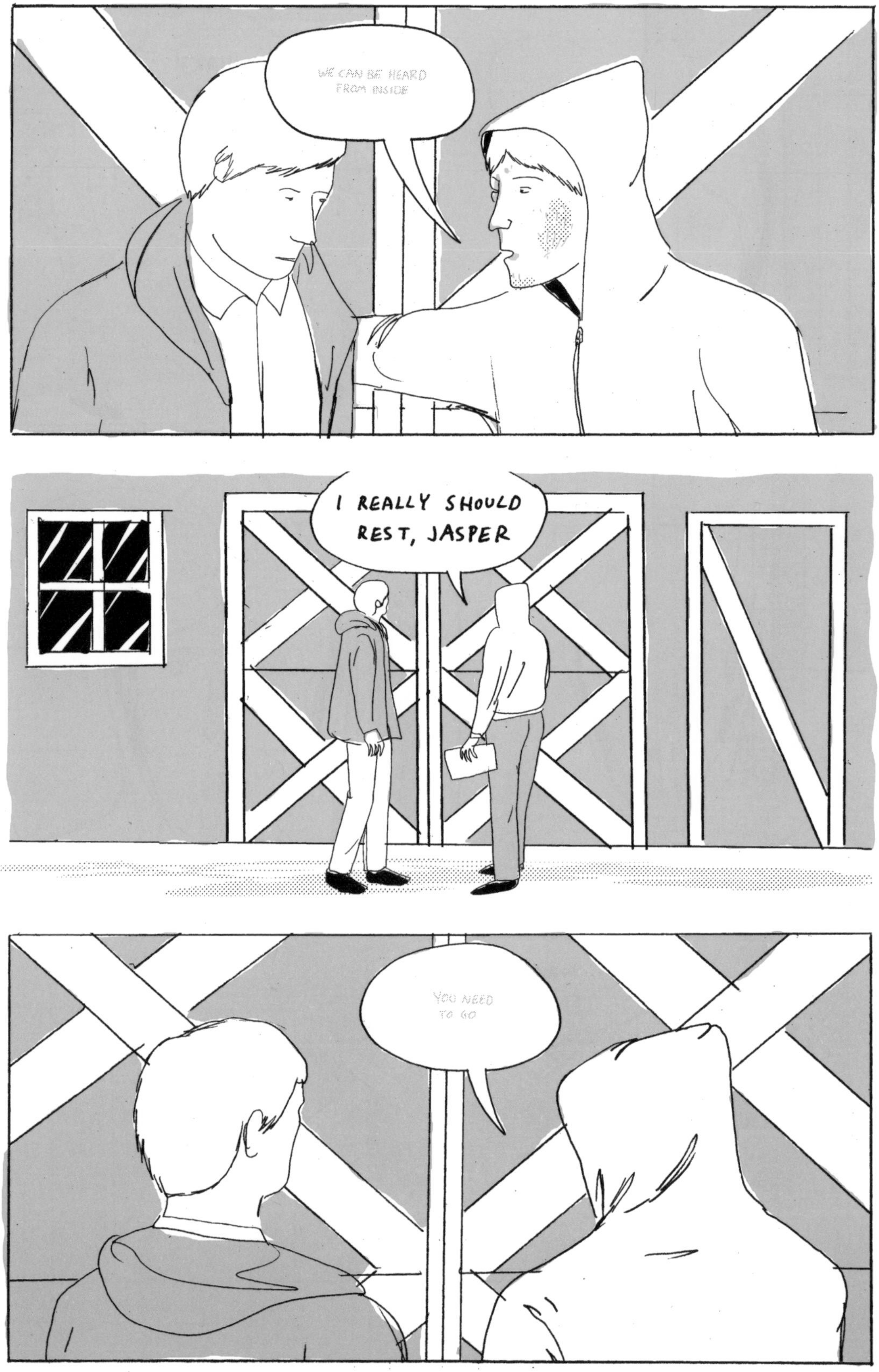
WE CAN BE HEARD FROM INSIDE
I REALLY SHOULD REST, JASPER
YOU NEED TO GO

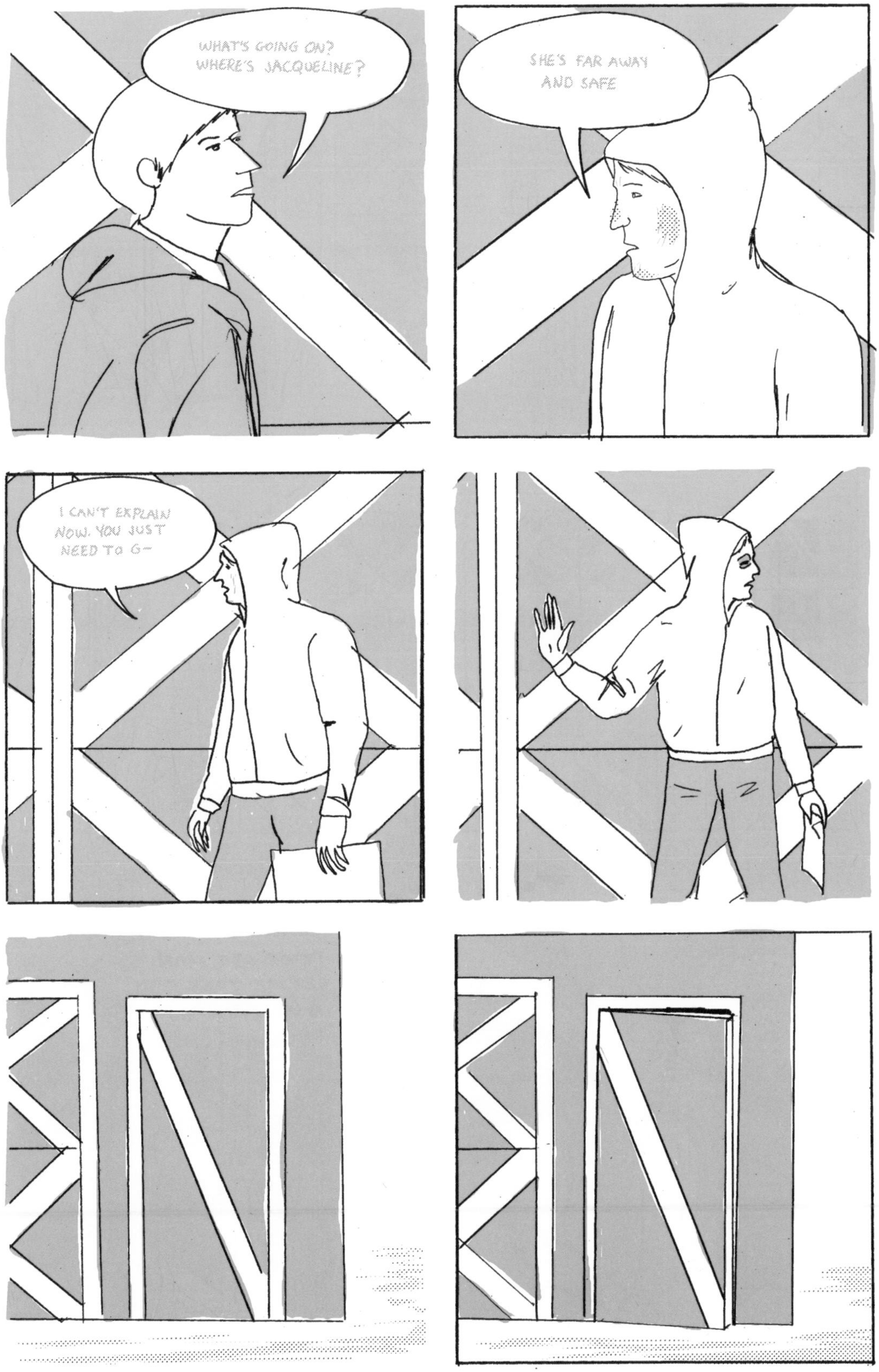
WHAT'S GOING ON? WHERE'S JACQUELINE?
SHE'S FAR AWAY AND SAFE
I CAN'T EXPLAIN NOW. YOU JUST NEED TO G-

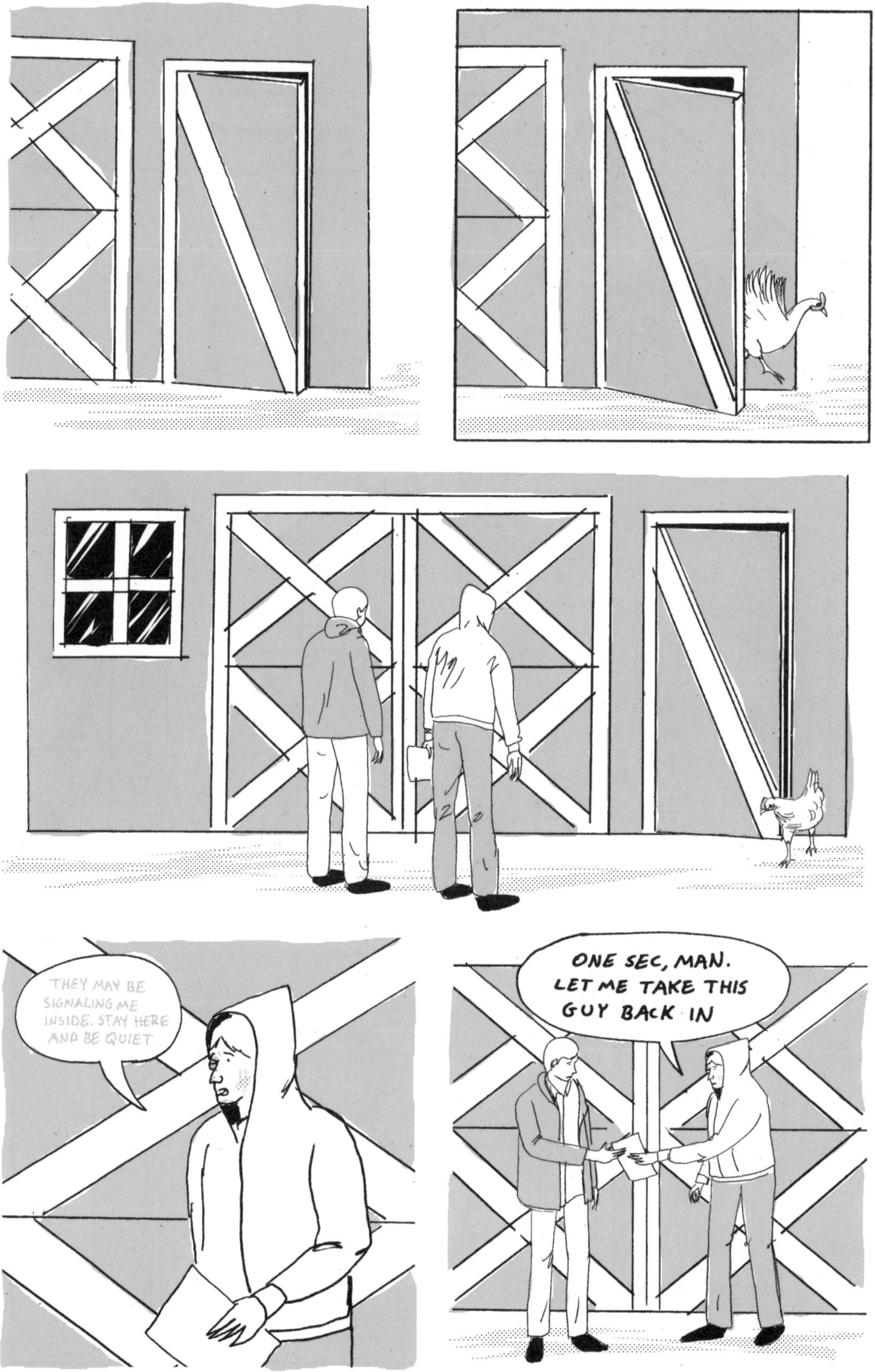
THEY MAY BE SIGNALING ME INSIDE. STAY HERE AND BE QUIET
ONE SEC, MAN. LET ME TAKE THIS GUY BACK IN

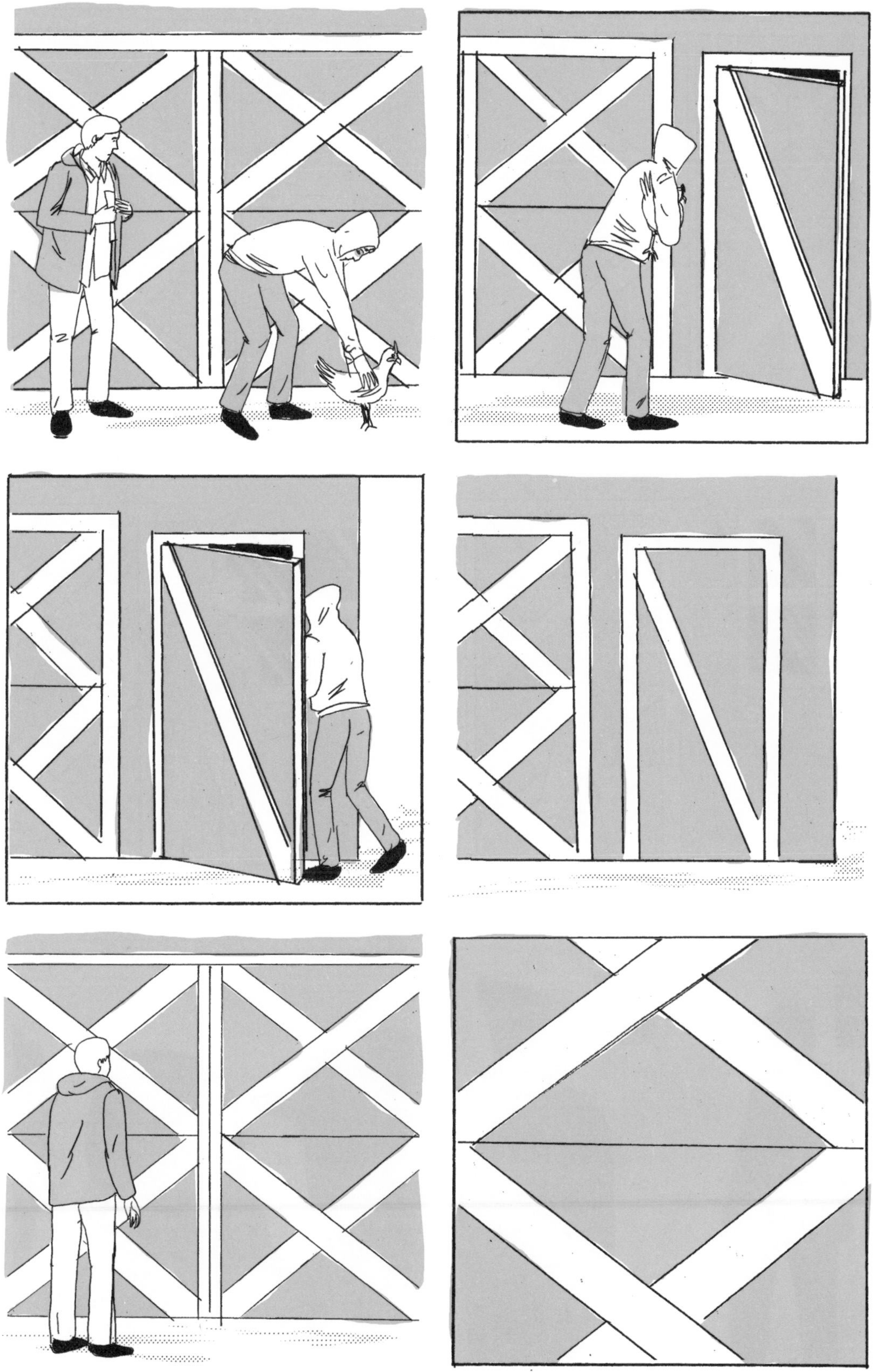

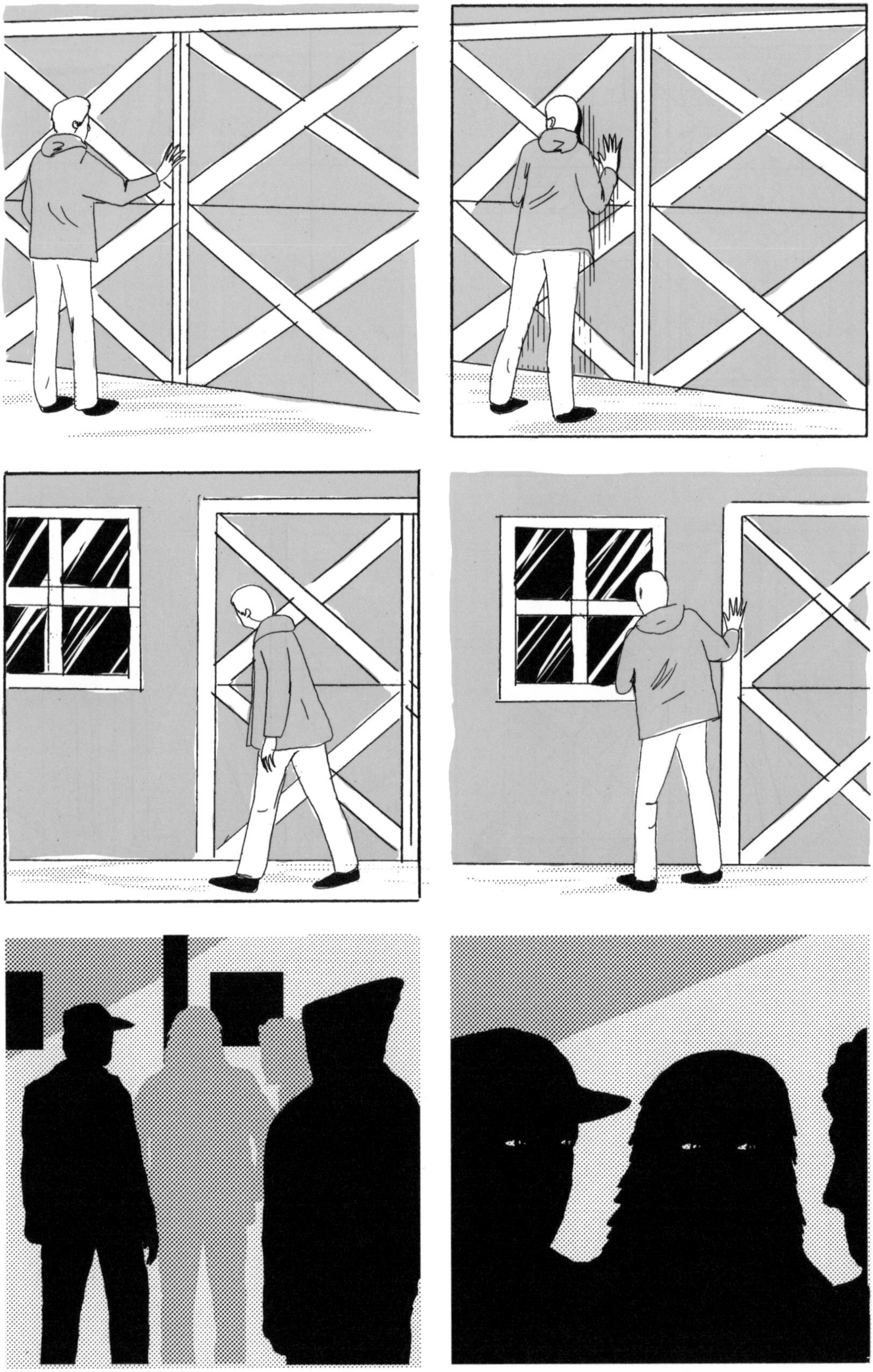

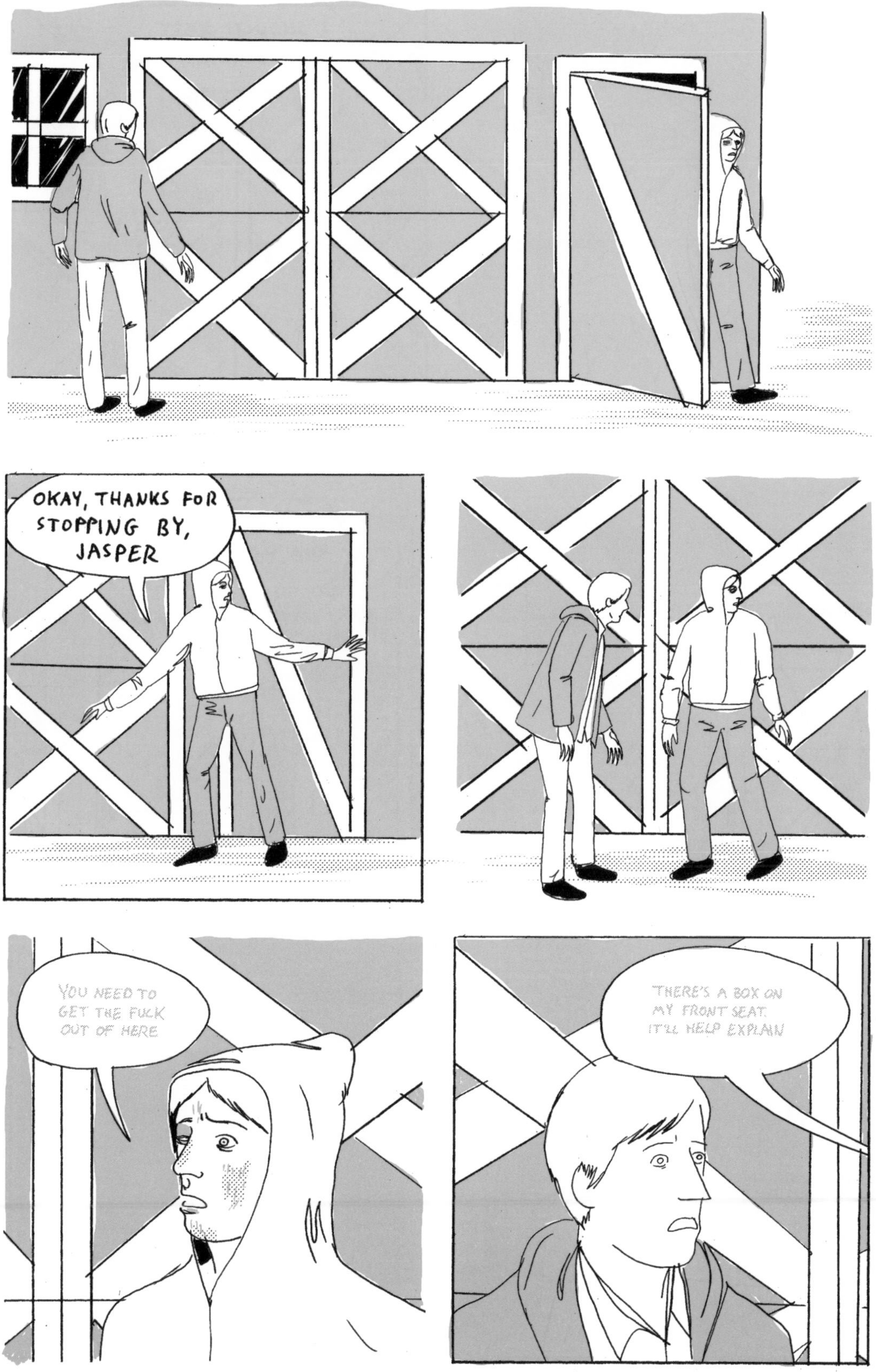
OKAY, THANKS FOR STOPPING BY, JASPER
YOU NEED TO GET THE FUCK OUT OF HERE
THERE'S A BOX ON MY FRONT SEAT. IT'LL HELP EXPLAIN

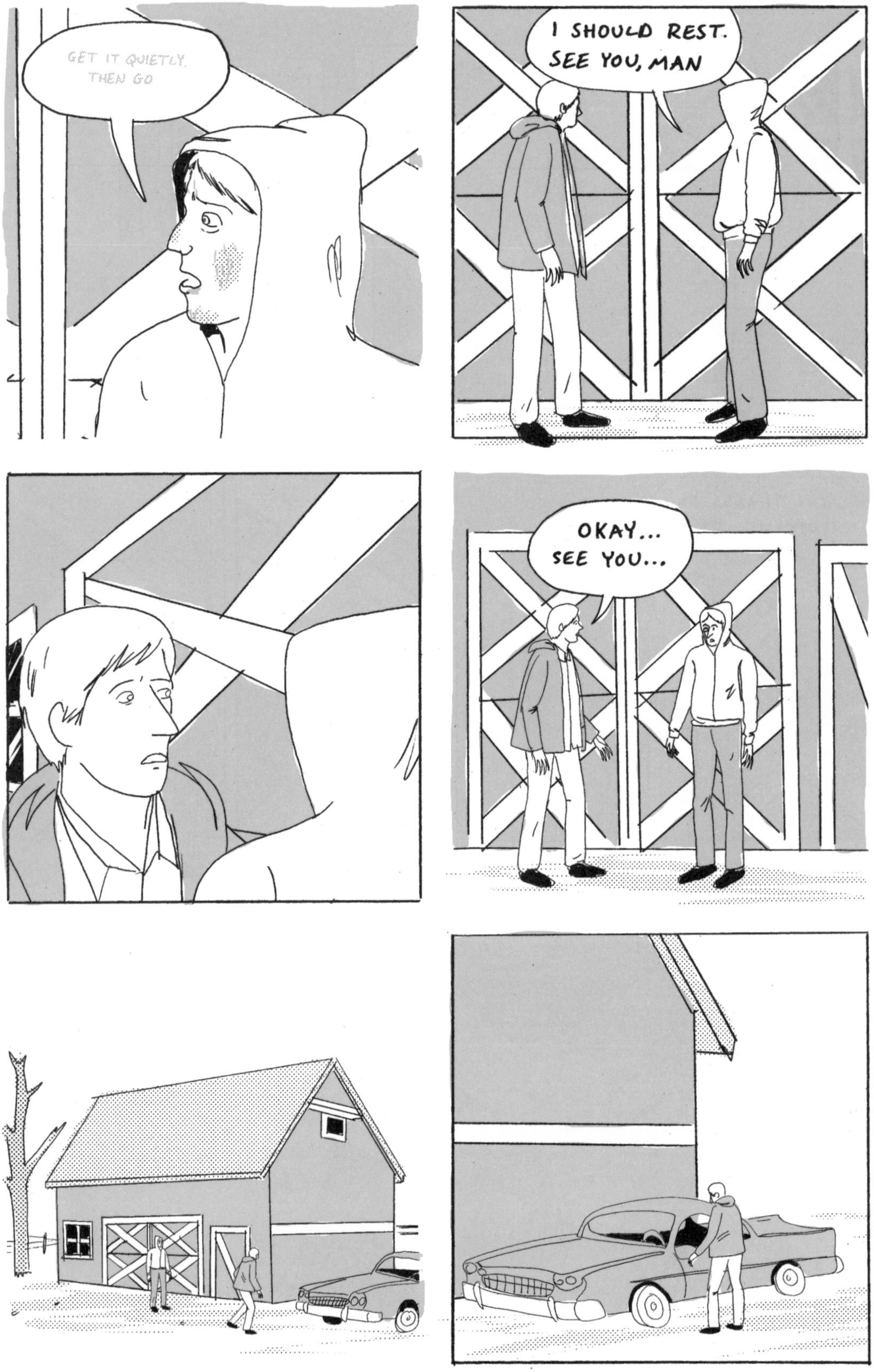
GET IT QUIETLY. THEN GO
I SHOULD REST. SEE YOU, MAN
OKAY... SEE YOU...

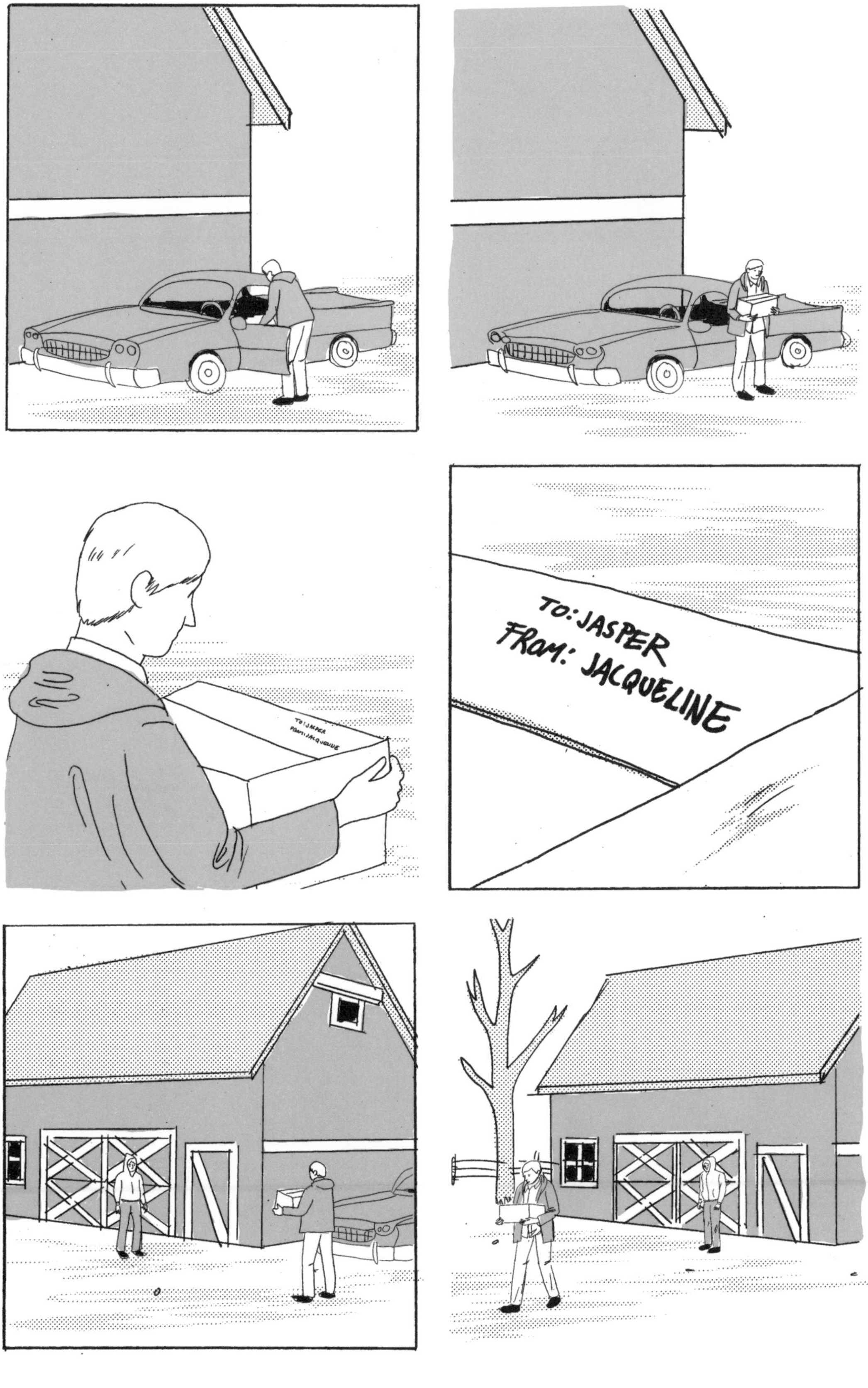
TO: JASPER
FROM: JACQUELINE

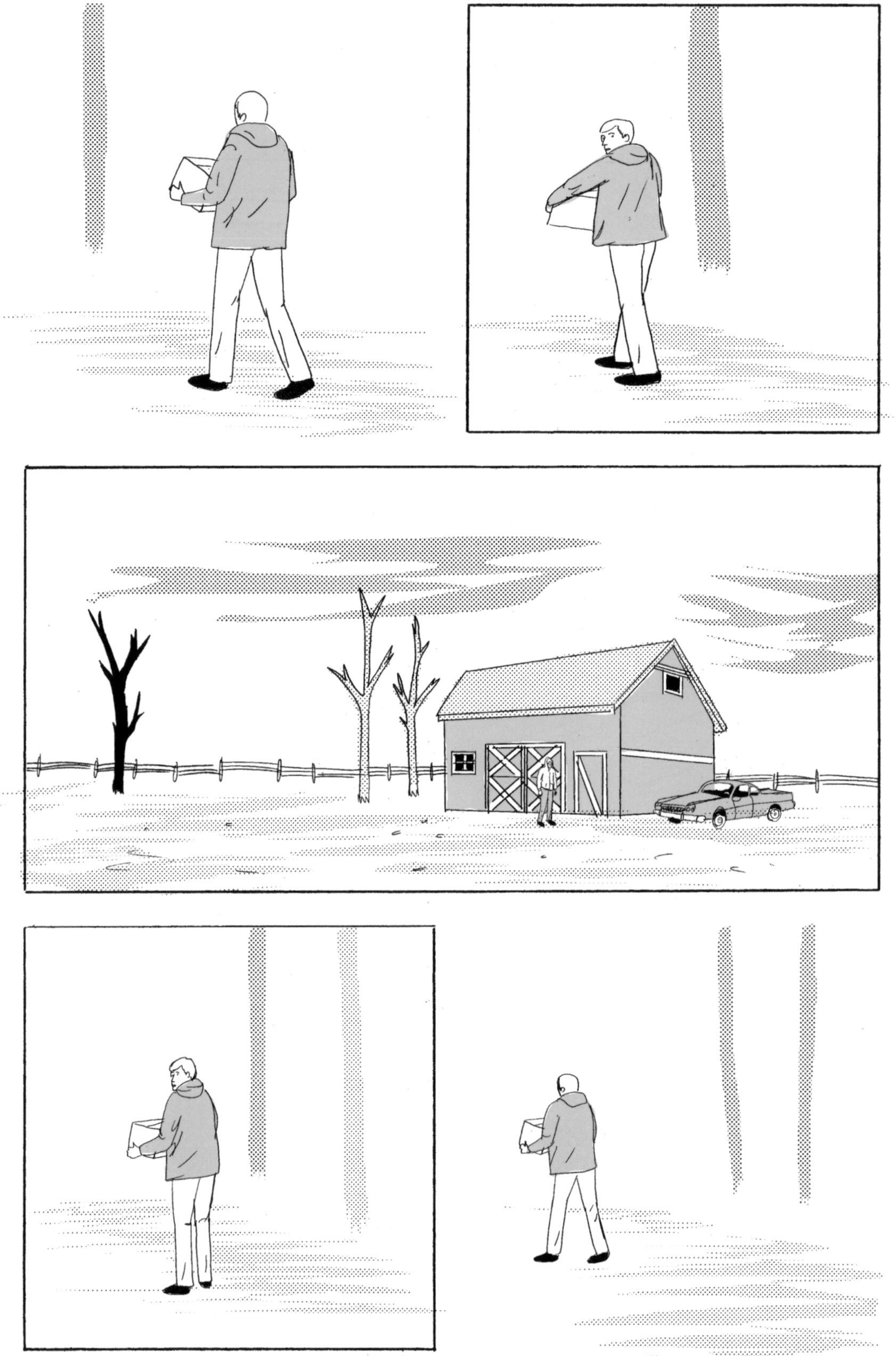

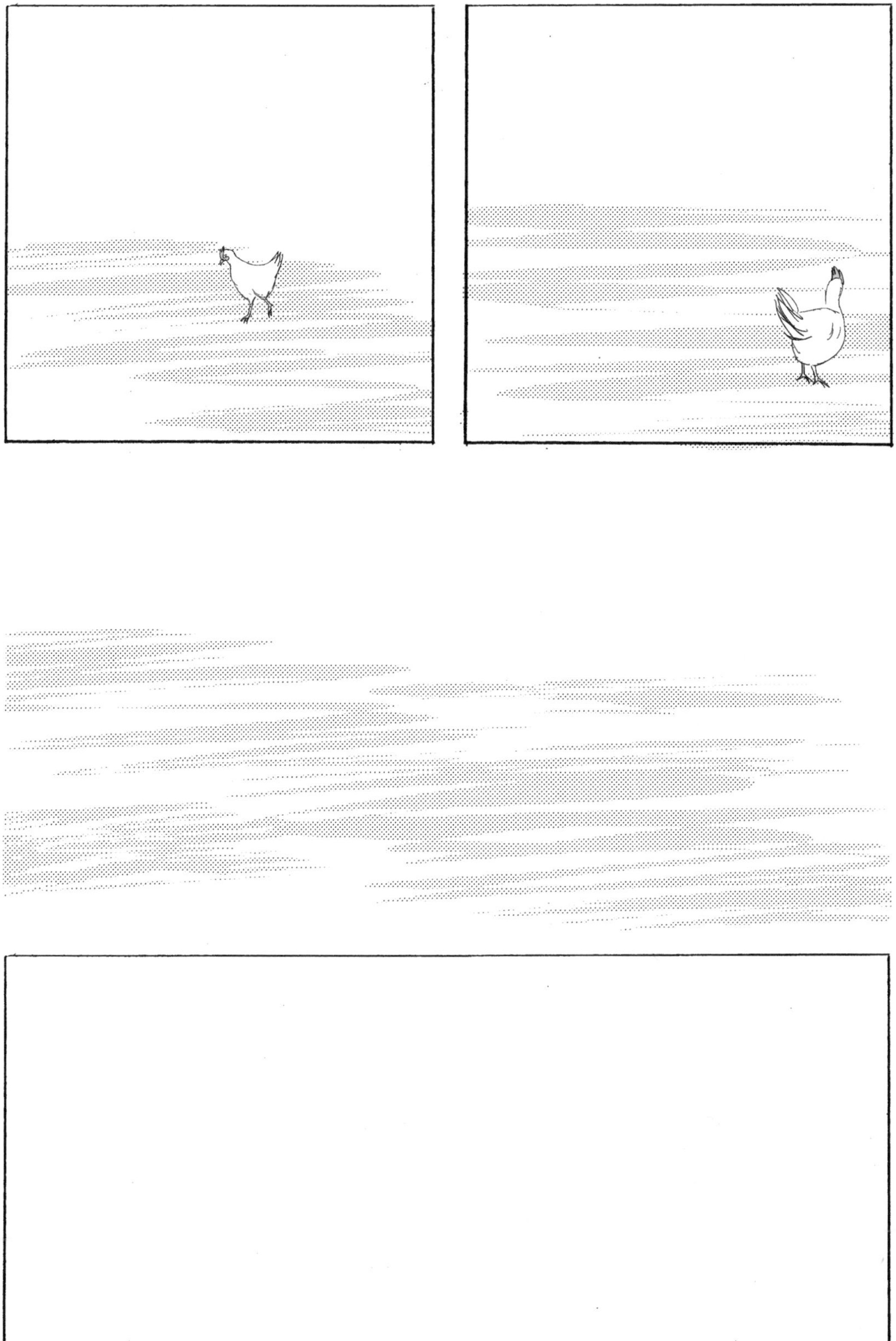

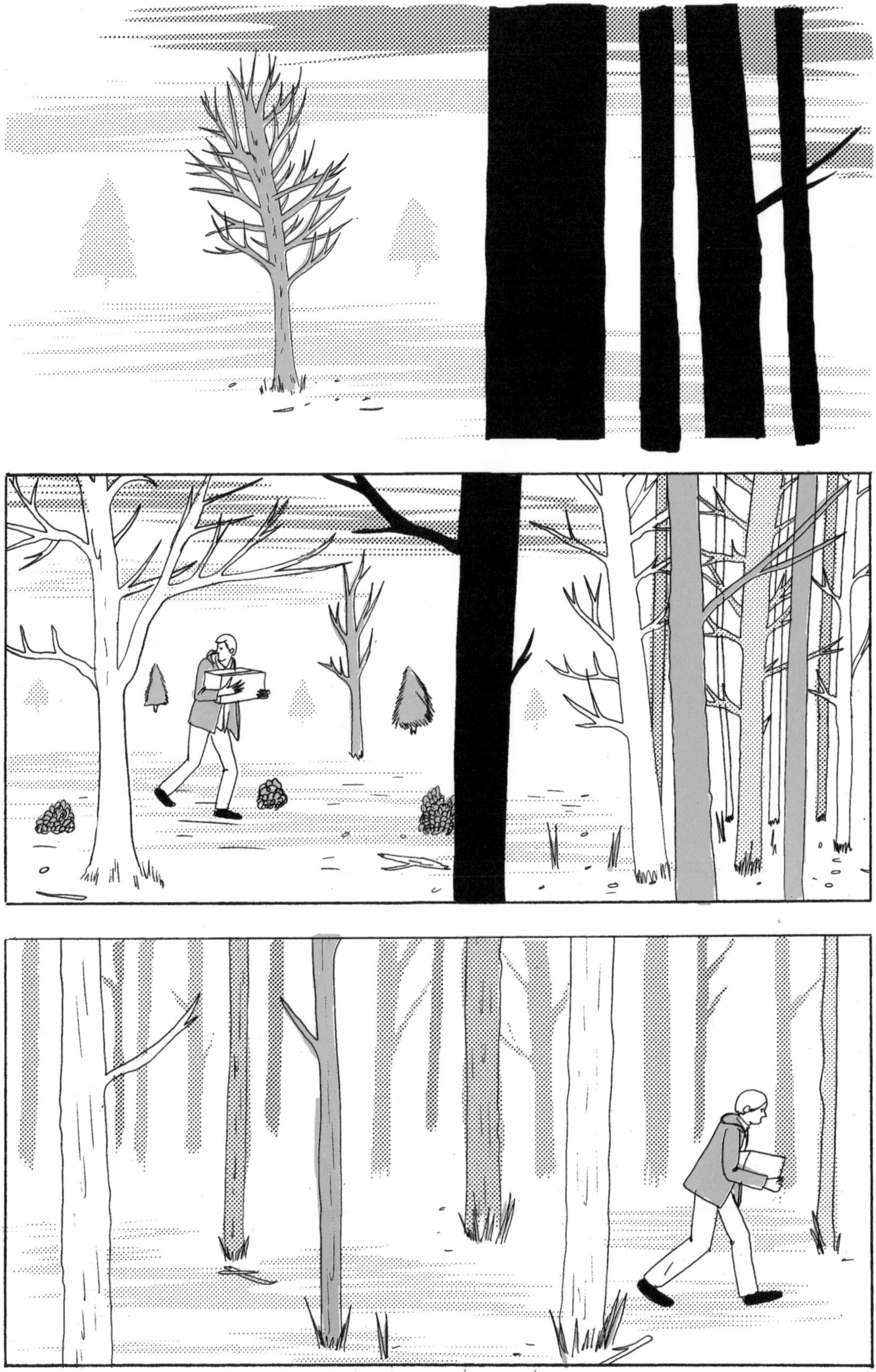

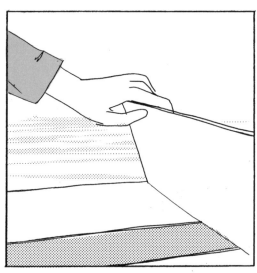
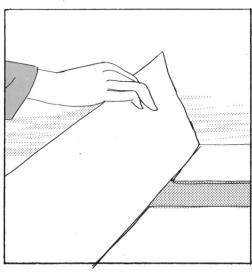

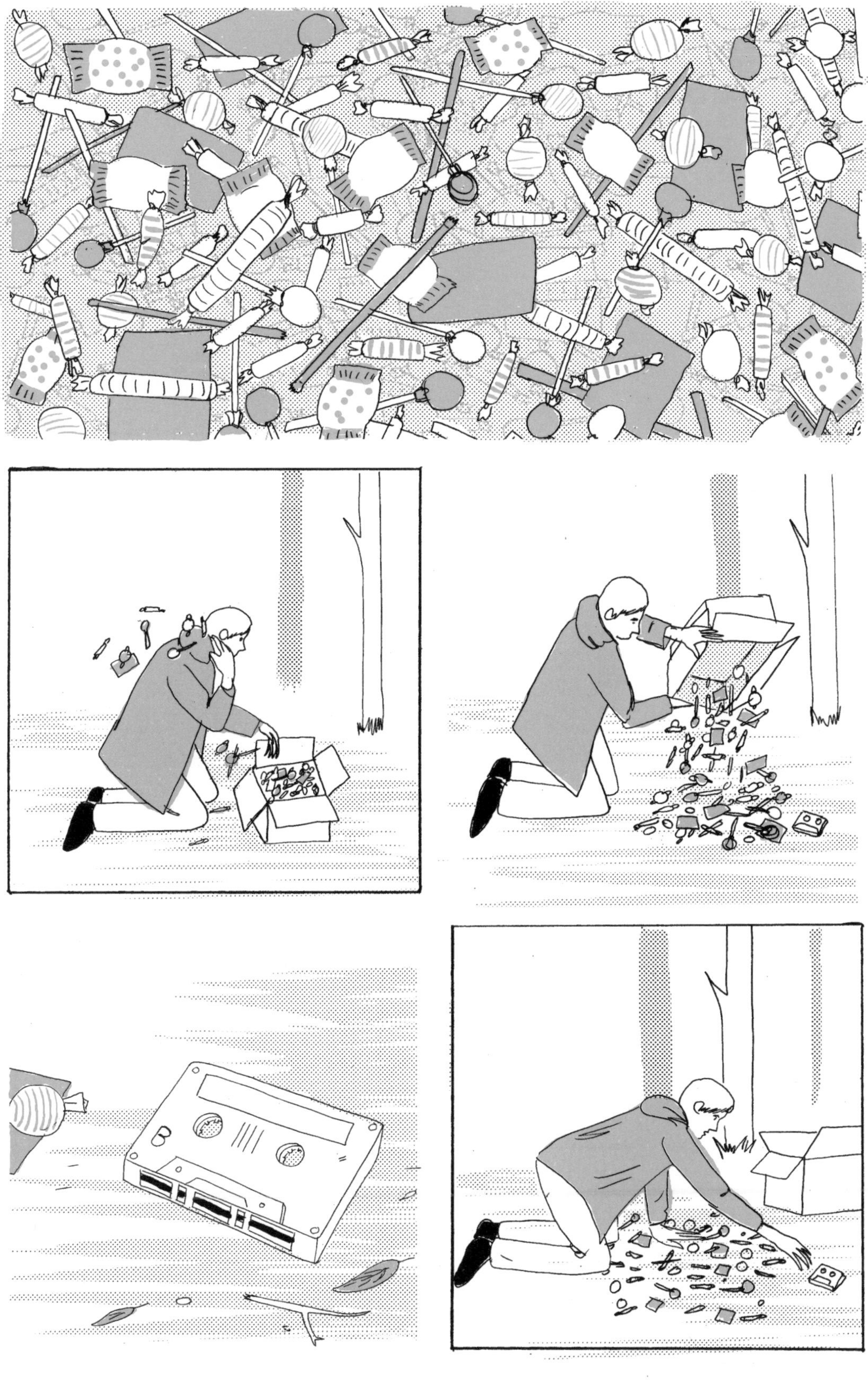
B

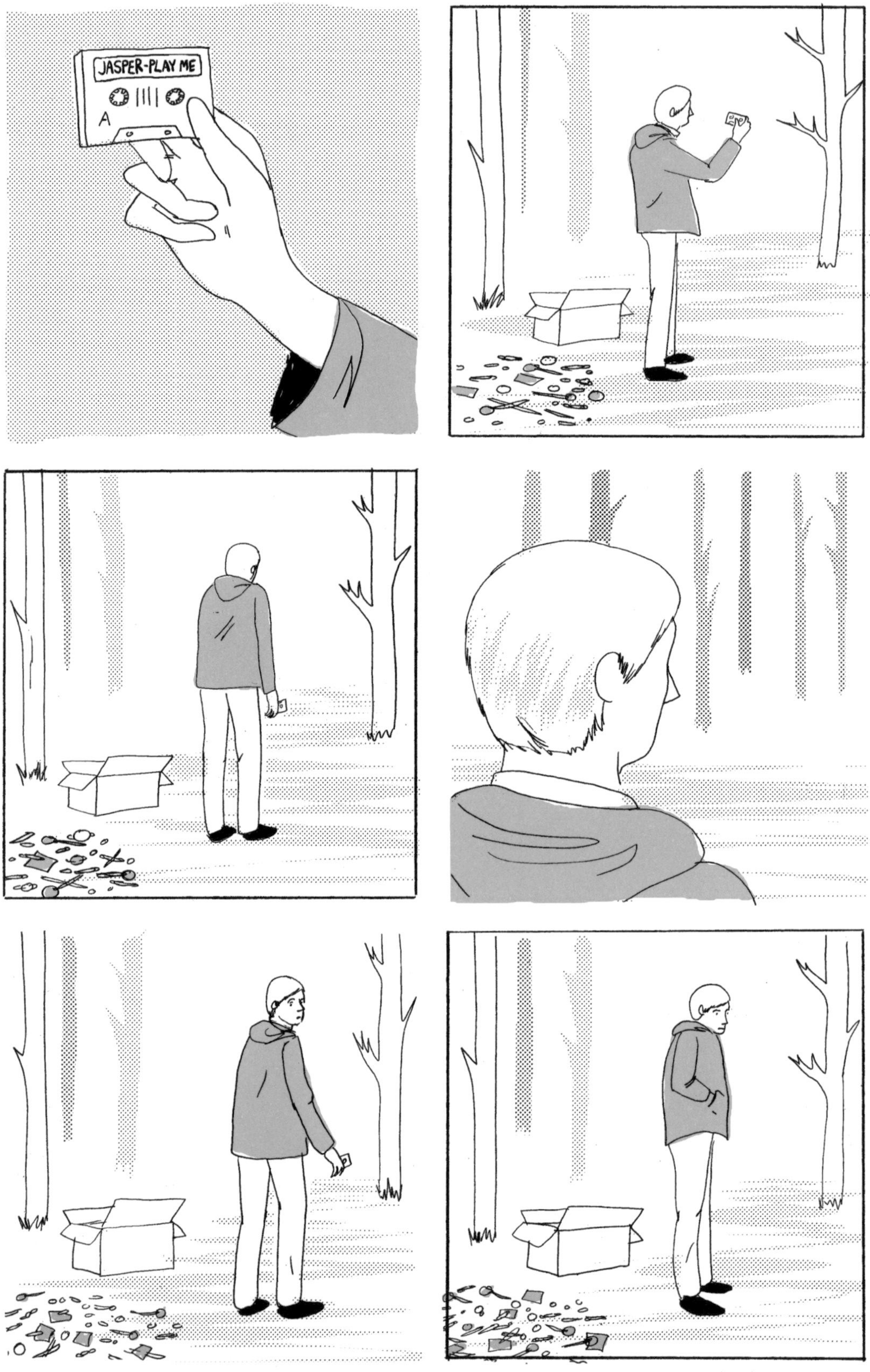
JASPER-PLAY ME
A

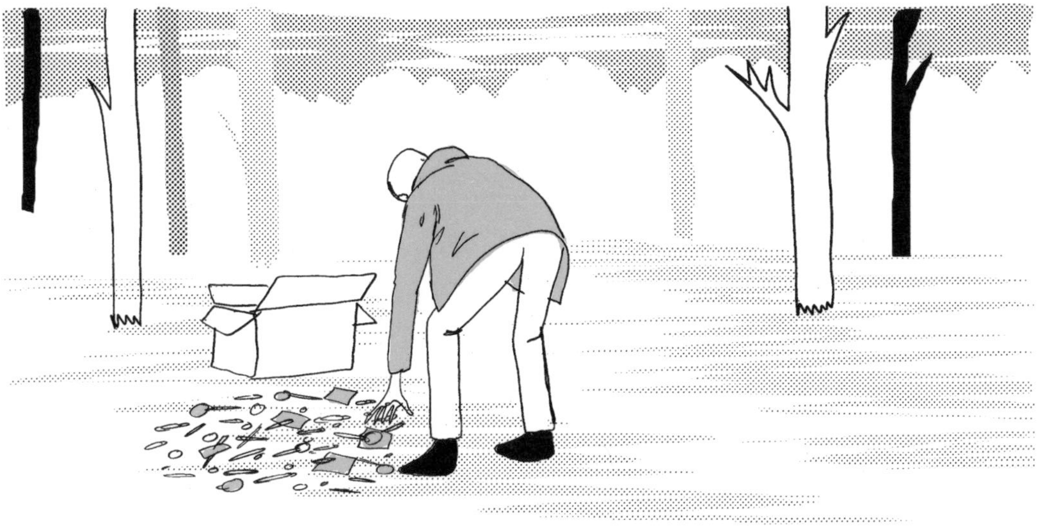
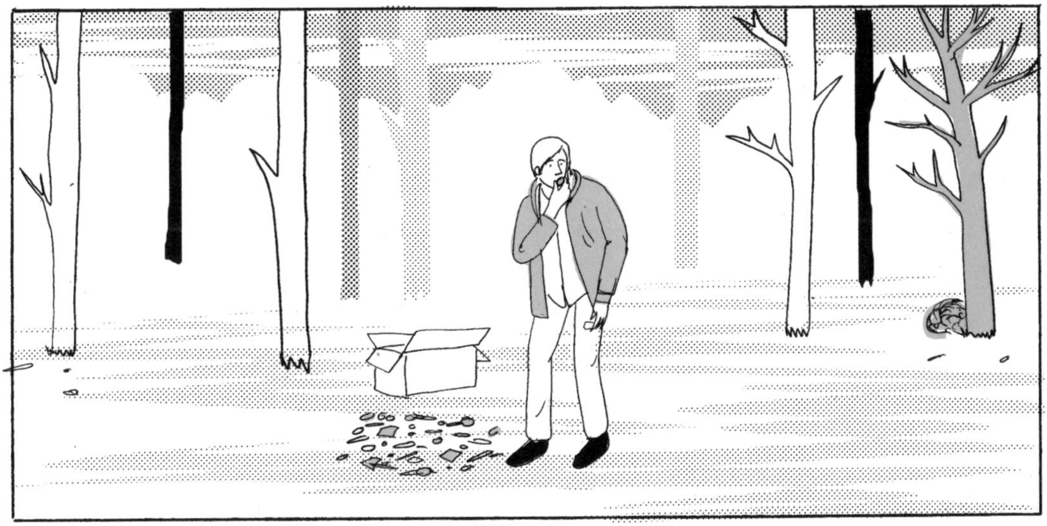
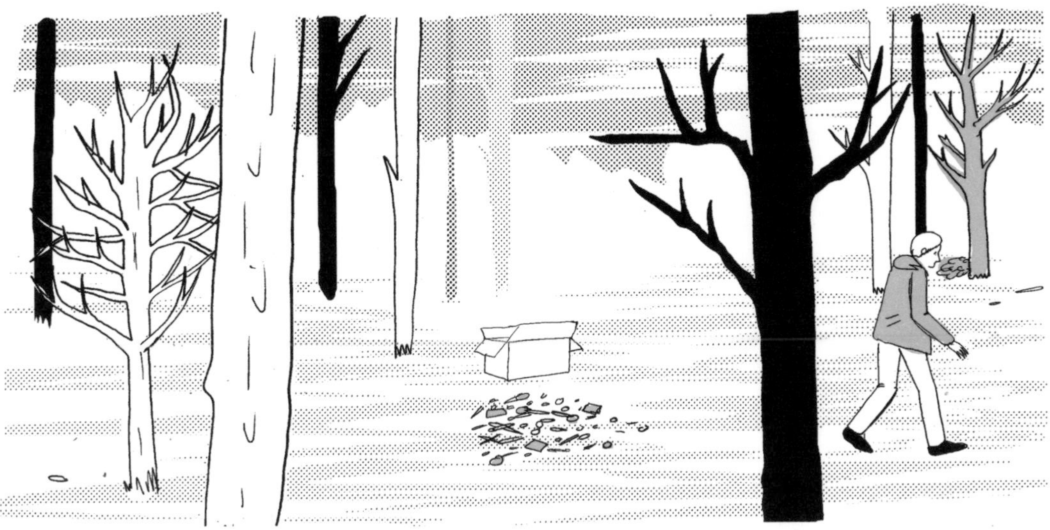

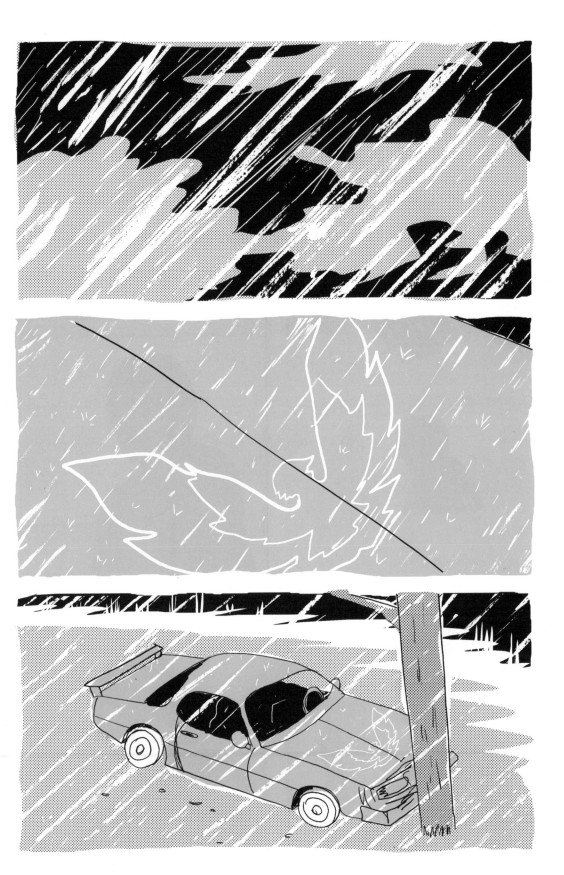

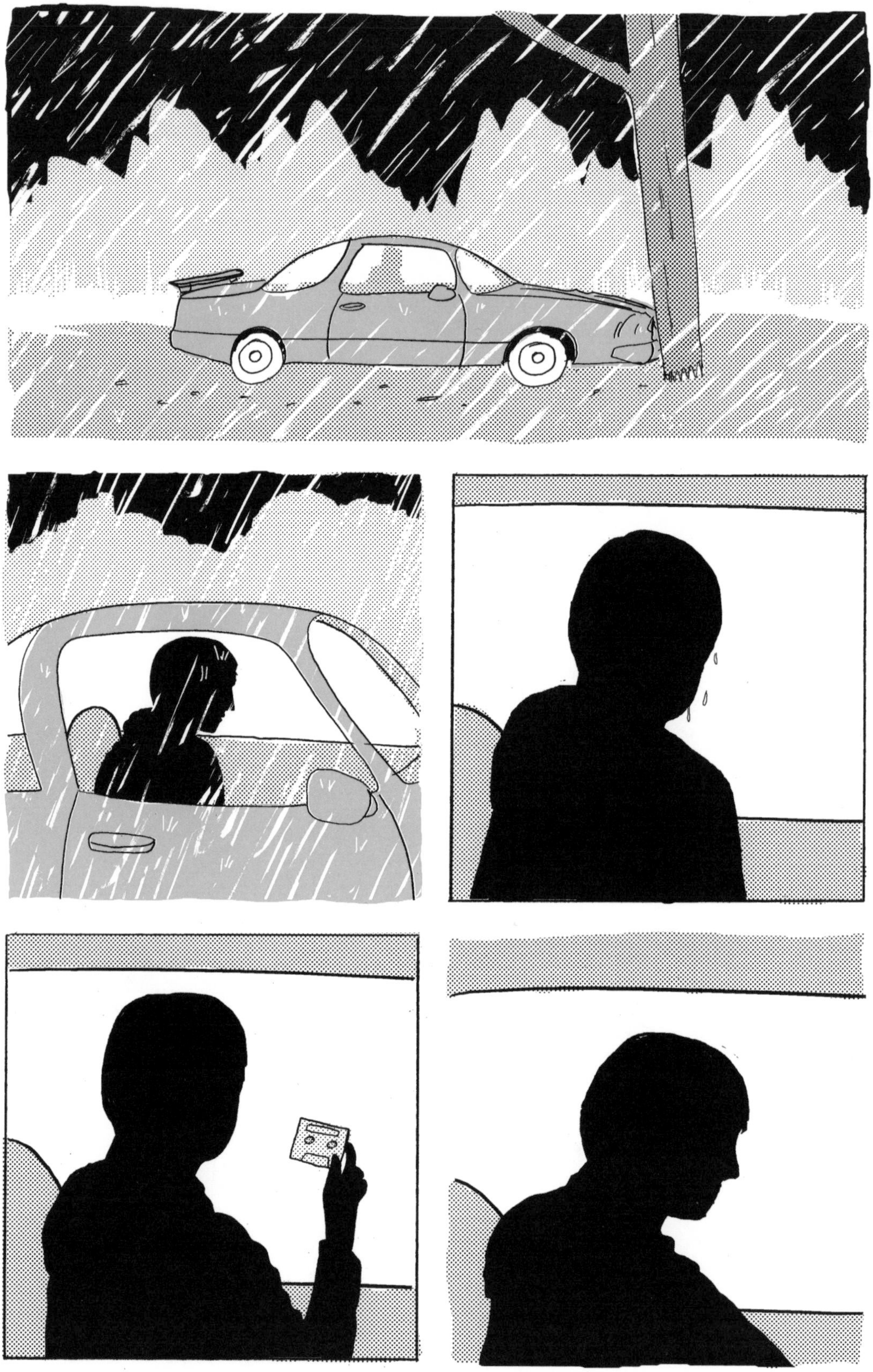

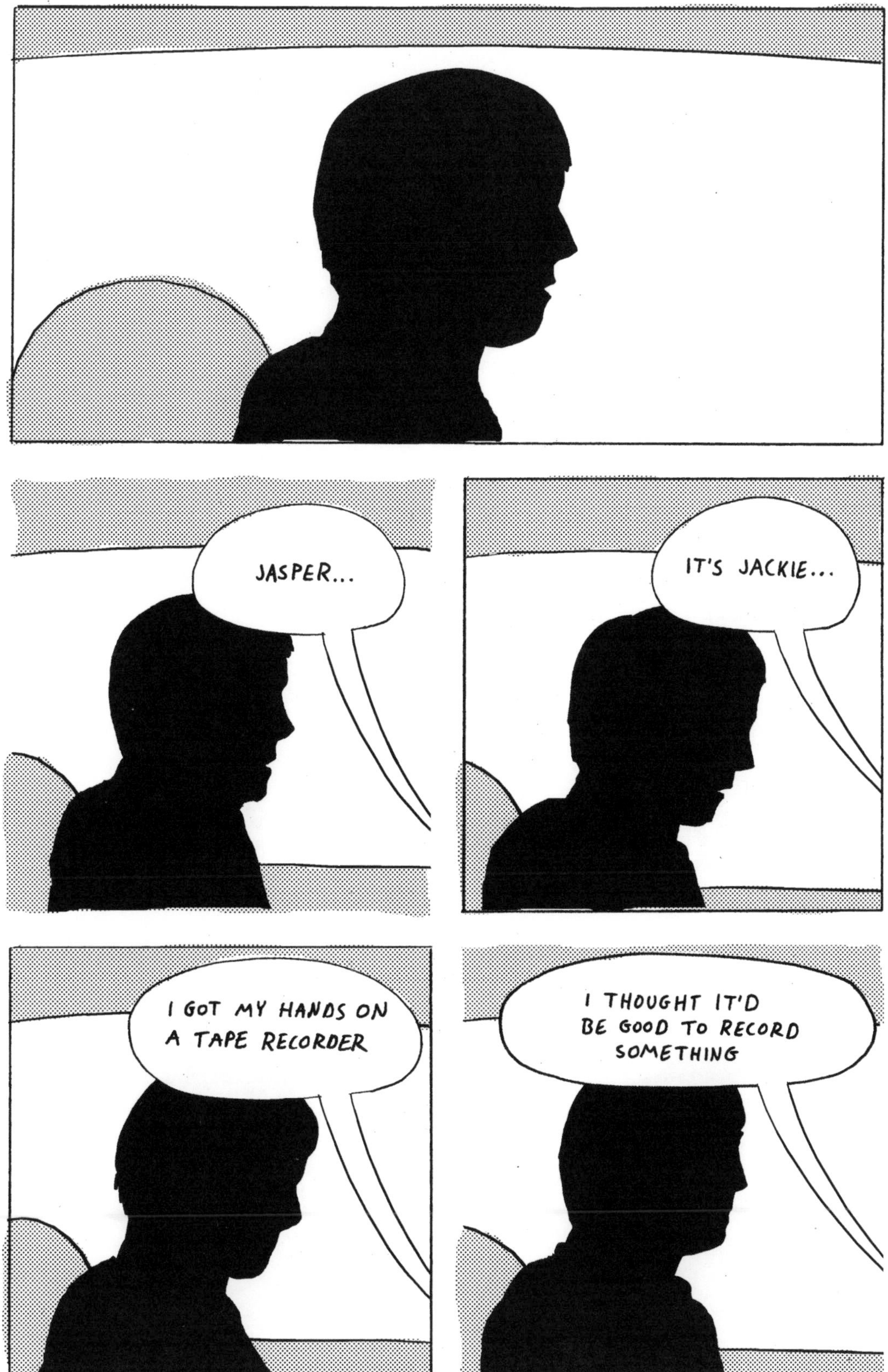
JASPER...
IT'S JACKIE...
I GOT MY HANDS ON A TAPE RECORDER
I THOUGHT IT'D BE GOOD TO RECORD SOMETHING

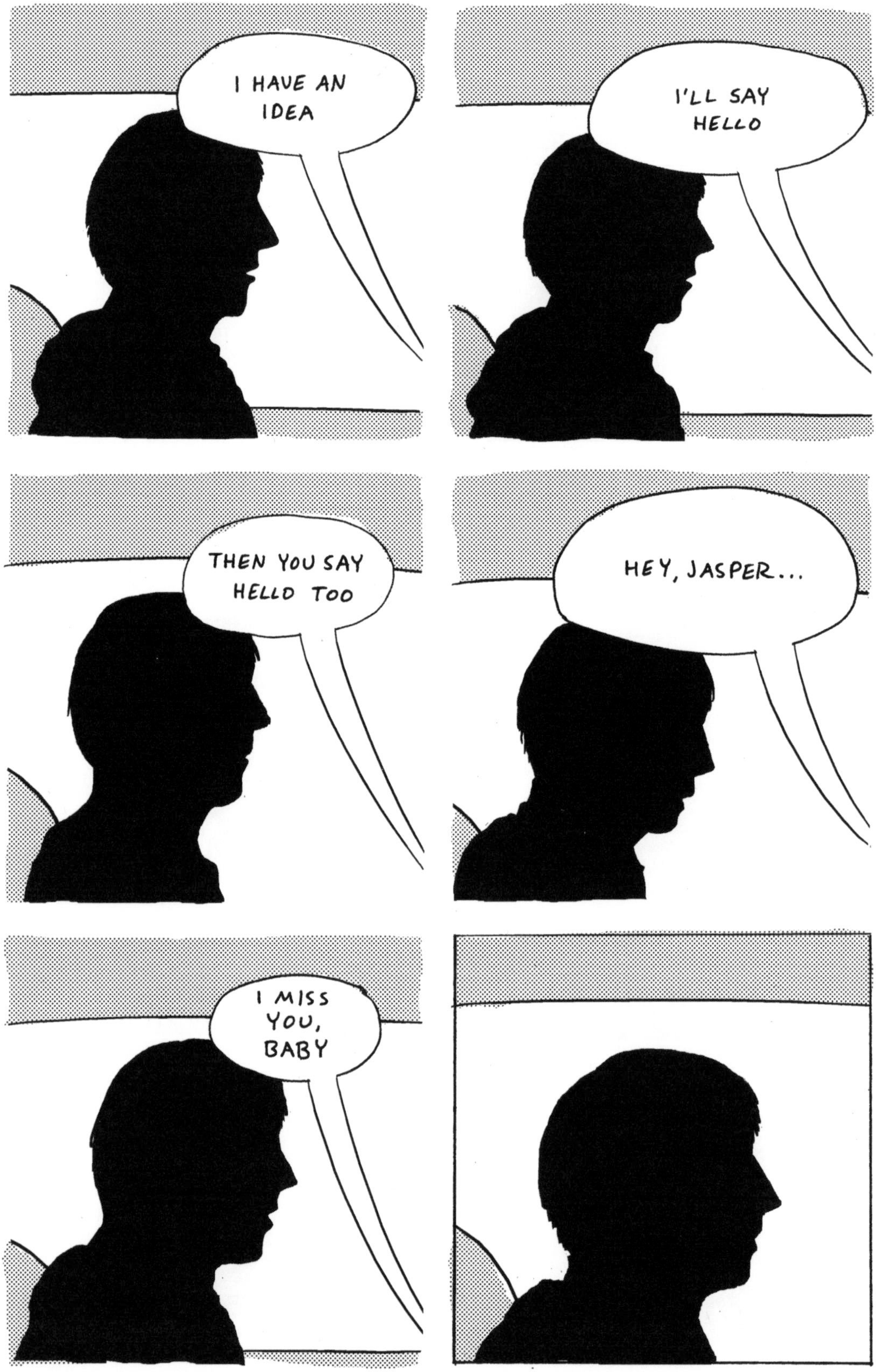
I HAVE AN IDEA
I'LL SAY HELLO
THEN YOU SAY HELLO TOO
HEY, JASPER...
I MISS YOU, BABY

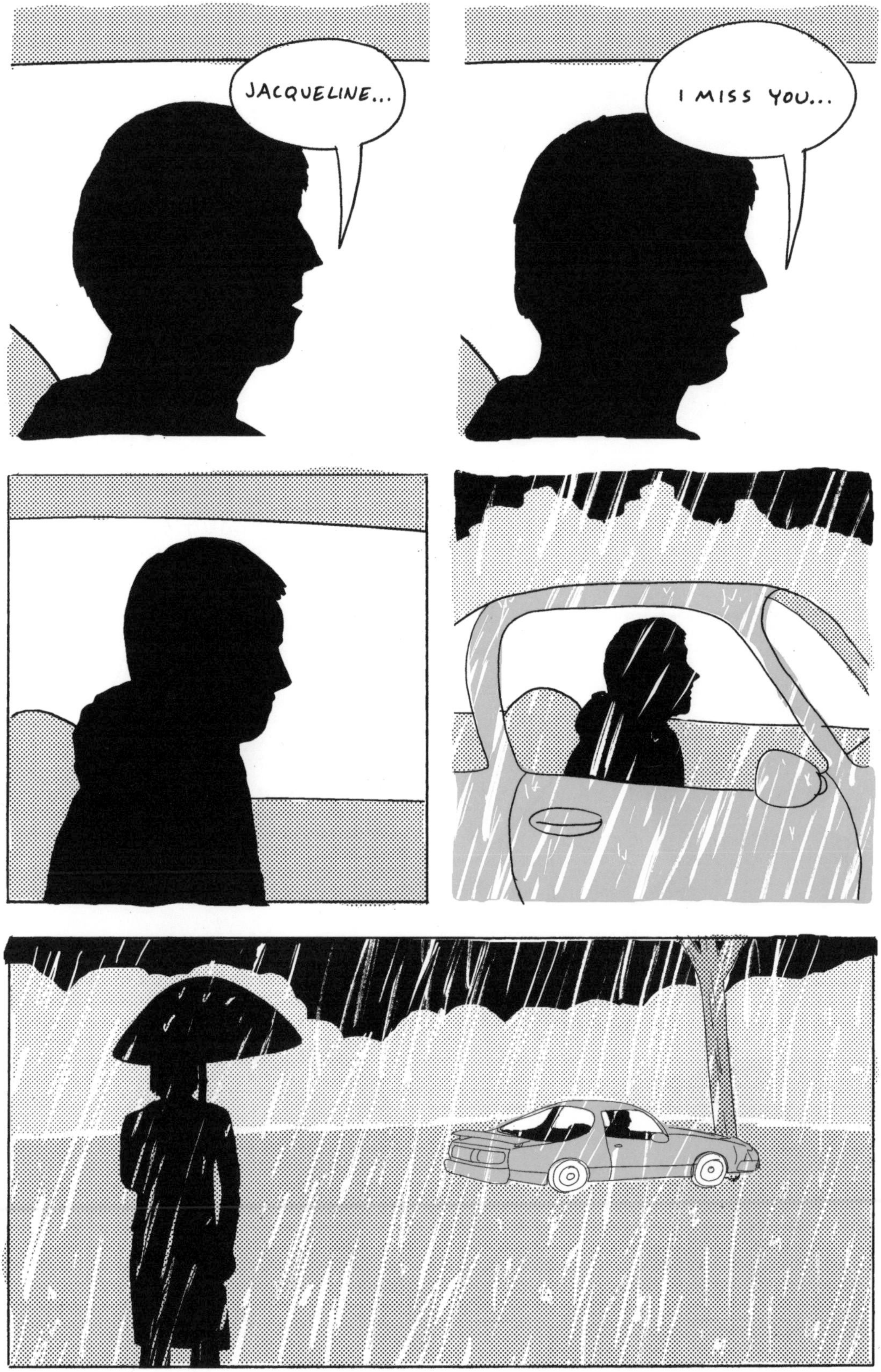
JACQUELINE...
I MISS YOU...

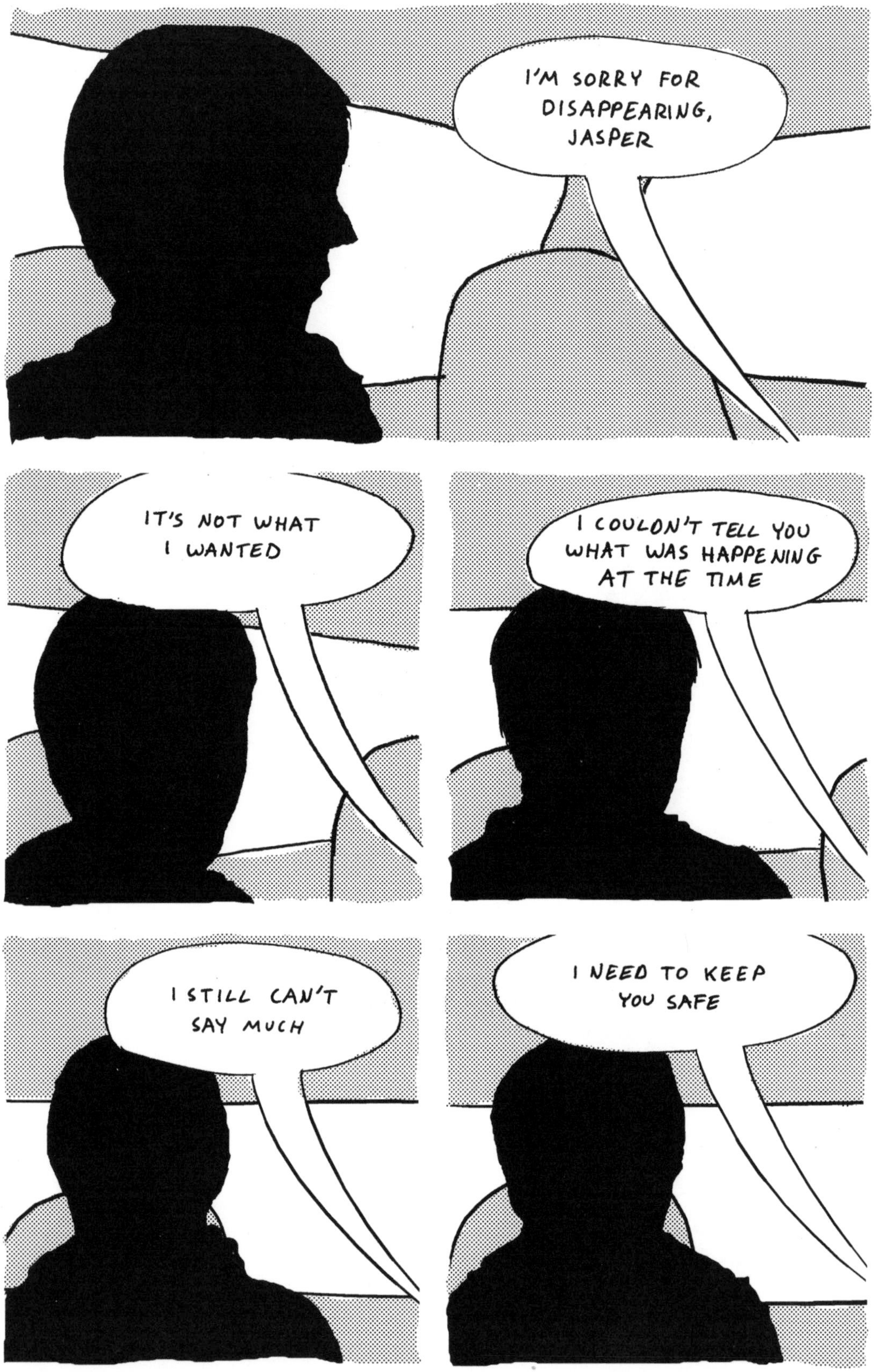
I'M SORRY FOR DISAPPEARING, JASPER
IT'S NOT WHAT I WANTED
I COULDN'T TELL YOU WHAT WAS HAPPENING AT THE TIME
I STILL CAN'T SAY MUCH
I NEED TO KEEP YOU SAFE

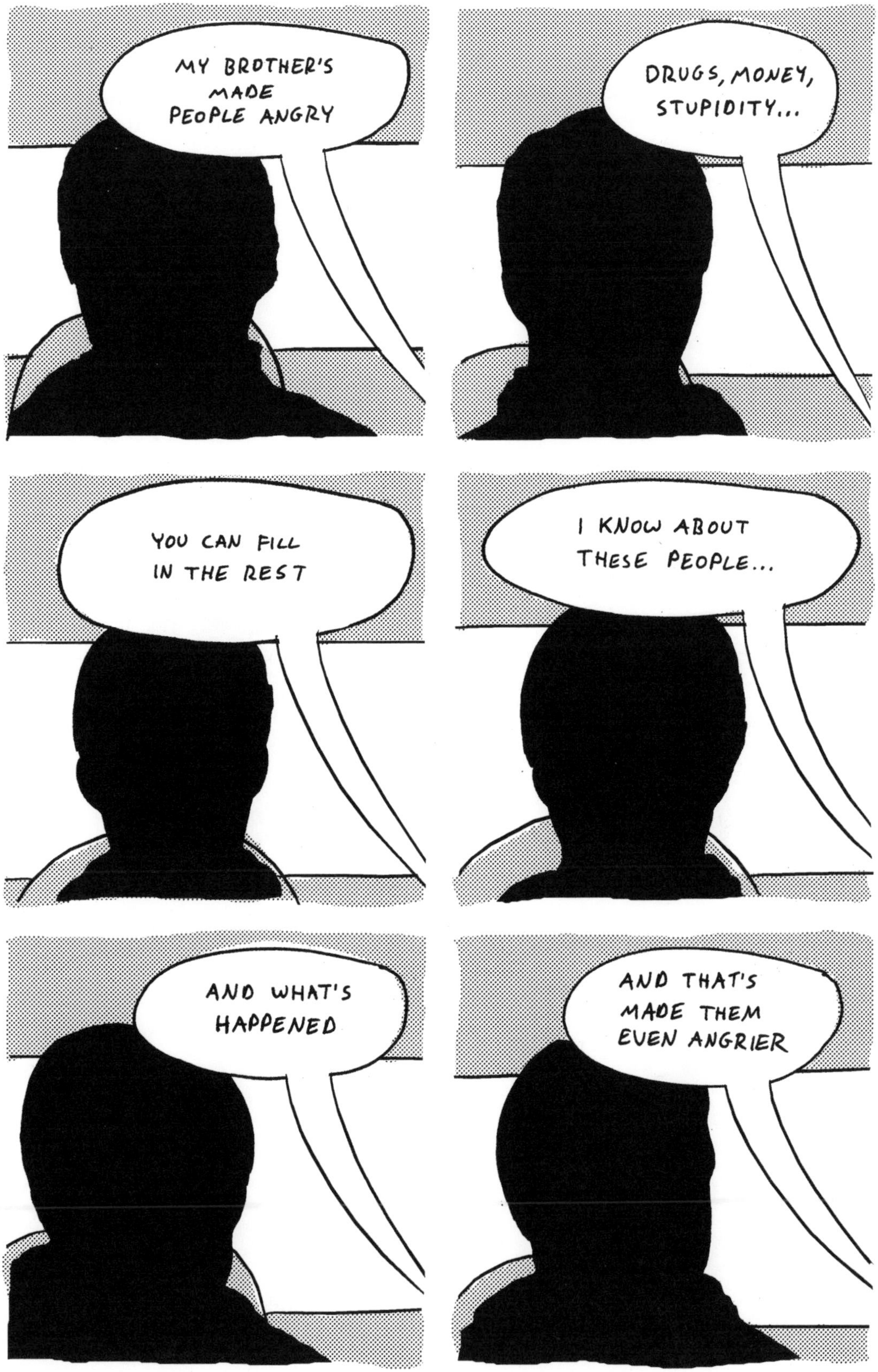
MY BROTHER'S MADE PEOPLE ANGRY
DRUGS, MONEY, STUPIDITY...
YOU CAN FILL IN THE REST
I KNOW ABOUT THESE PEOPLE...
AND WHAT'S HAPPENED
AND THAT'S MADE THEM EVEN ANGRIER

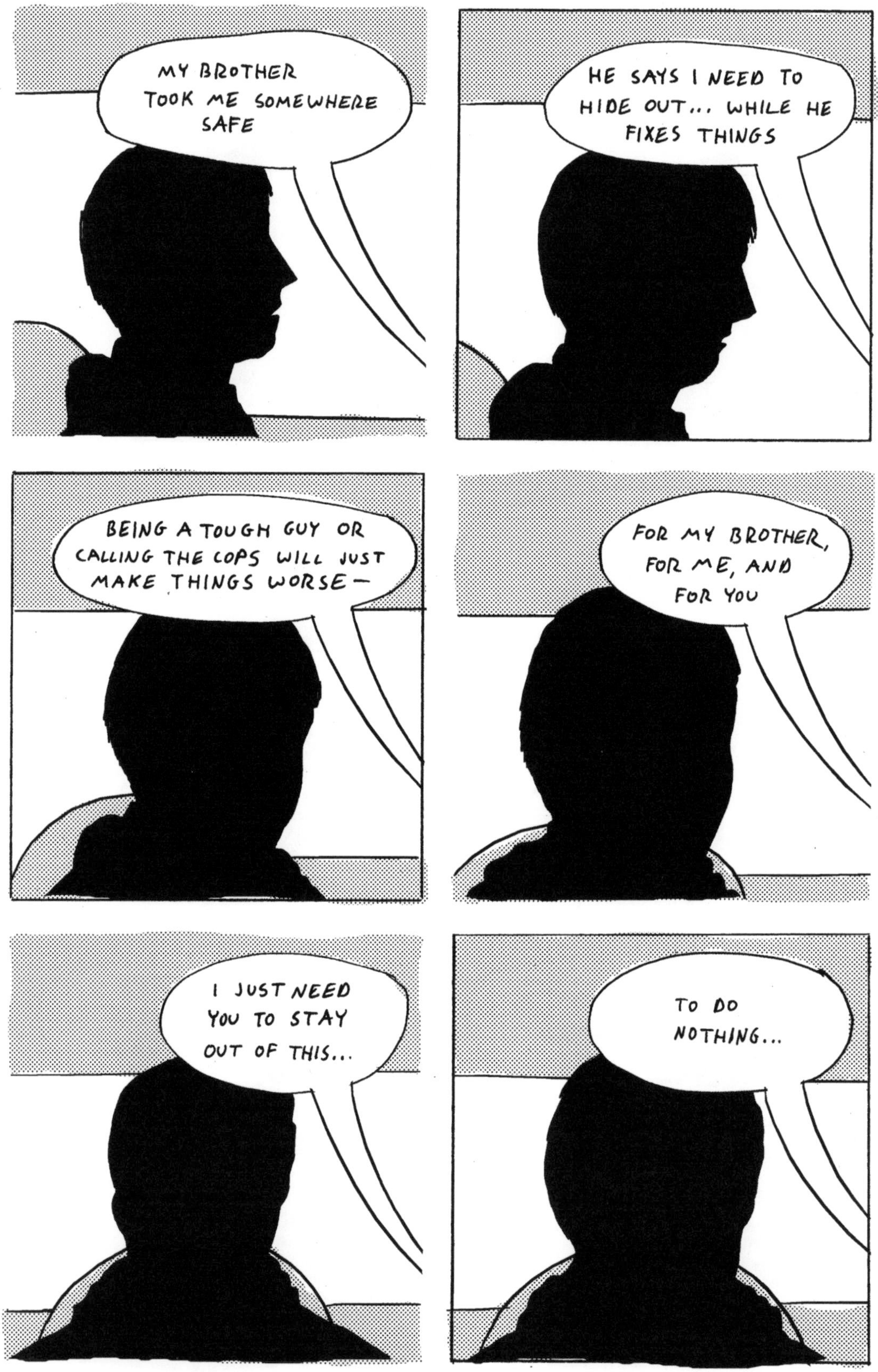
MY BROTHER TOOK ME SOMEWHERE SAFE
HE SAYS I NEED TO HIDE OUT... WHILE HE FIXES THINGS
BEING A TOUGH GUY OR CALLING THE COPS WILL JUST MAKE THINGS WORSE—
FOR MY BROTHER, FOR ME, AND FOR YOU
I JUST NEED YOU TO STAY OUT OF THIS...
TO DO NOTHING...

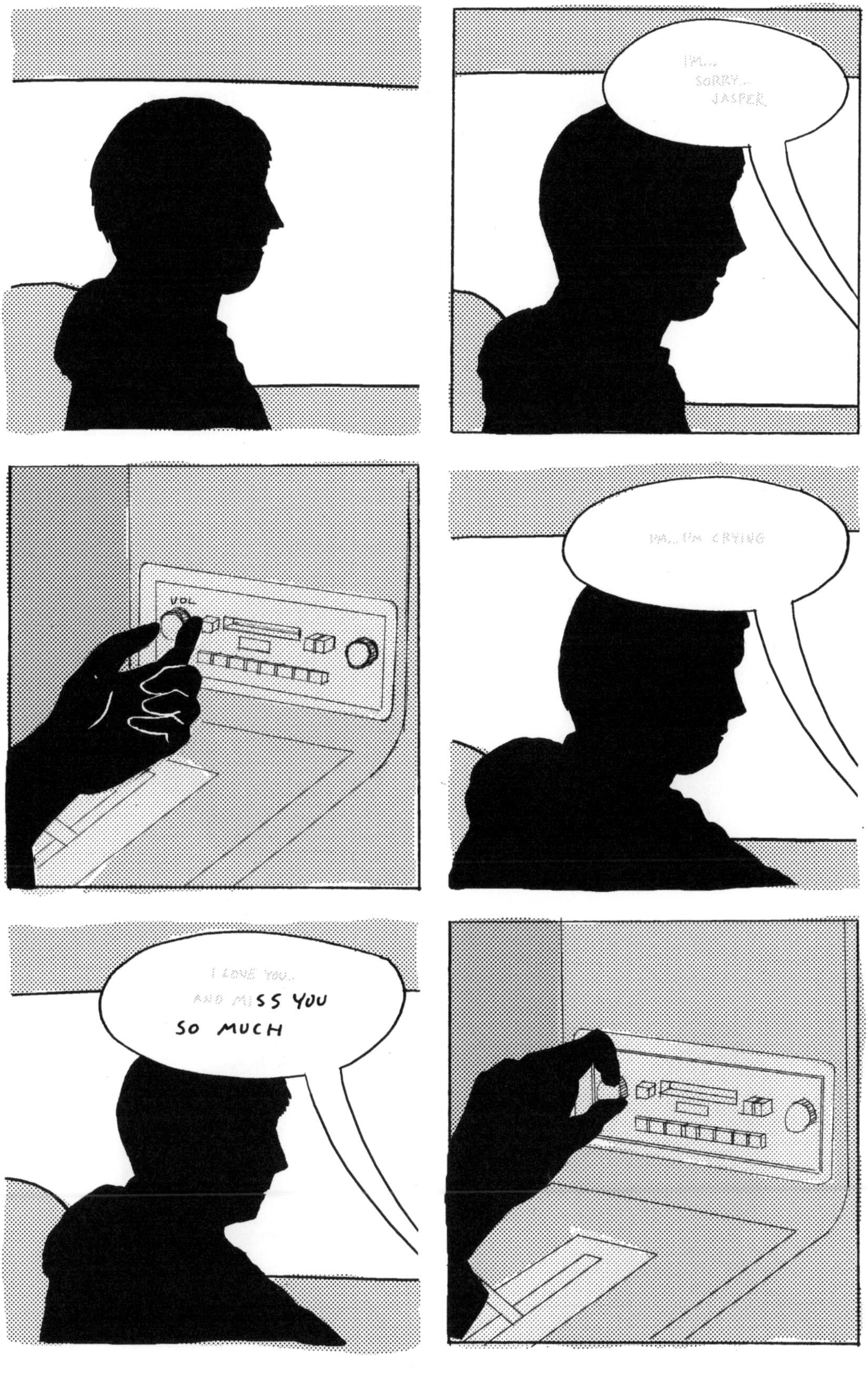
I'M...
SORRY...
JASPER
VOL
I'M...I'M CRYING
I LOVE YOU...
AND MISS YOU
SO MUCH

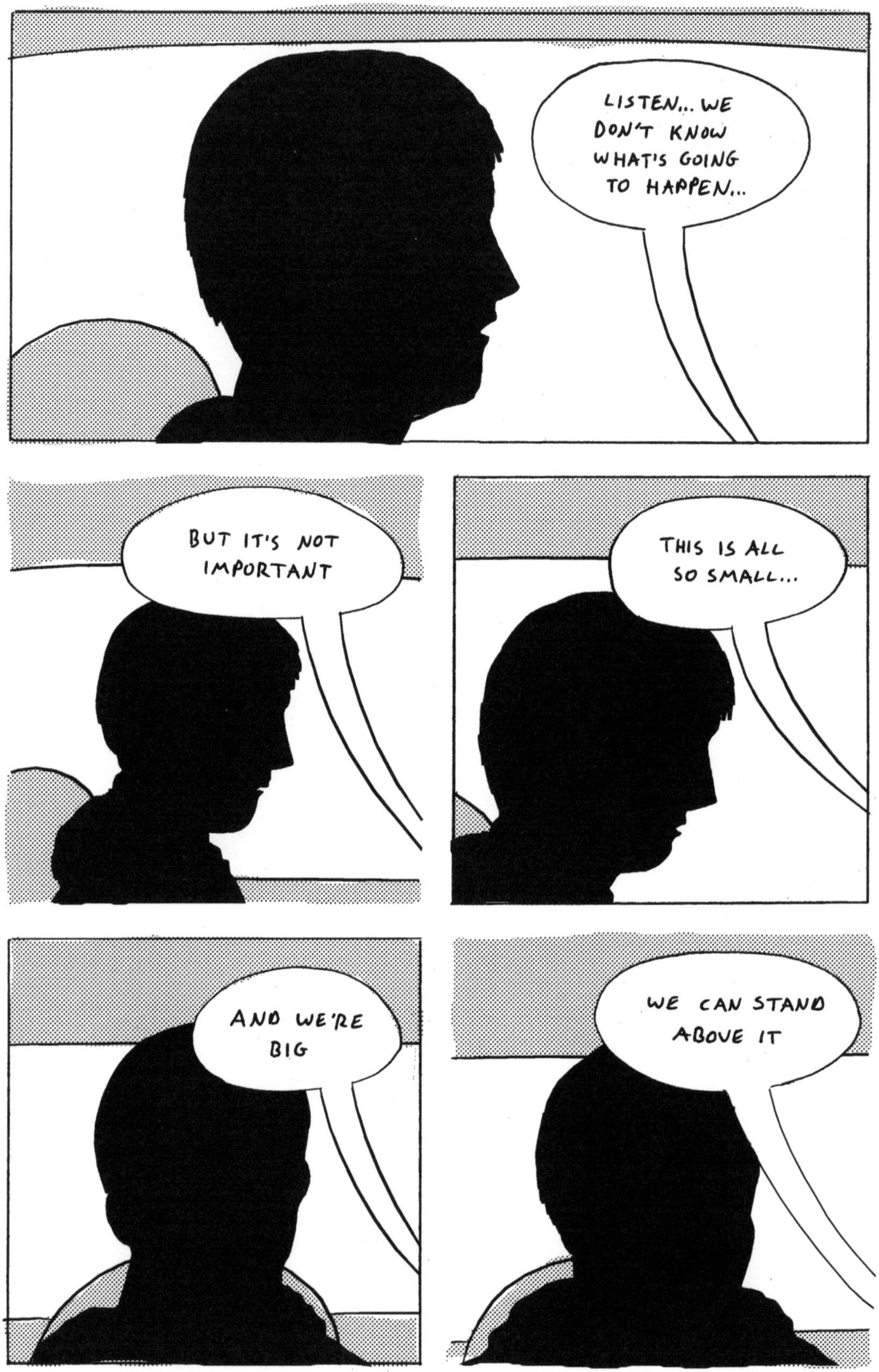
LISTEN... WE DON'T KNOW WHAT'S GOING TO HAPPEN...
BUT IT'S NOT IMPORTANT
THIS IS ALL SO SMALL...
AND WE'RE BIG
WE CAN STAND ABOVE IT

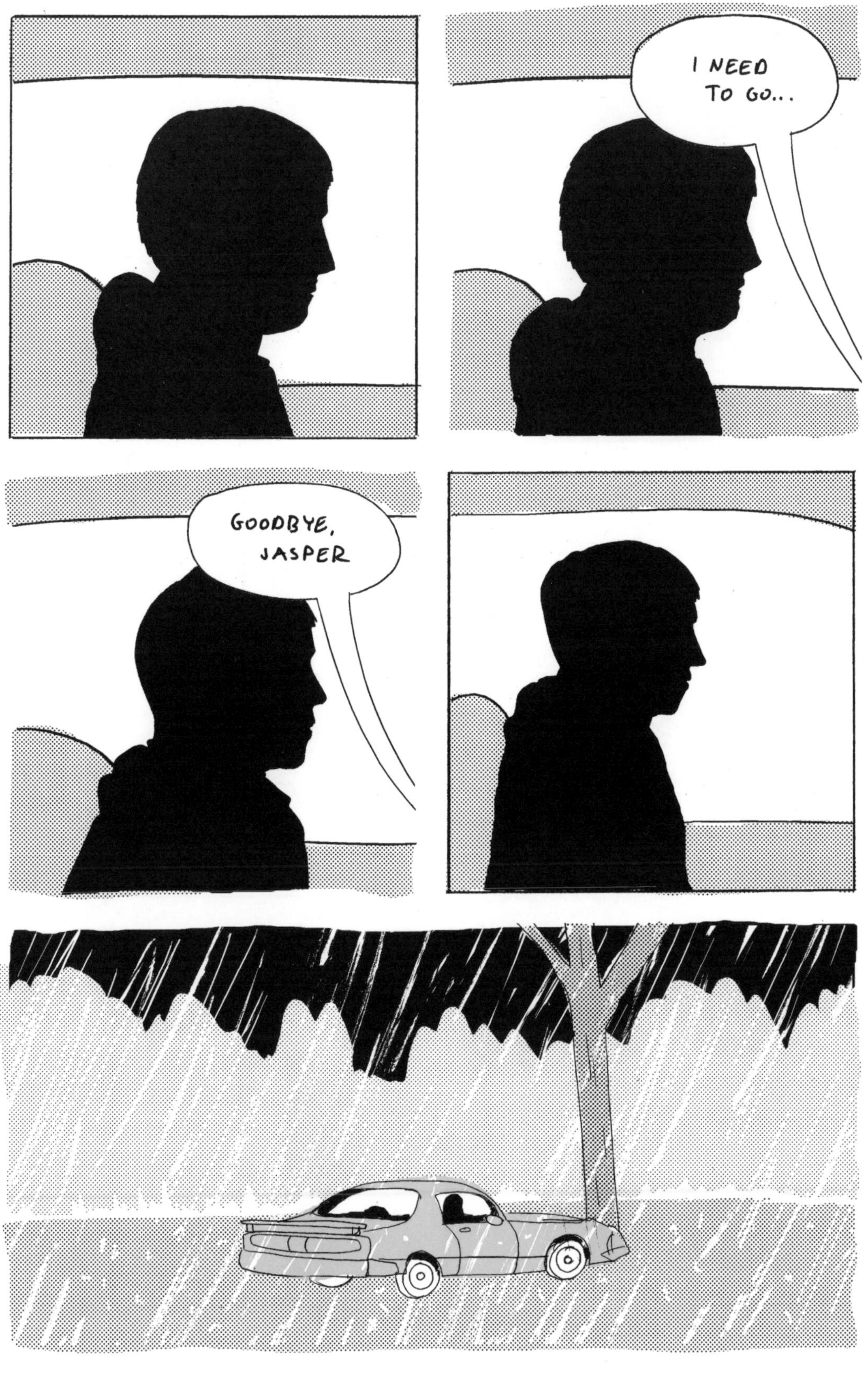
I NEED TO GO...
GOODBYE, JASPER

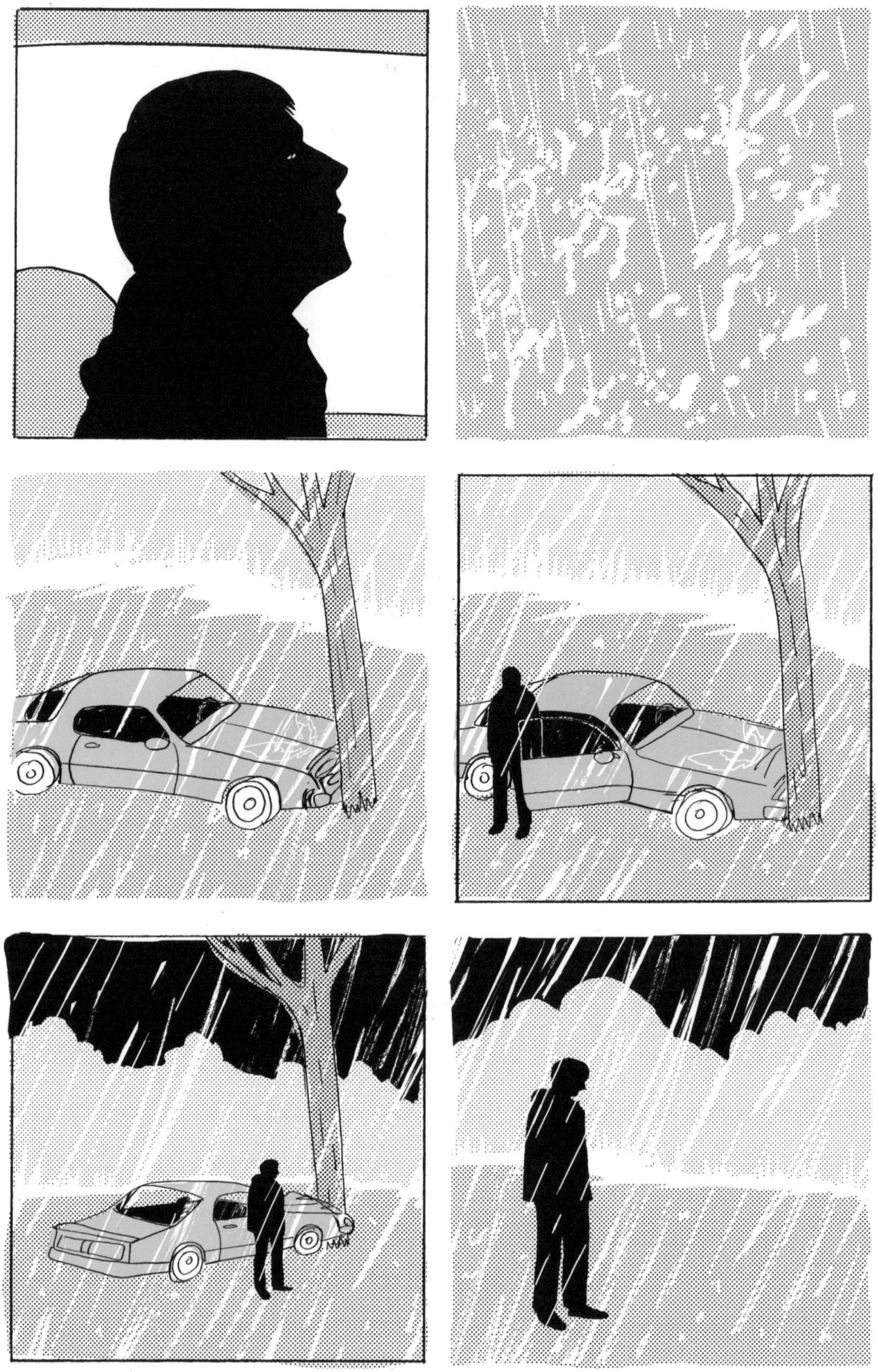

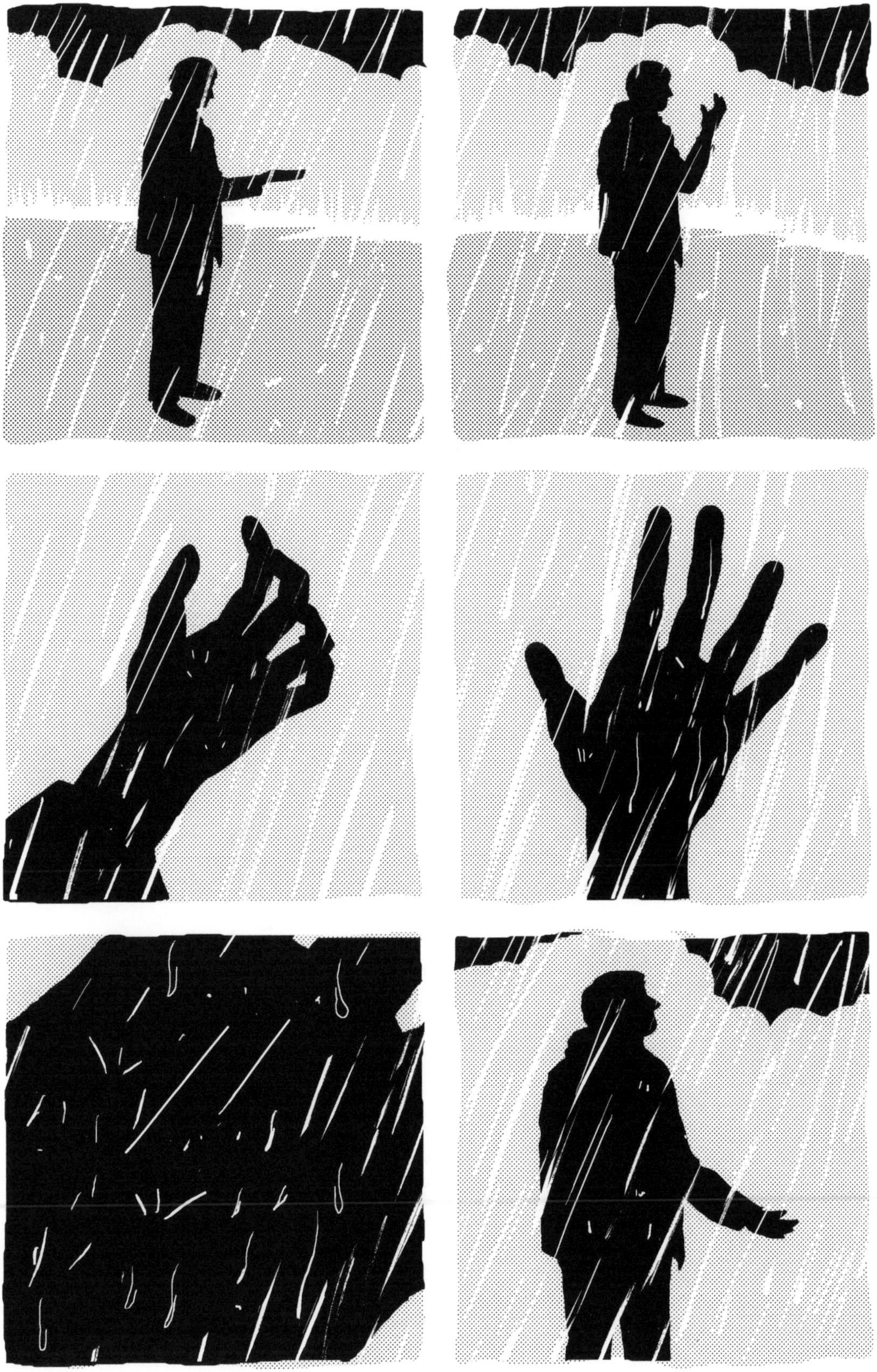

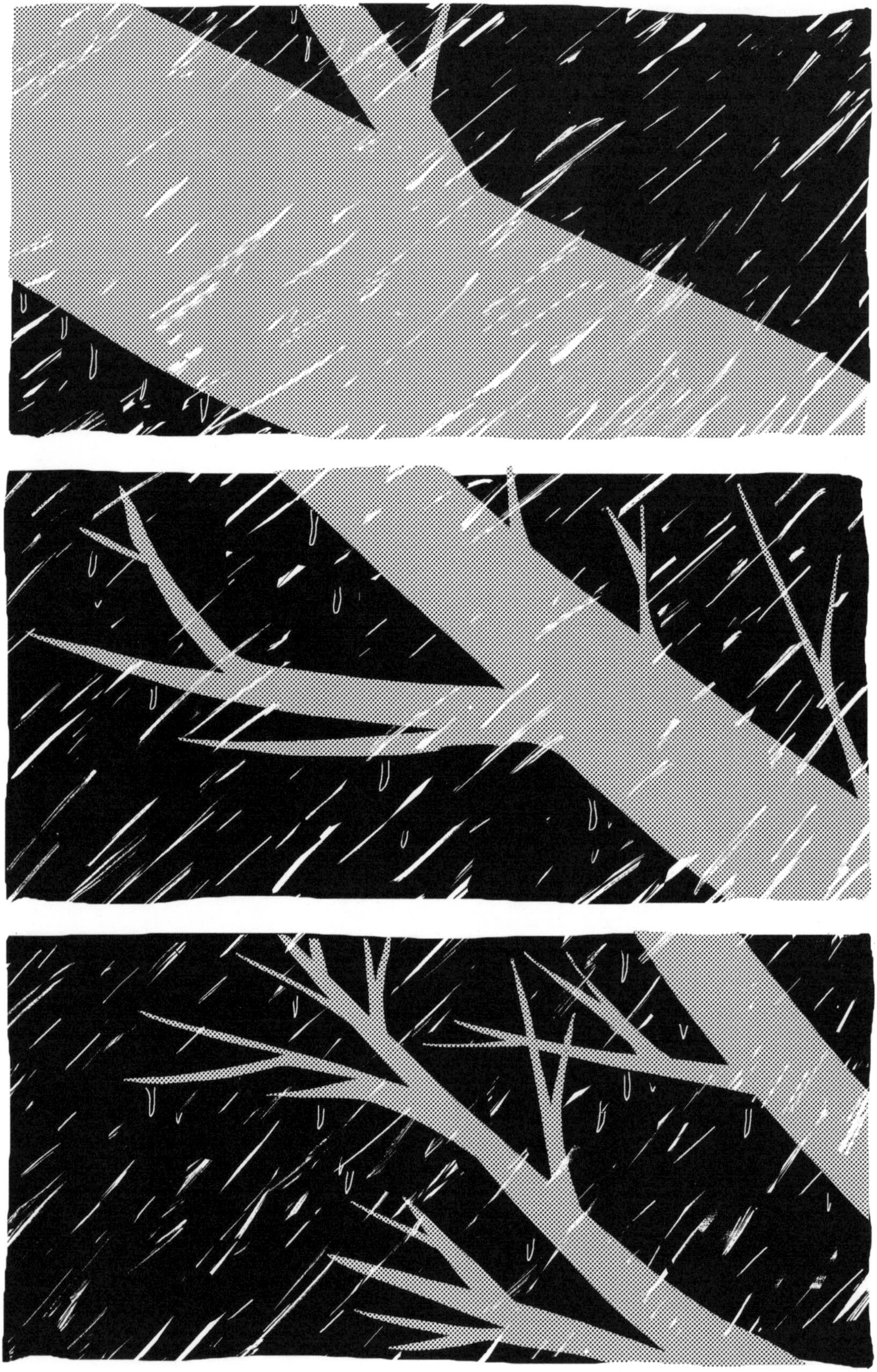

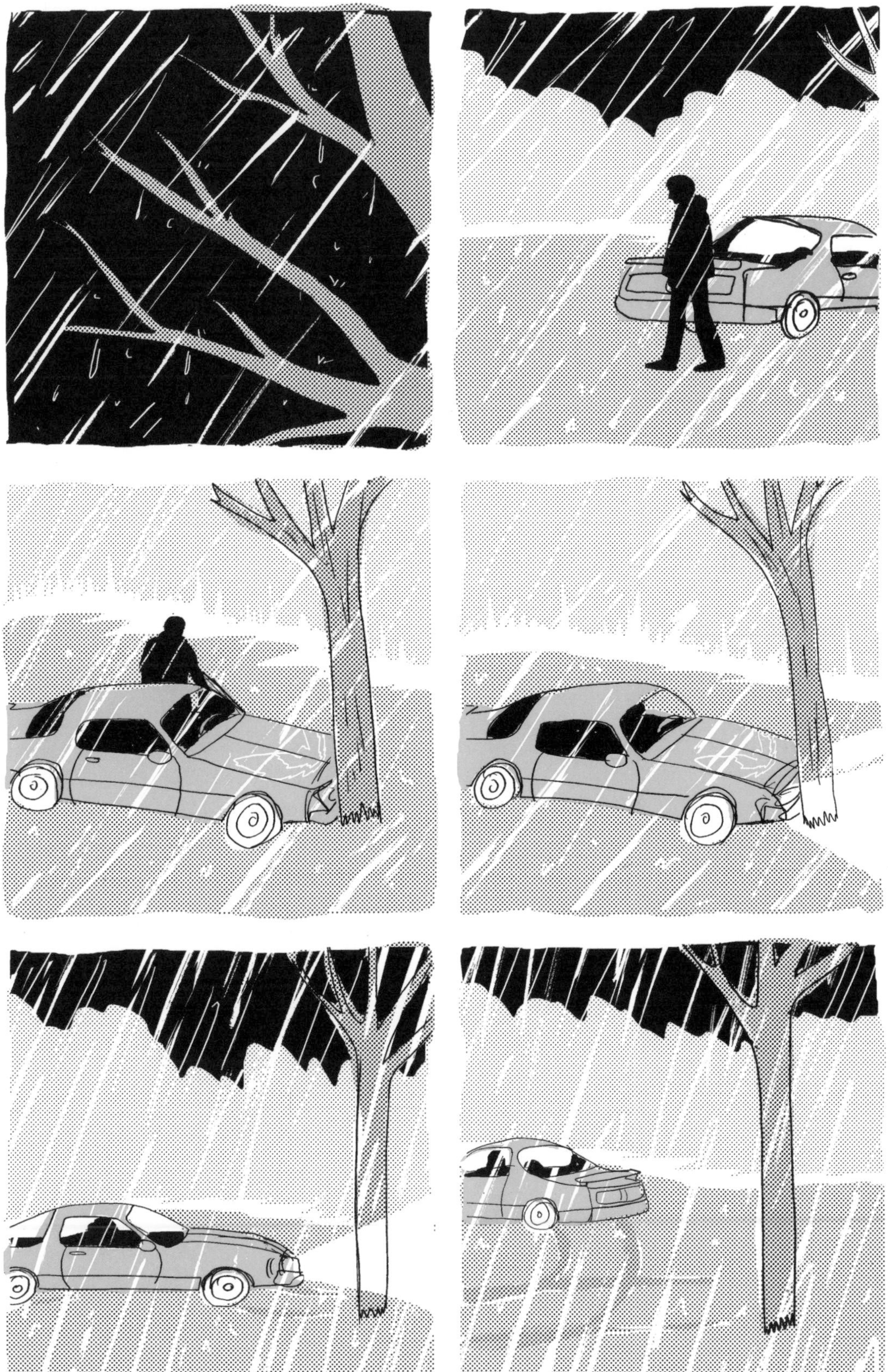

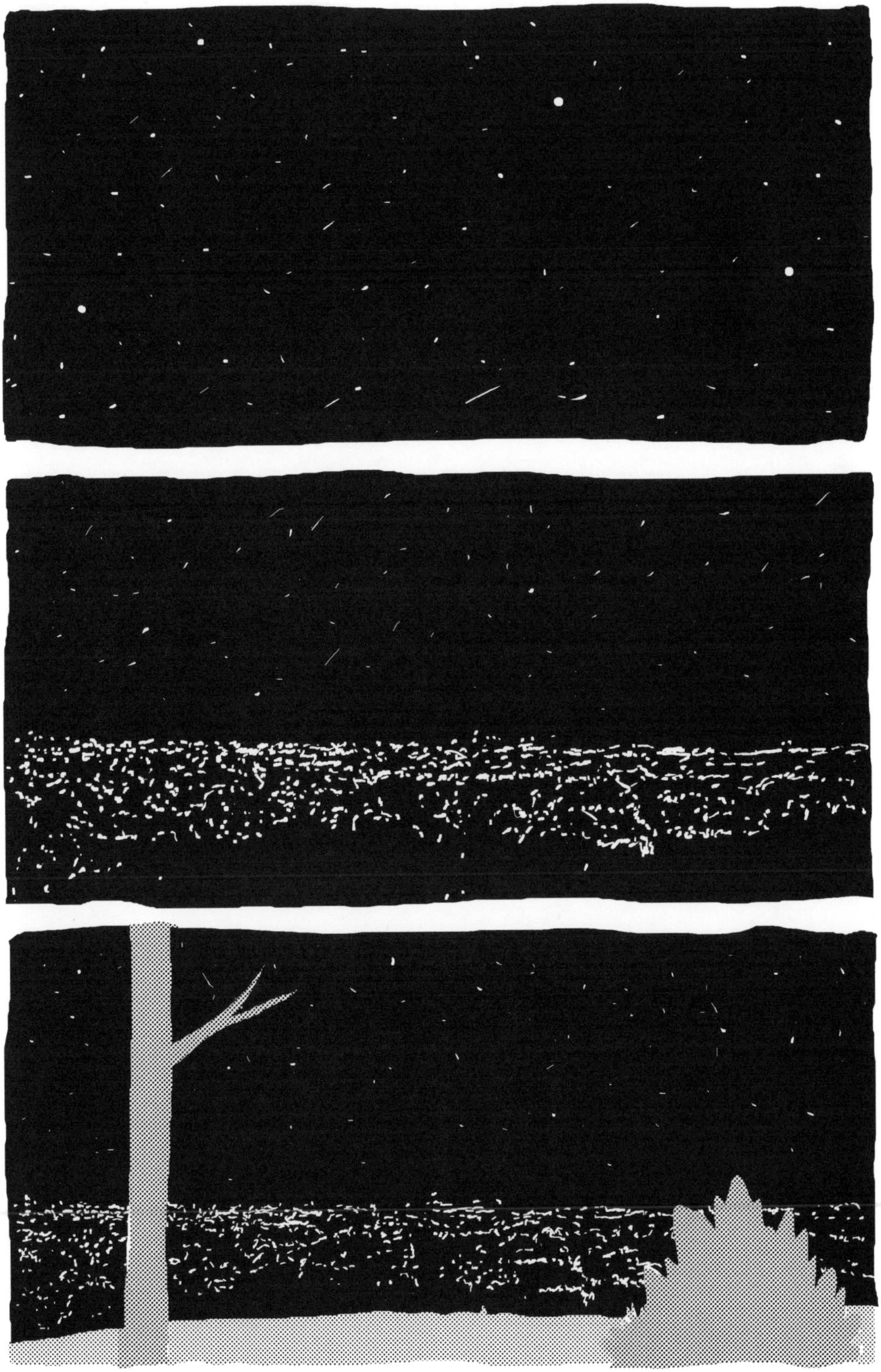

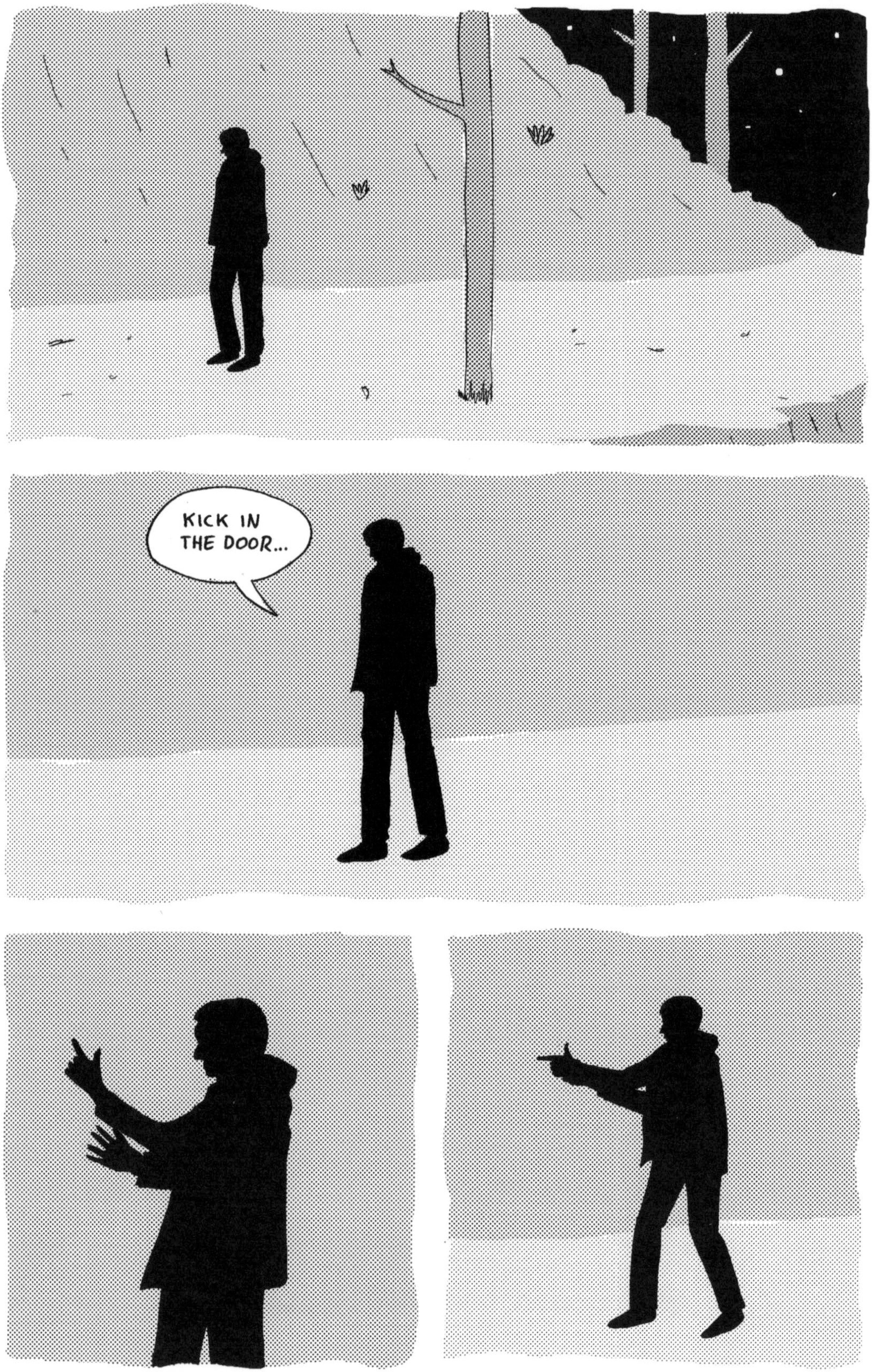
KICK IN THE DOOR...

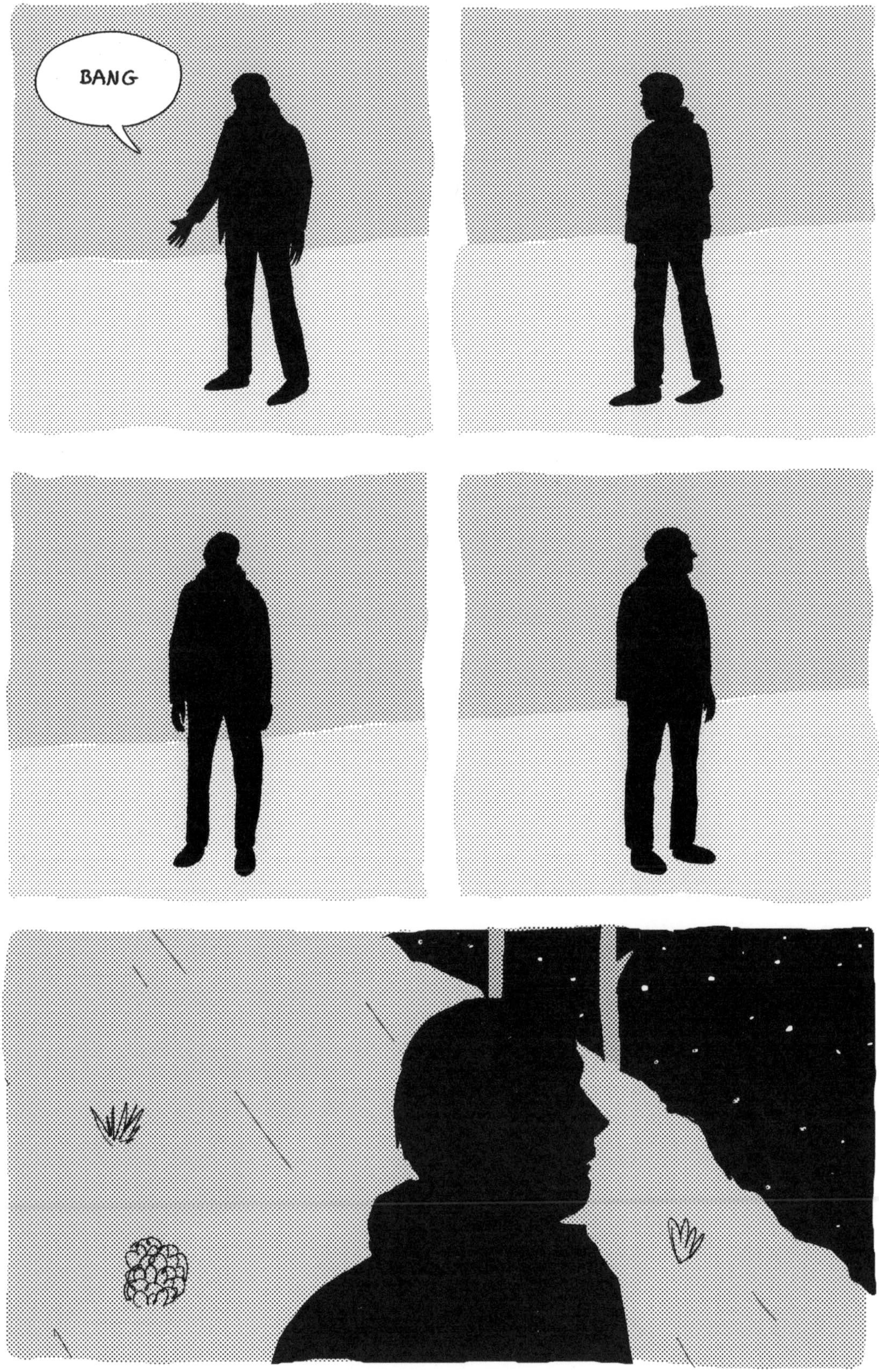
BANG

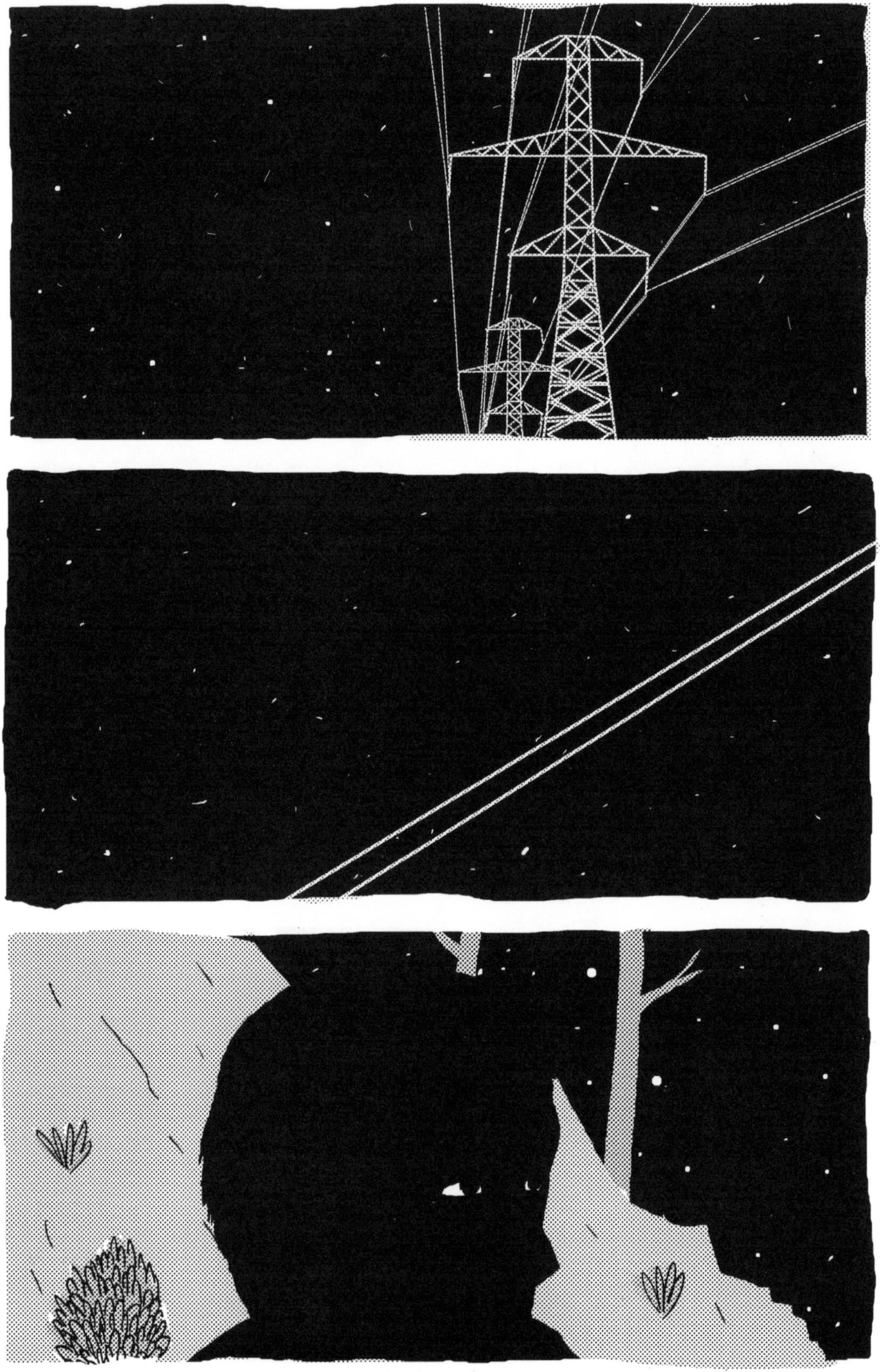

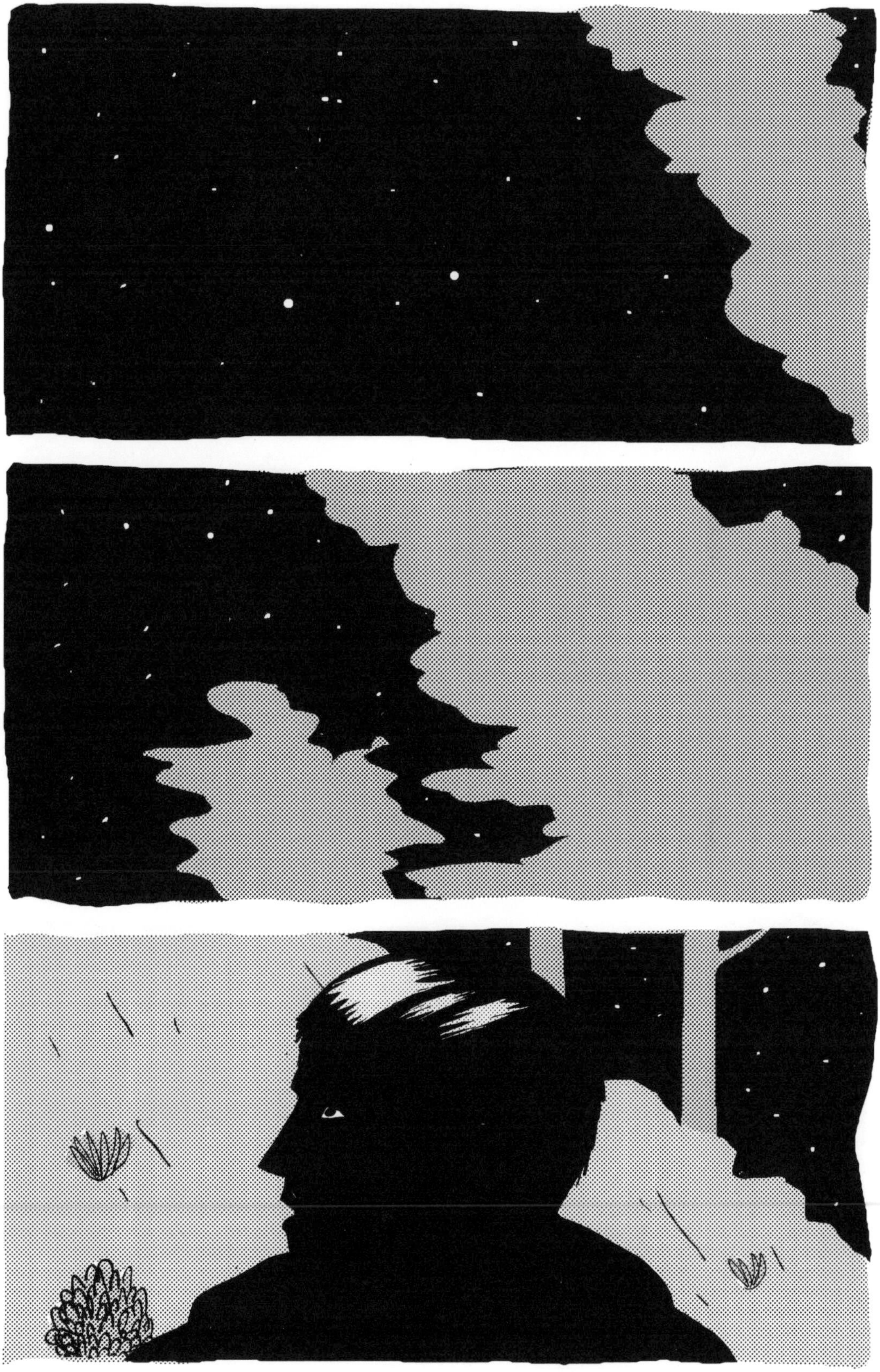

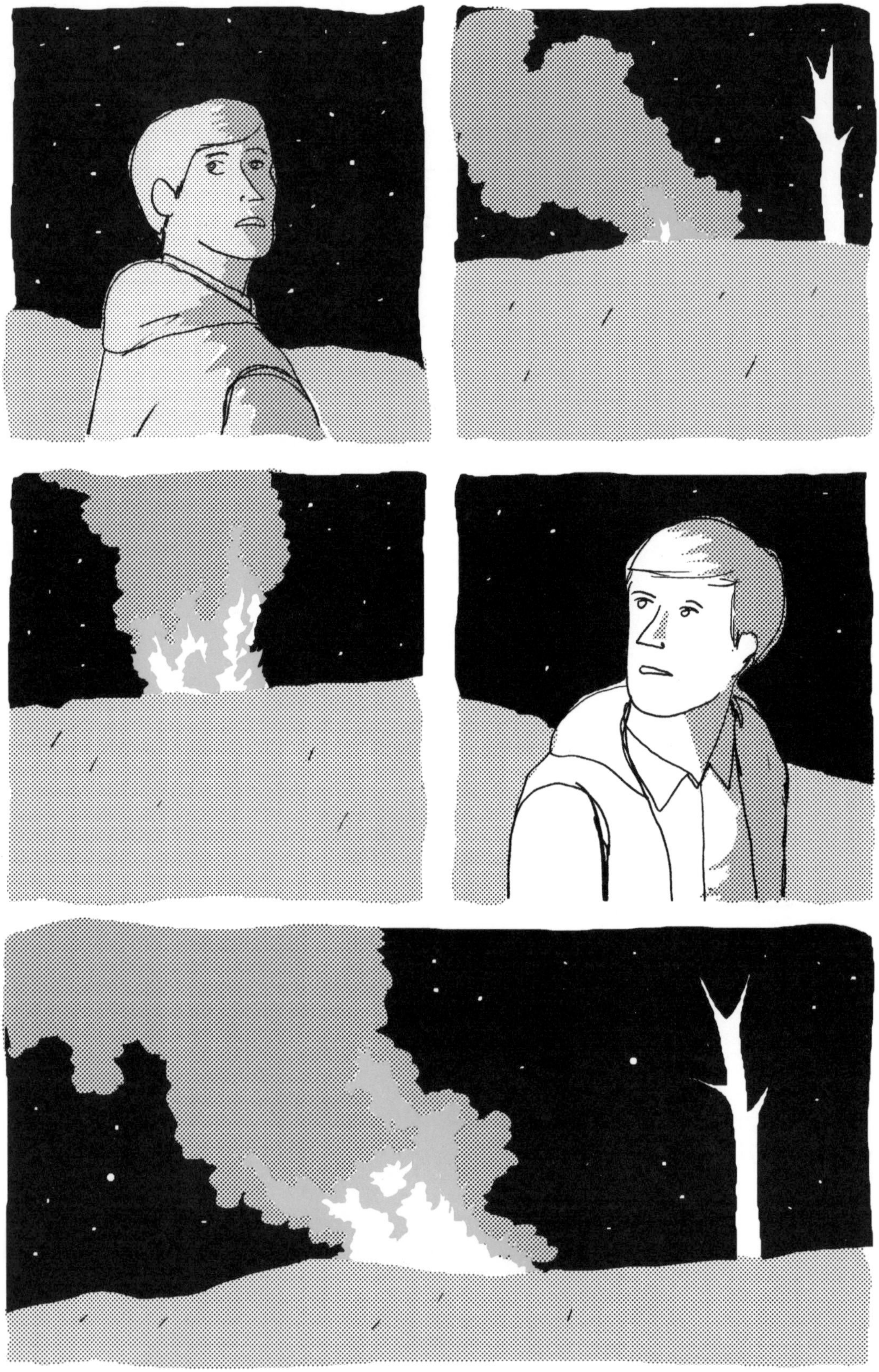

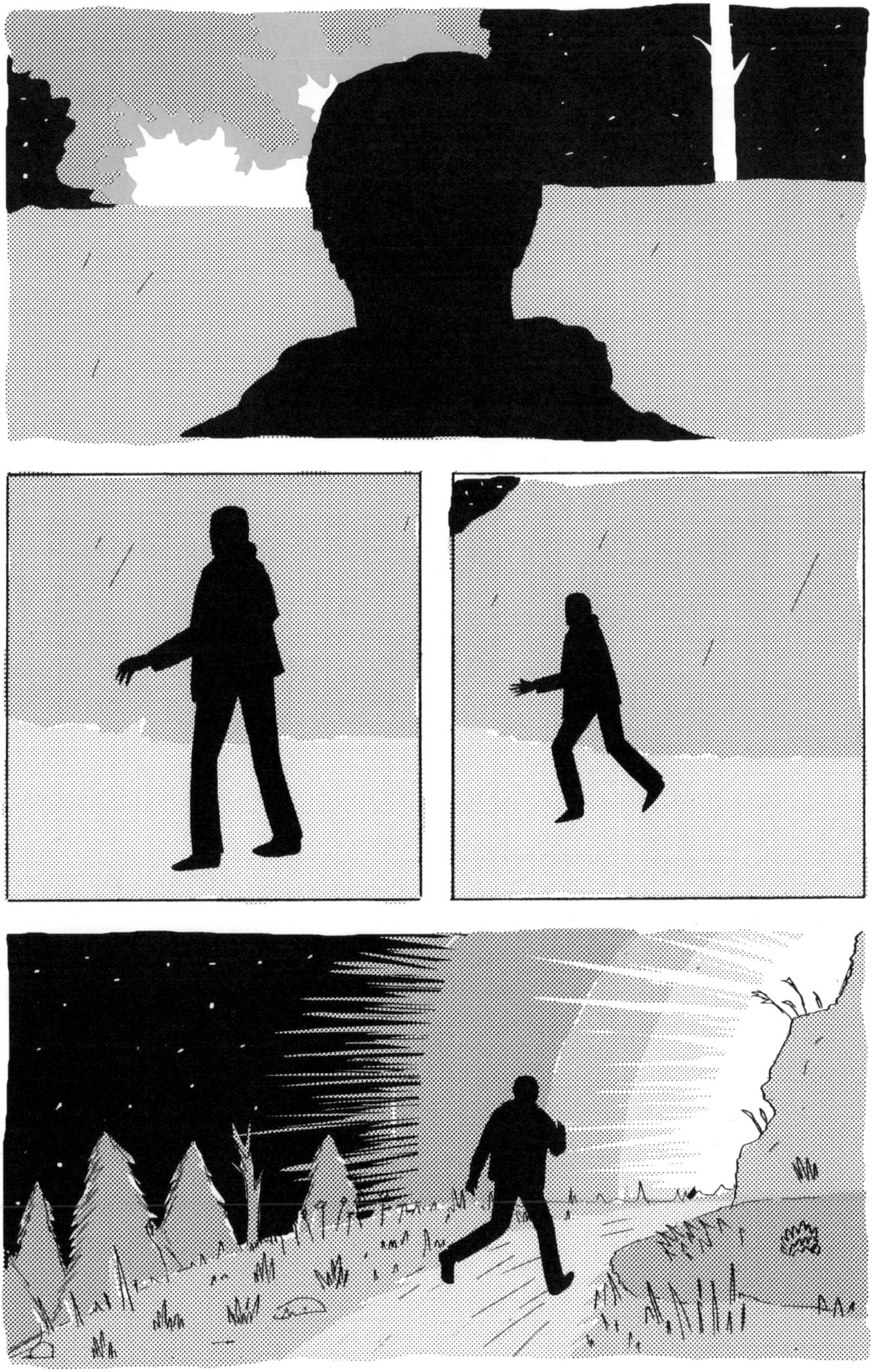

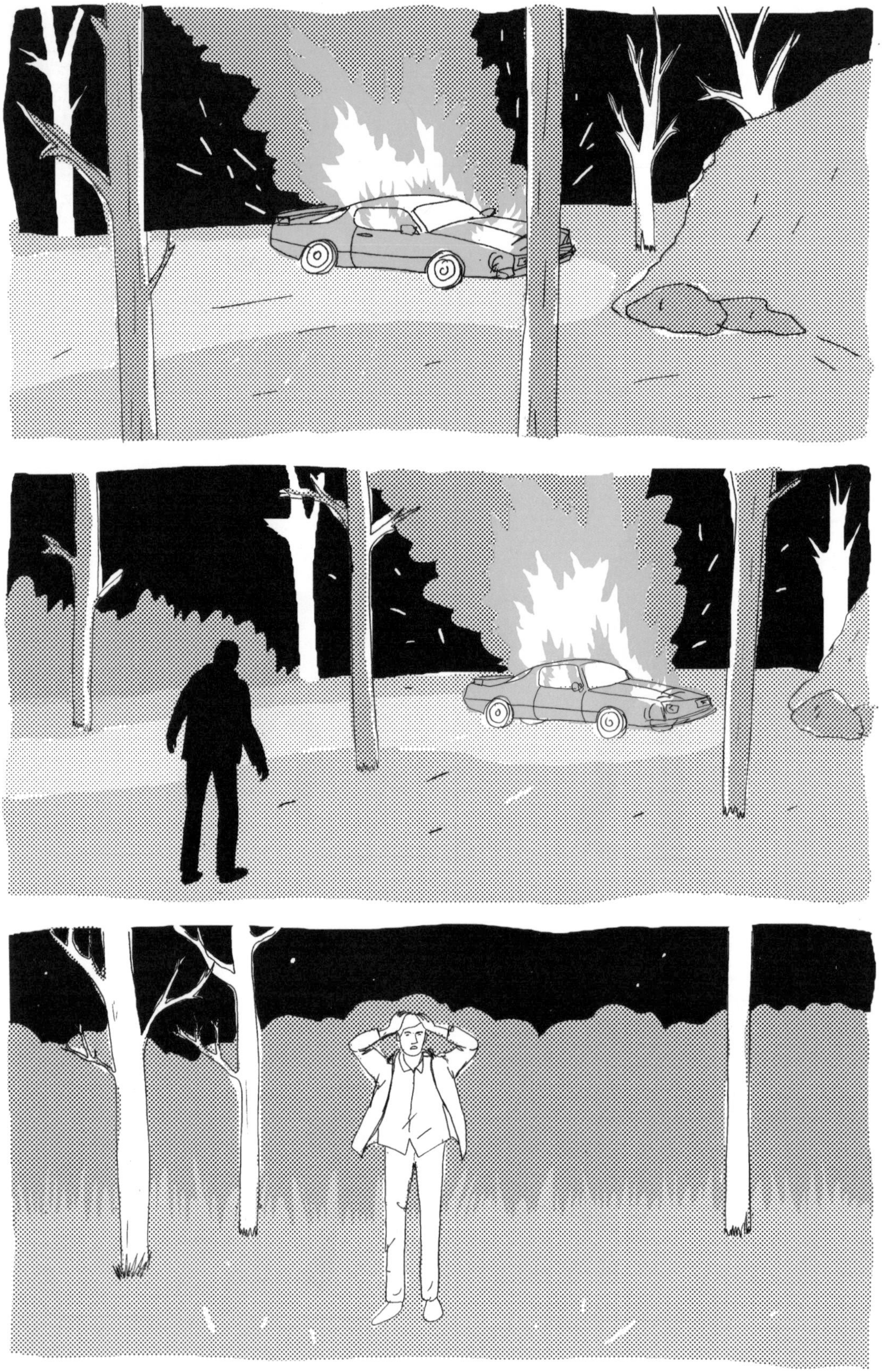

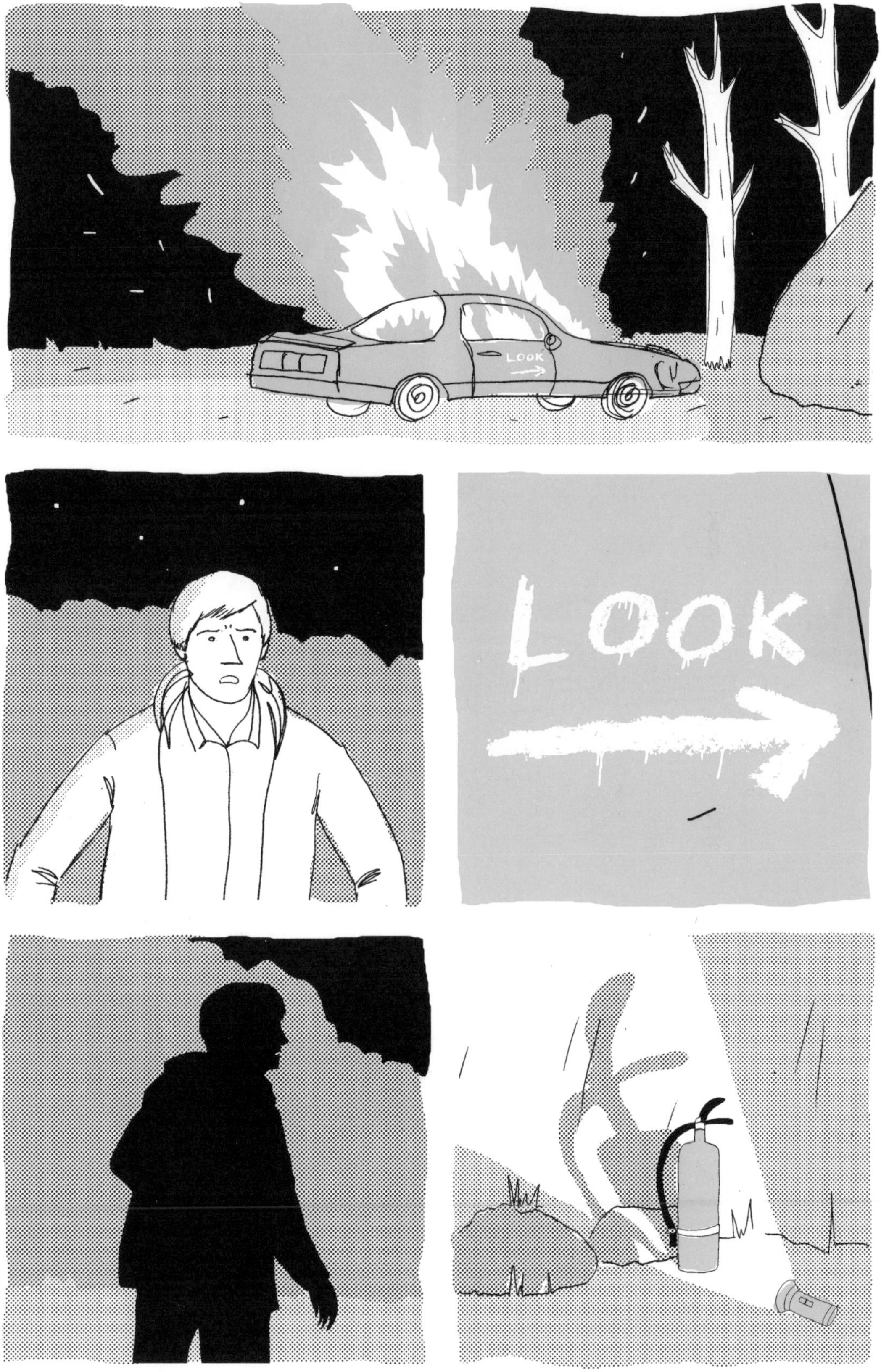
LOOK
LOOK

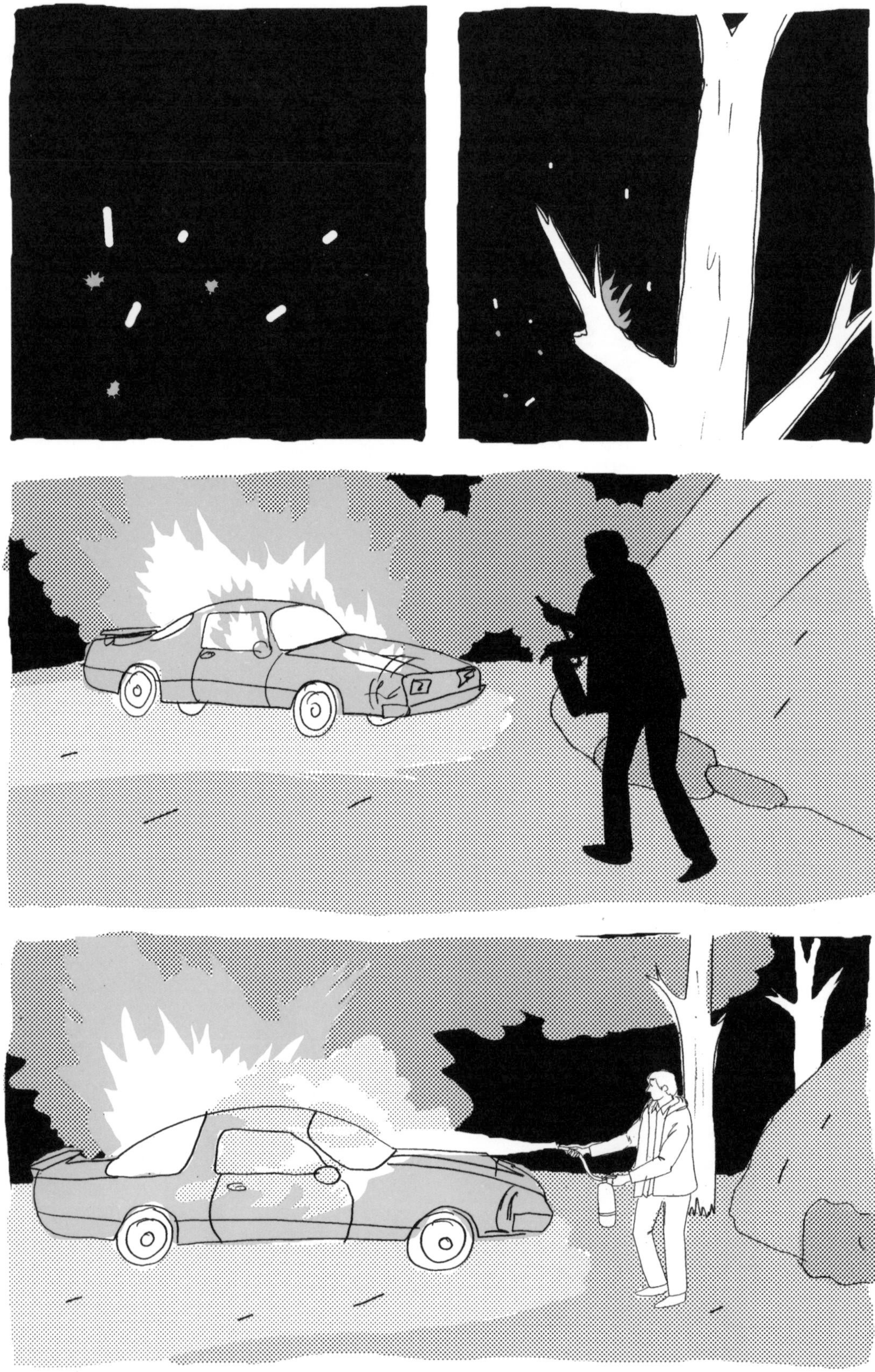

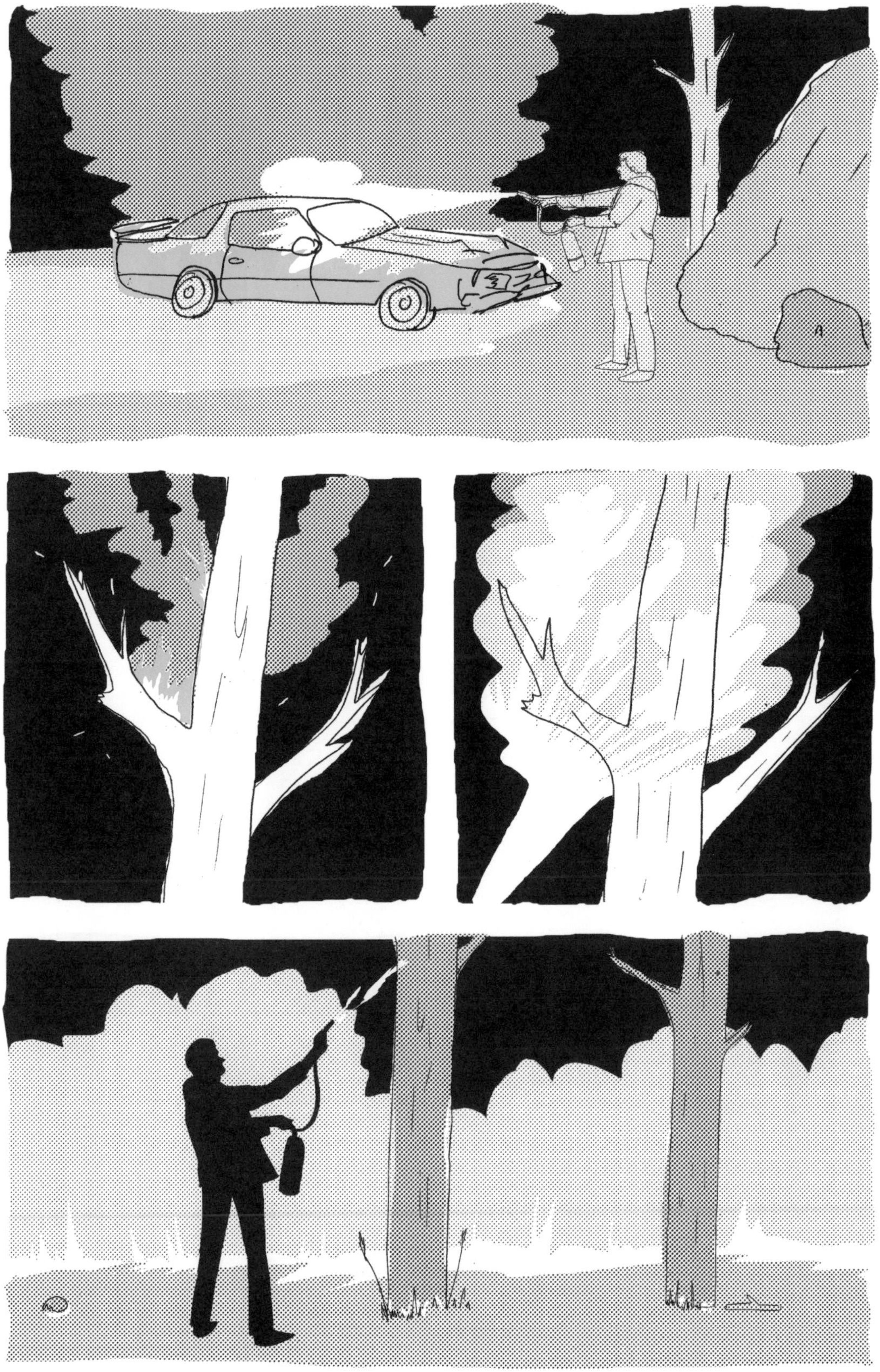

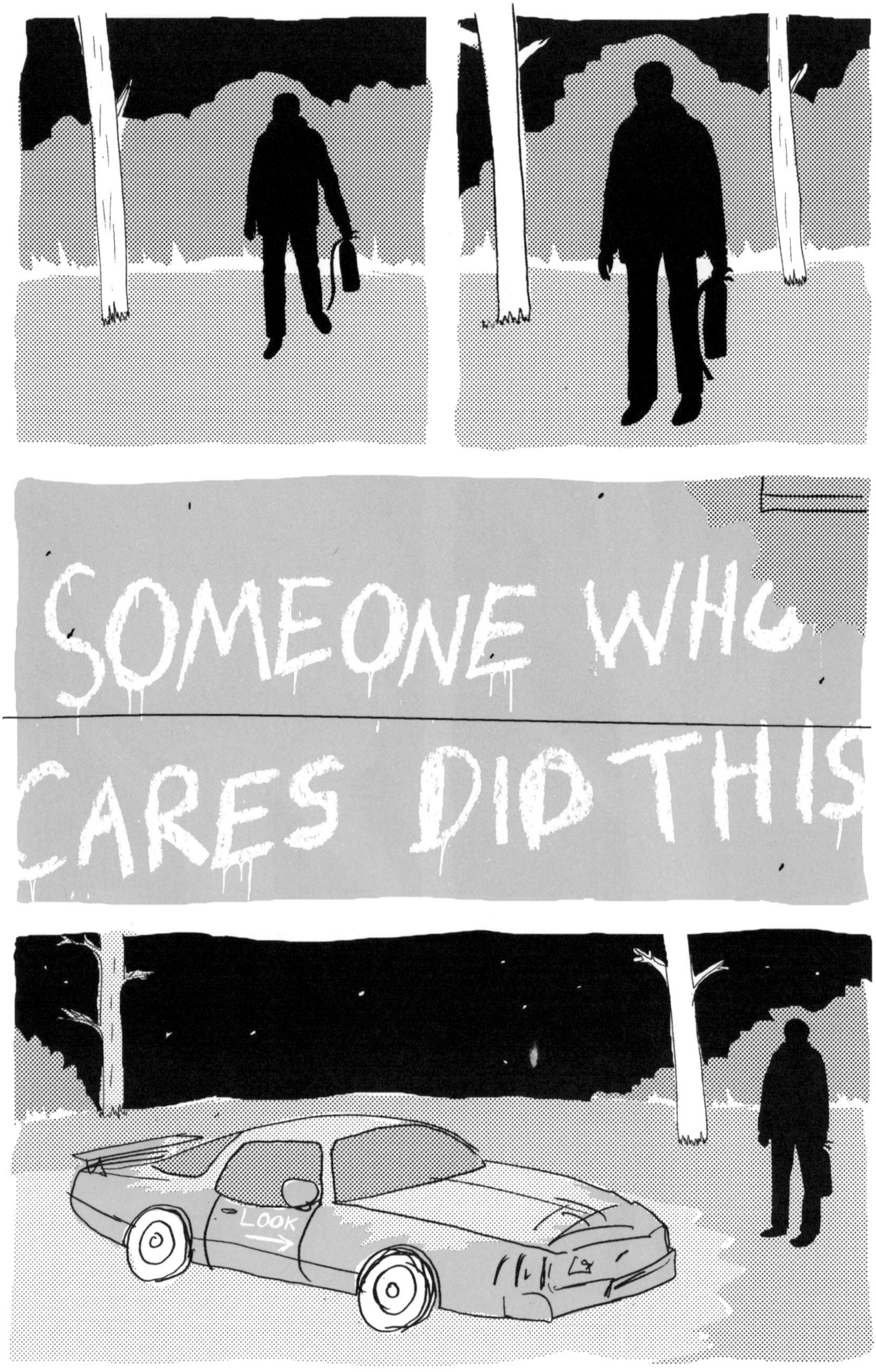
SOMEONE WHO
CARES DID THIS
LOOK

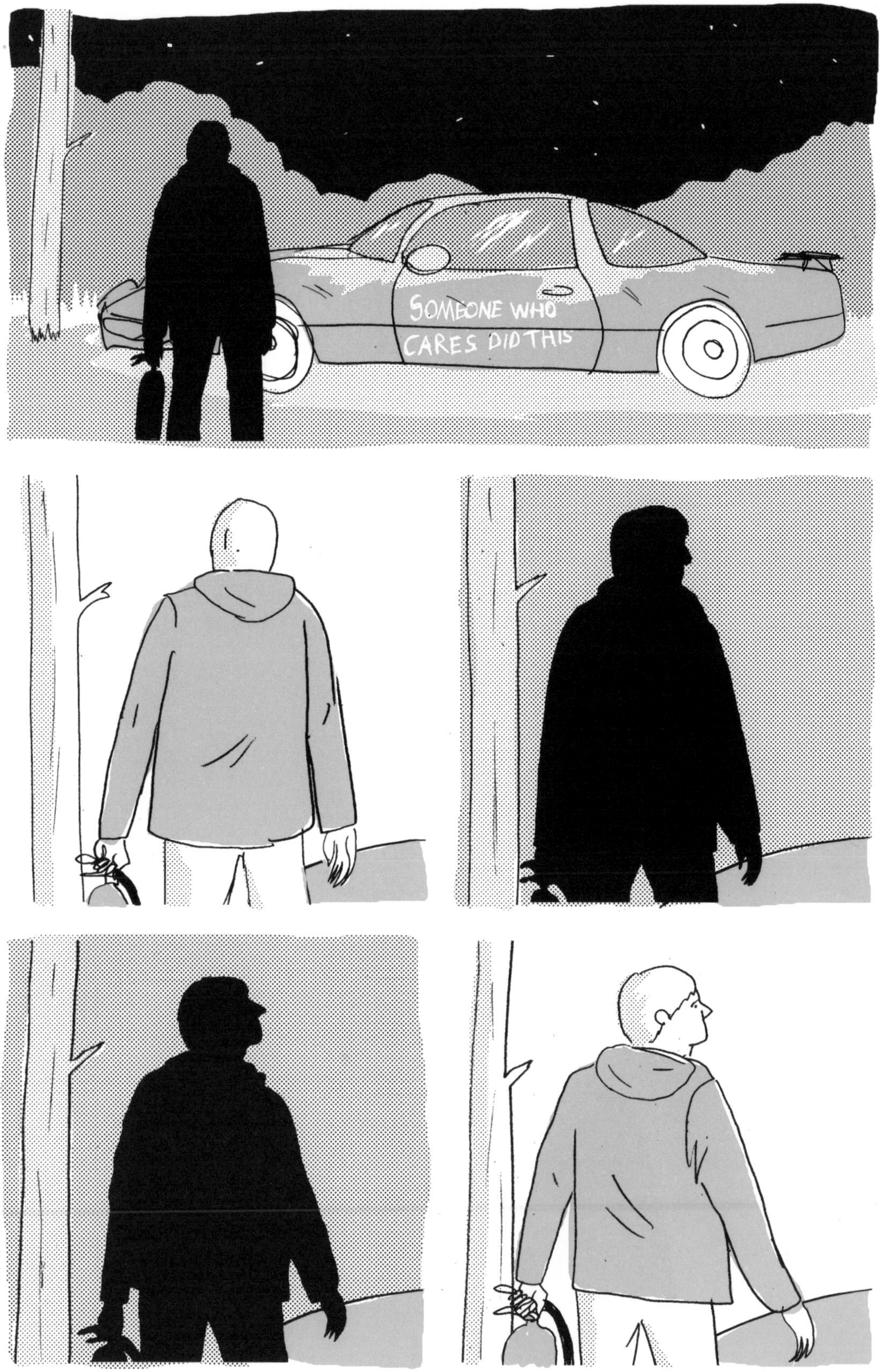
SOMEONE WHO
CARES DID THIS

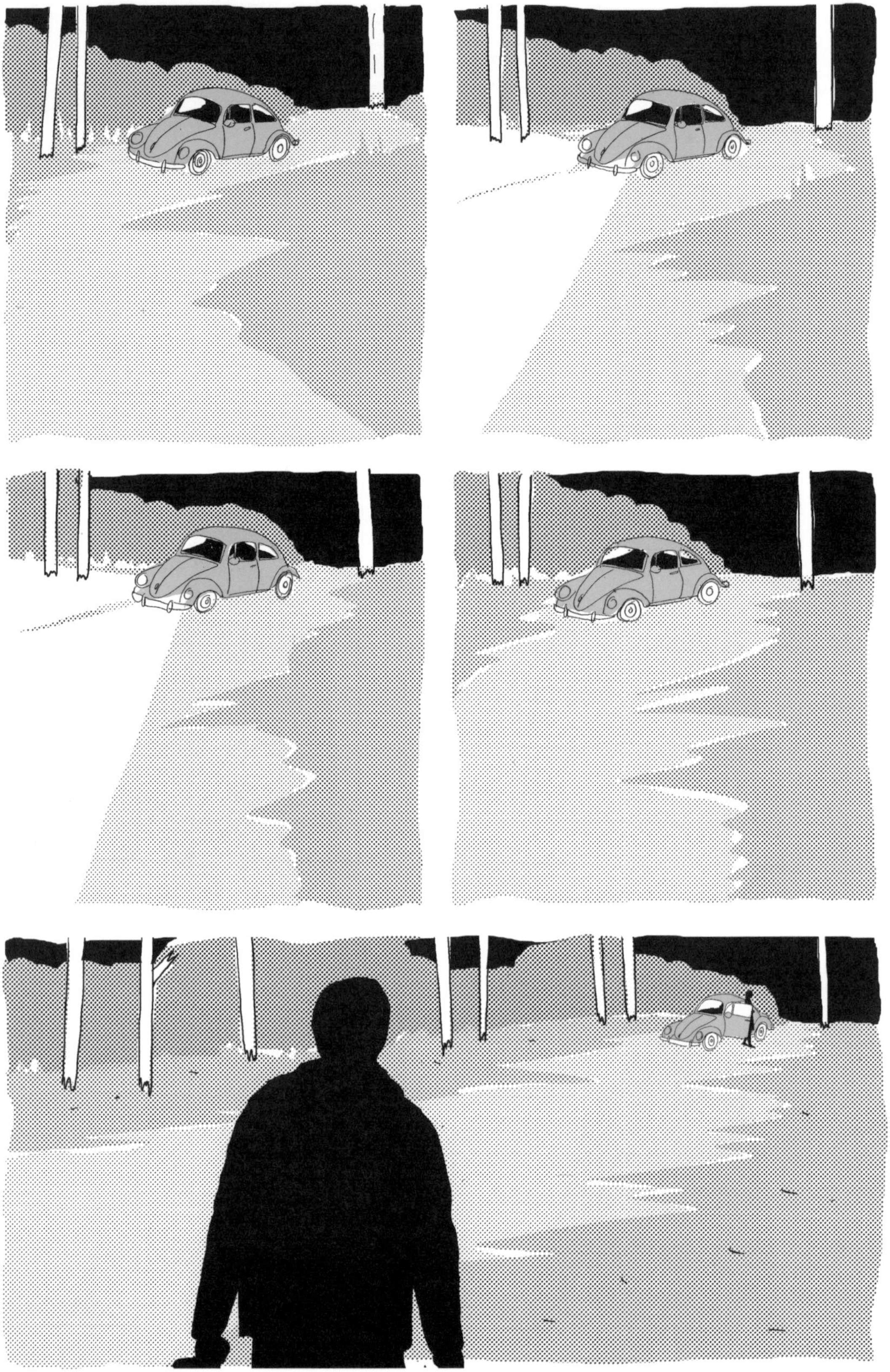

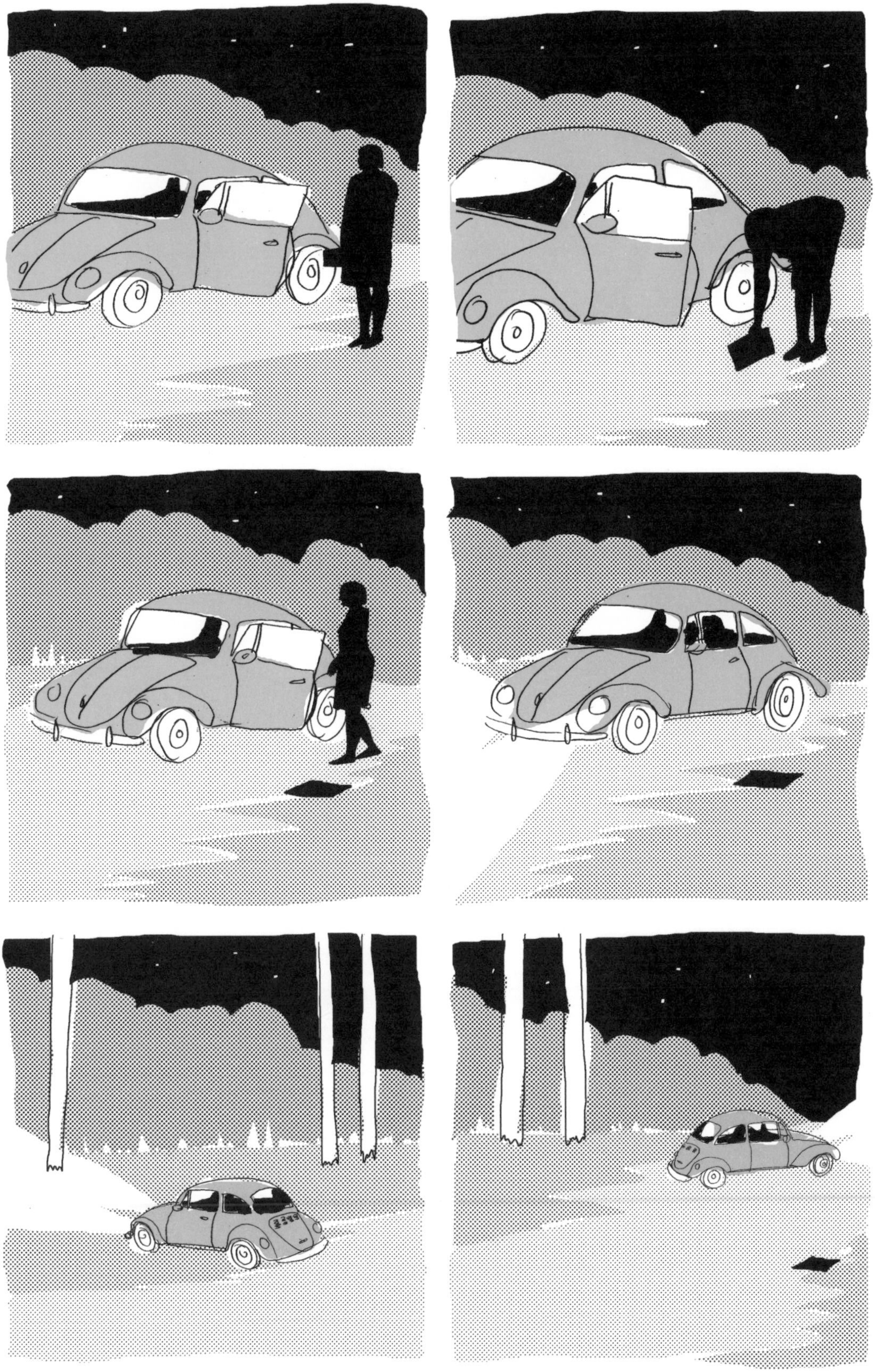

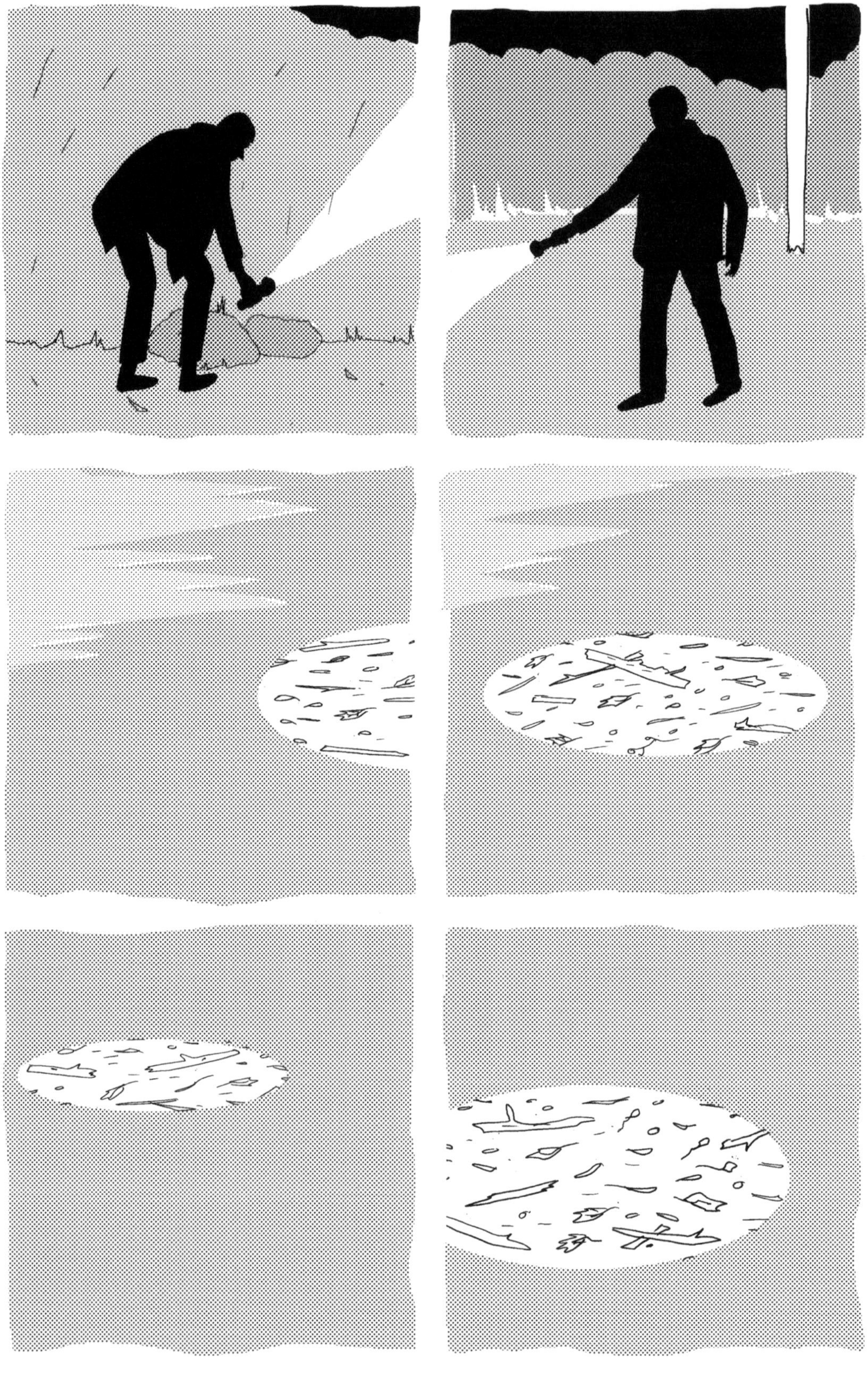

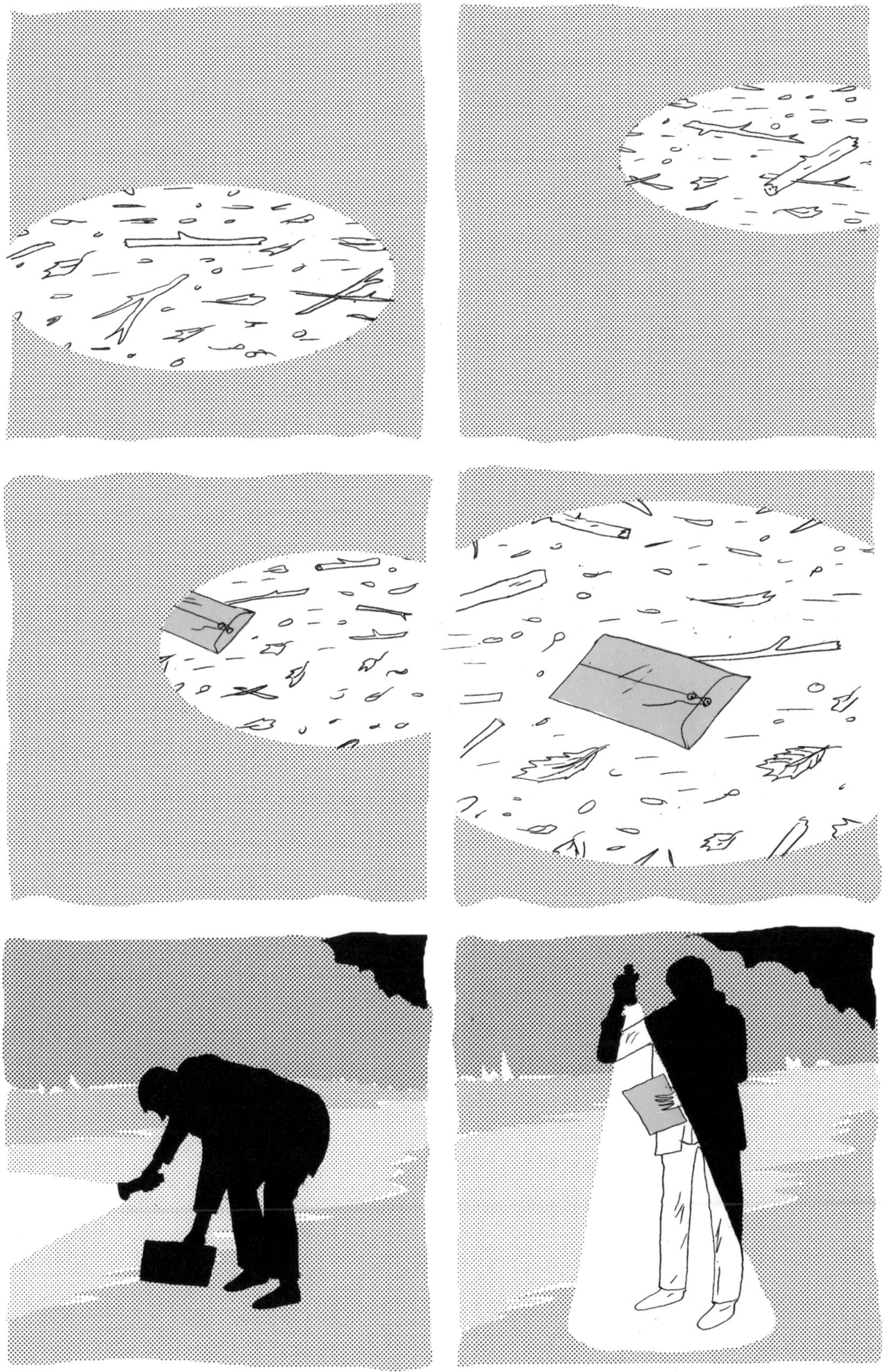

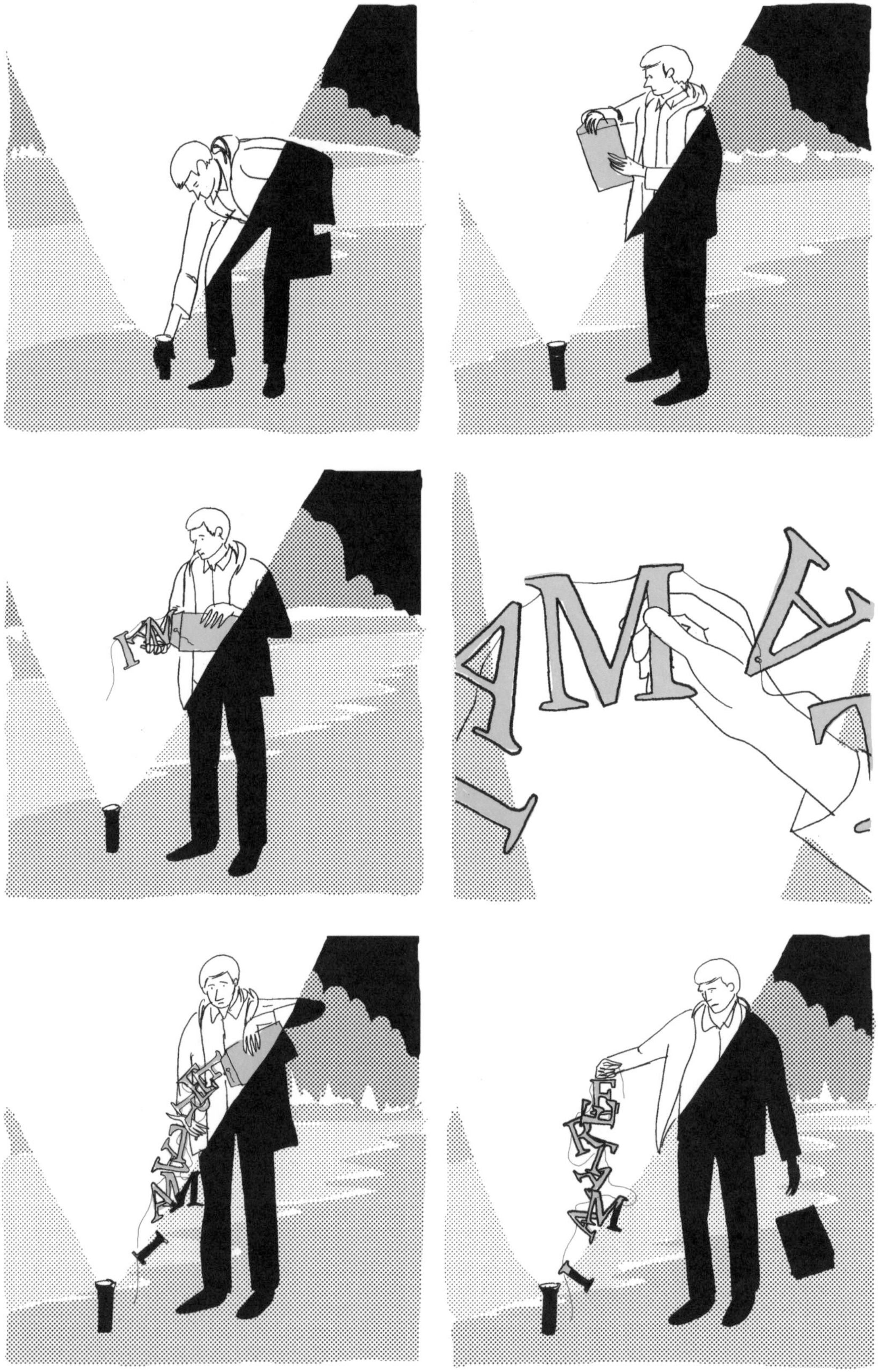
AM

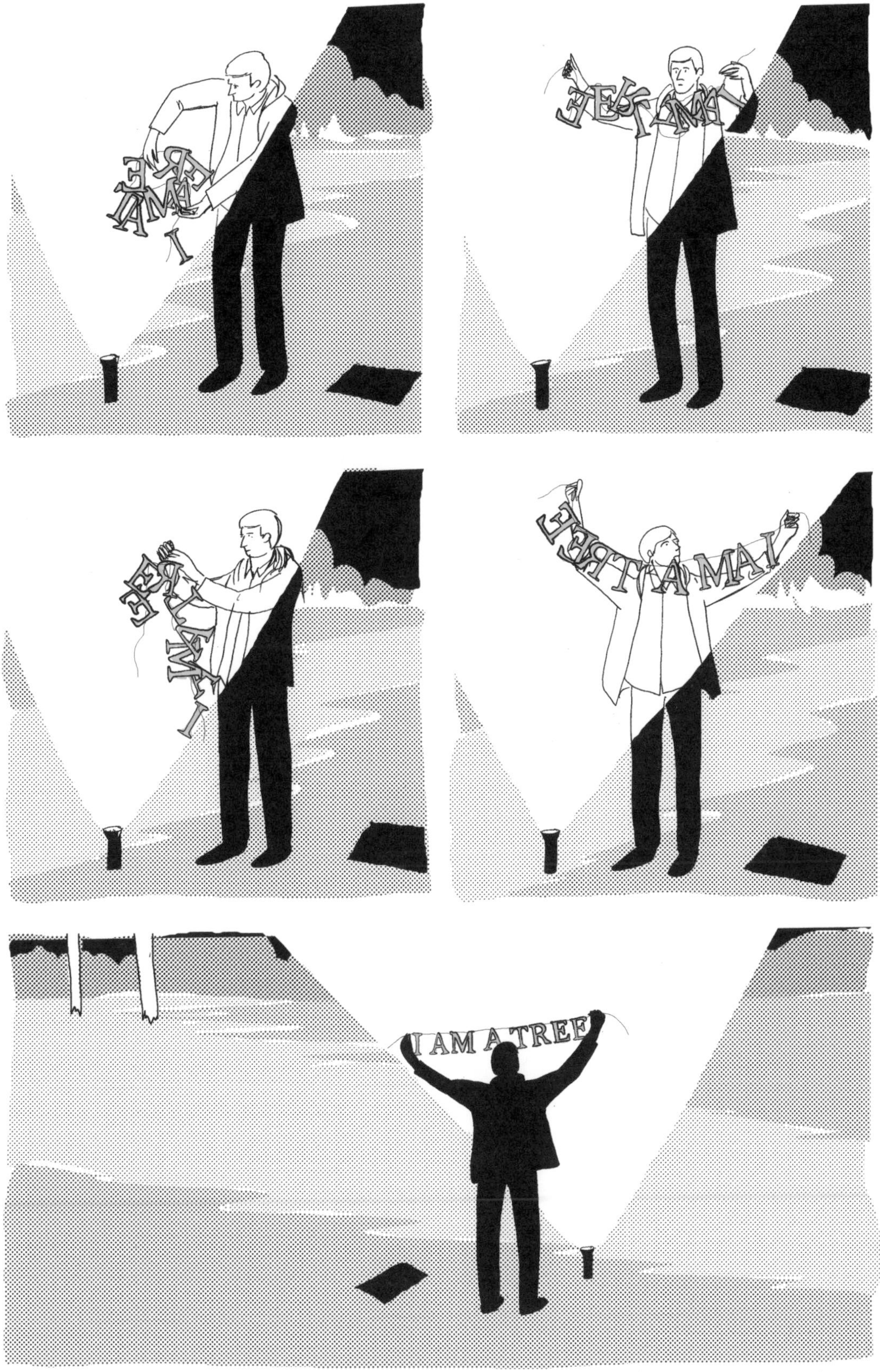
I AM A TREE

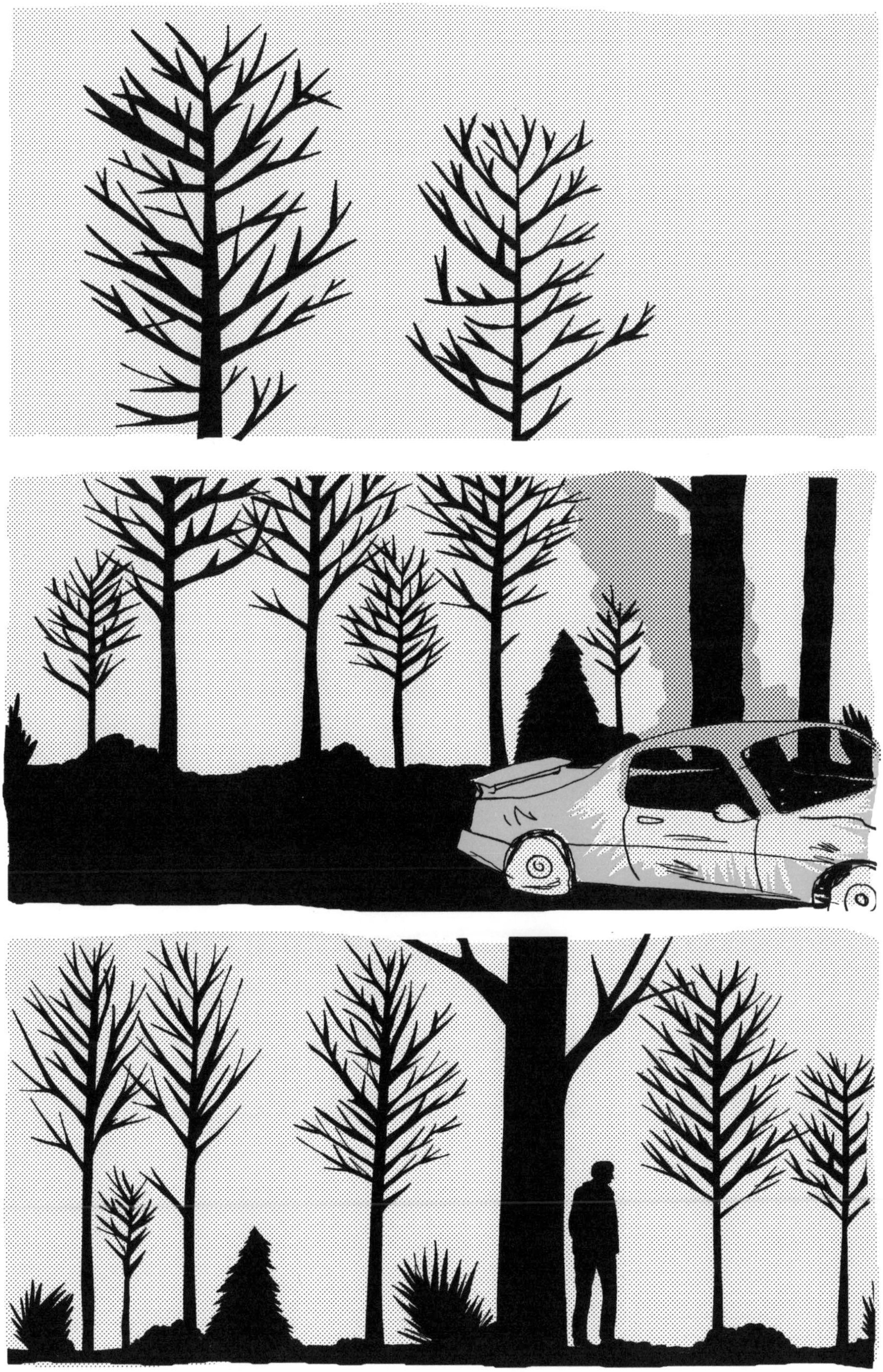

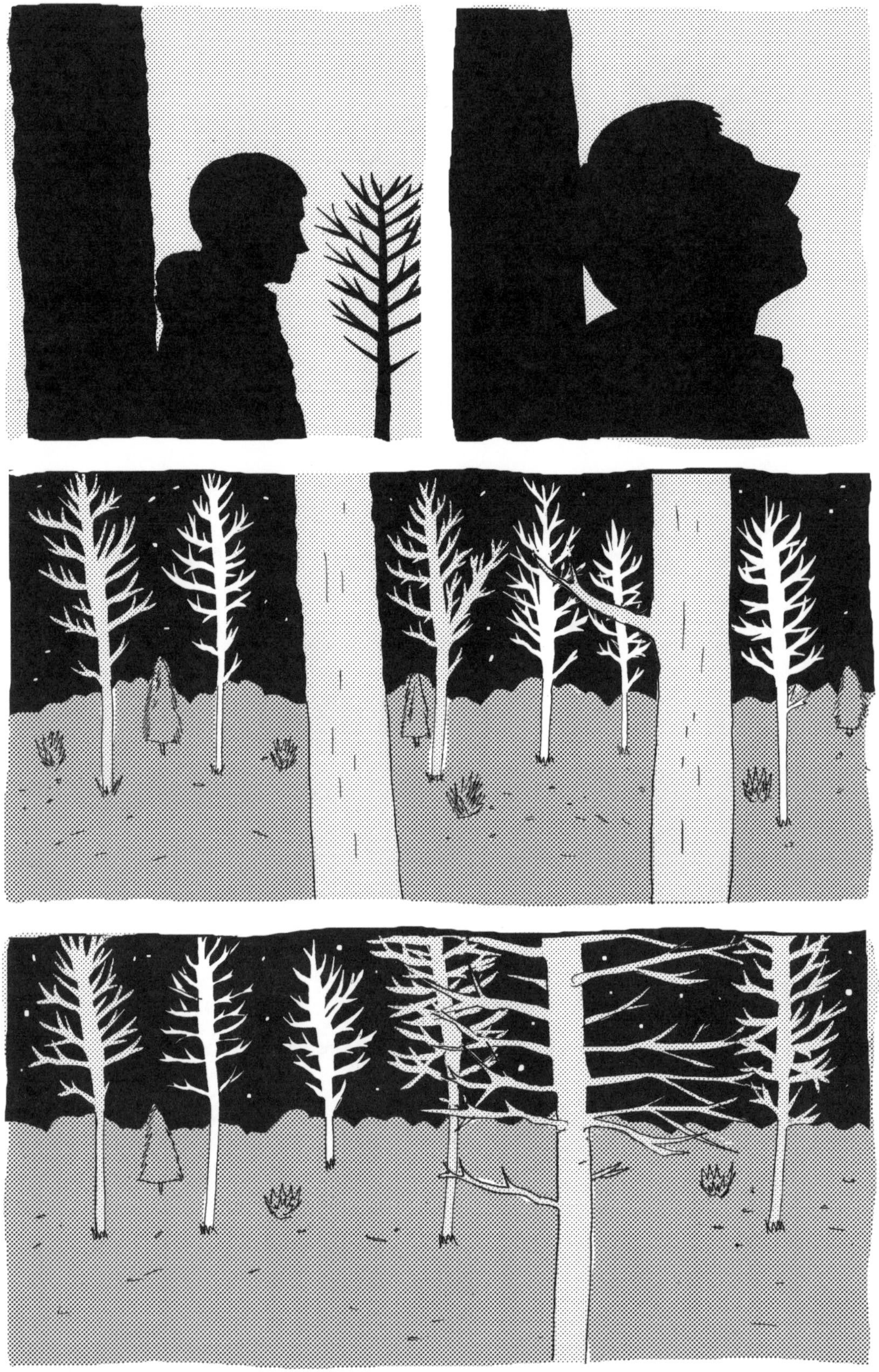

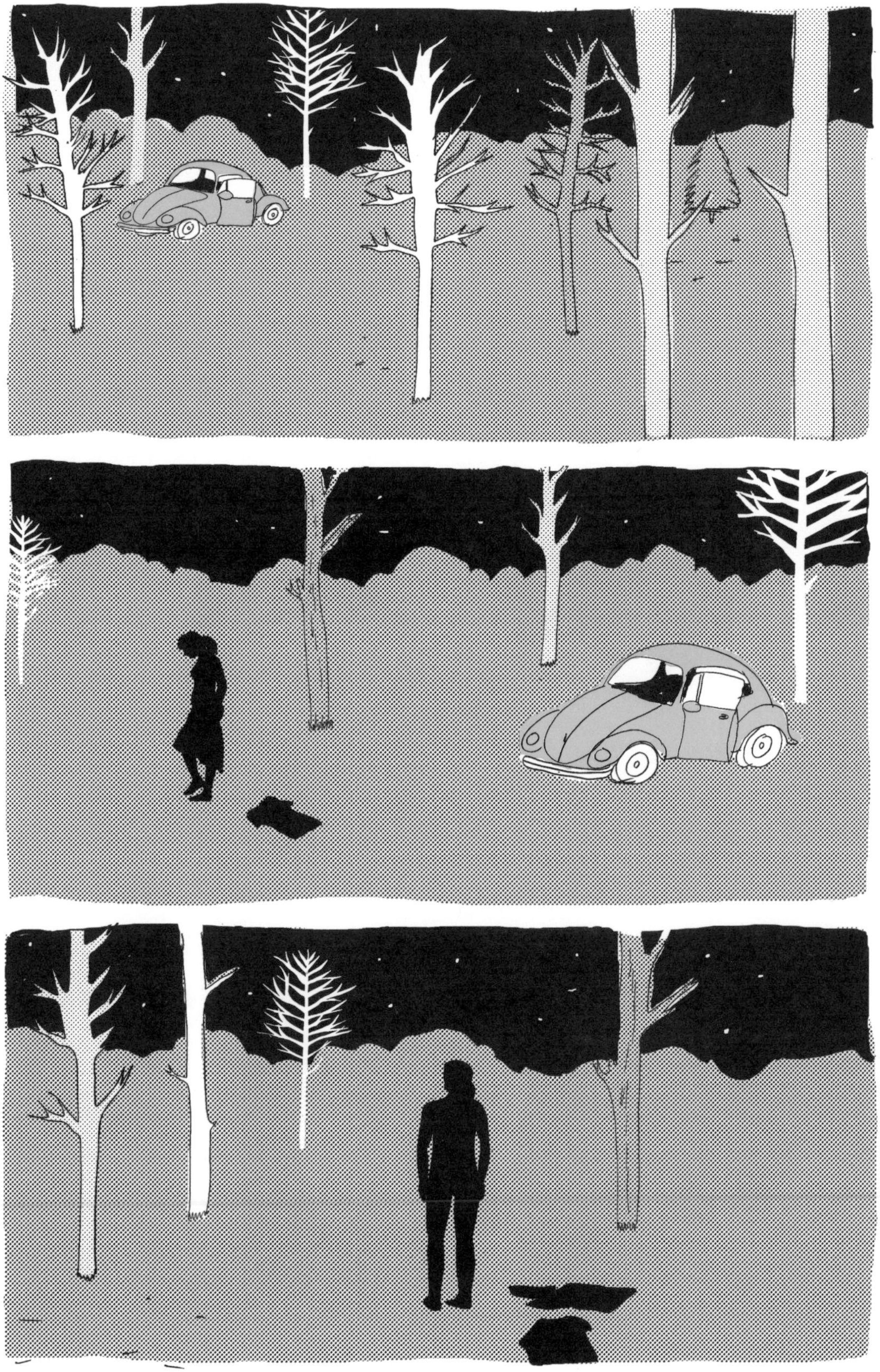

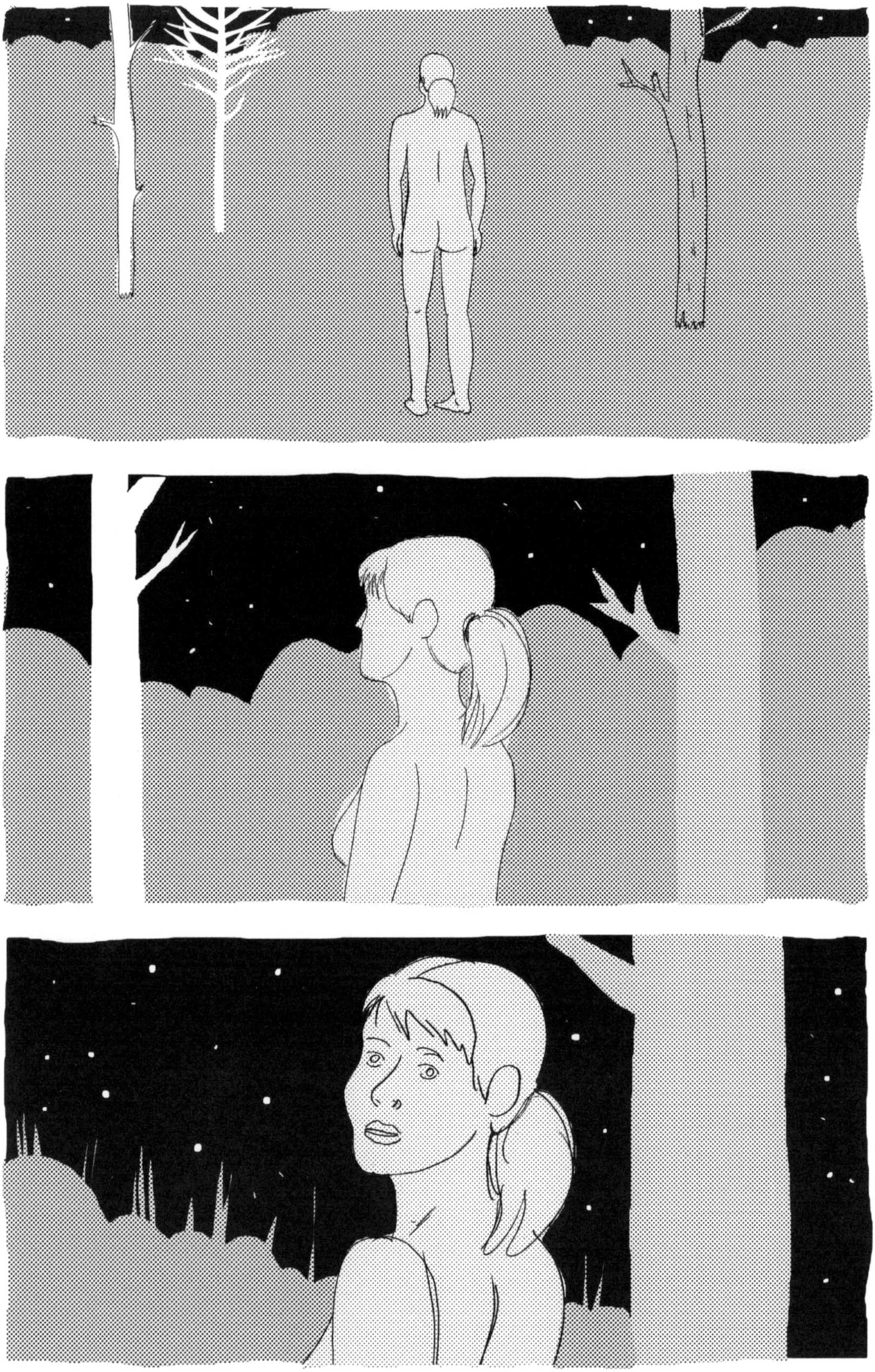

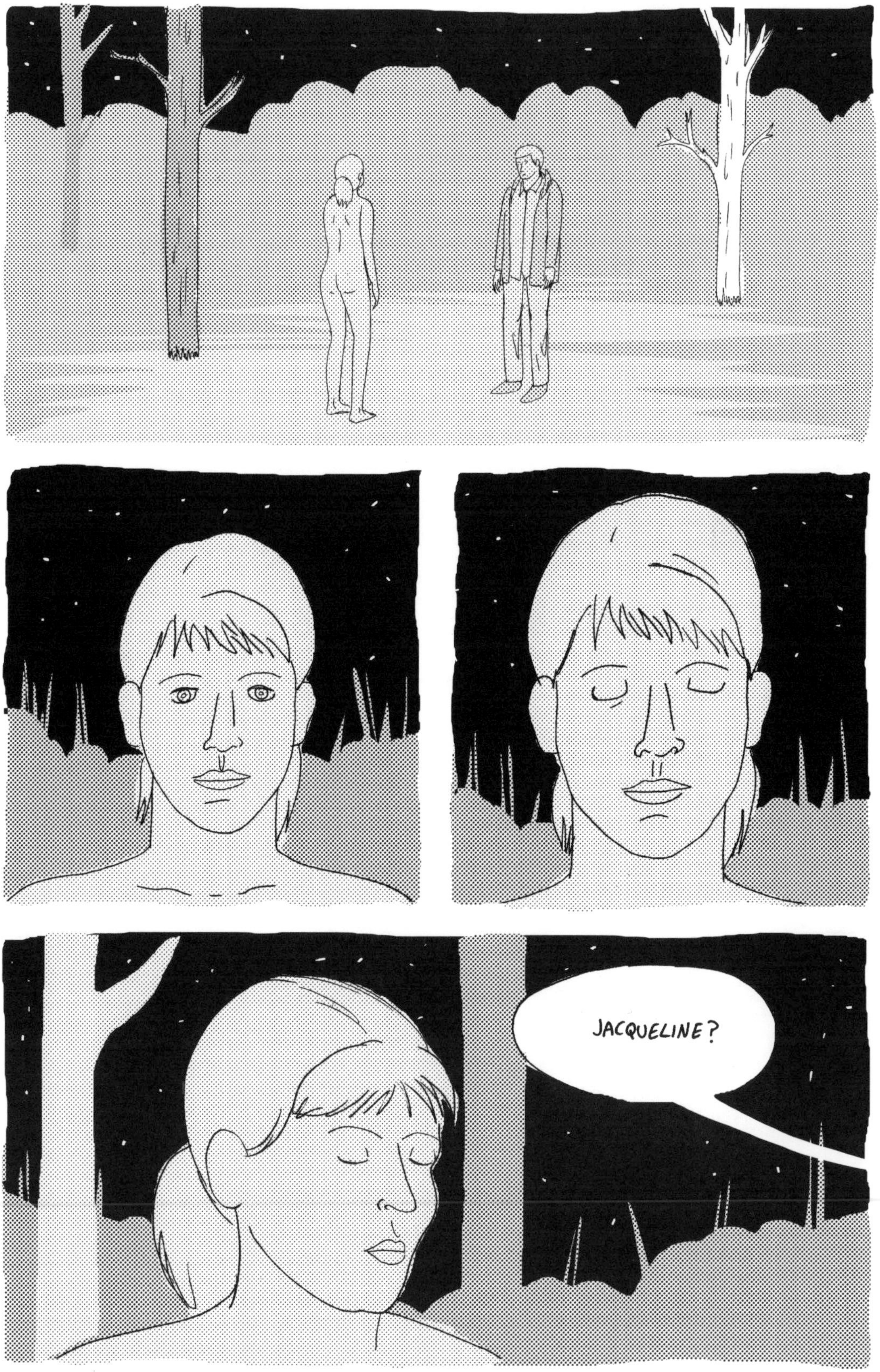
JACQUELINE?

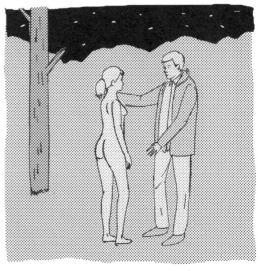

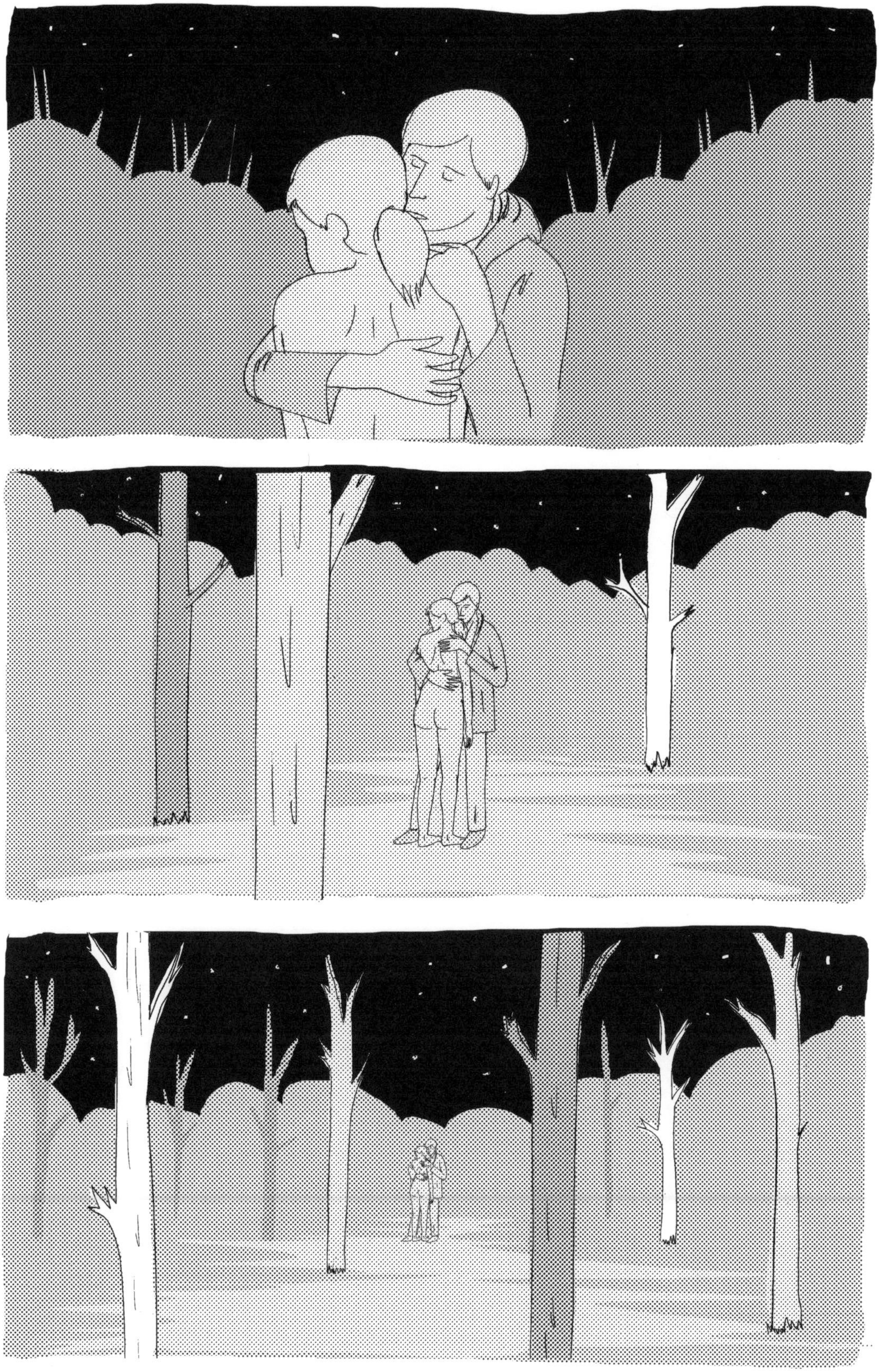

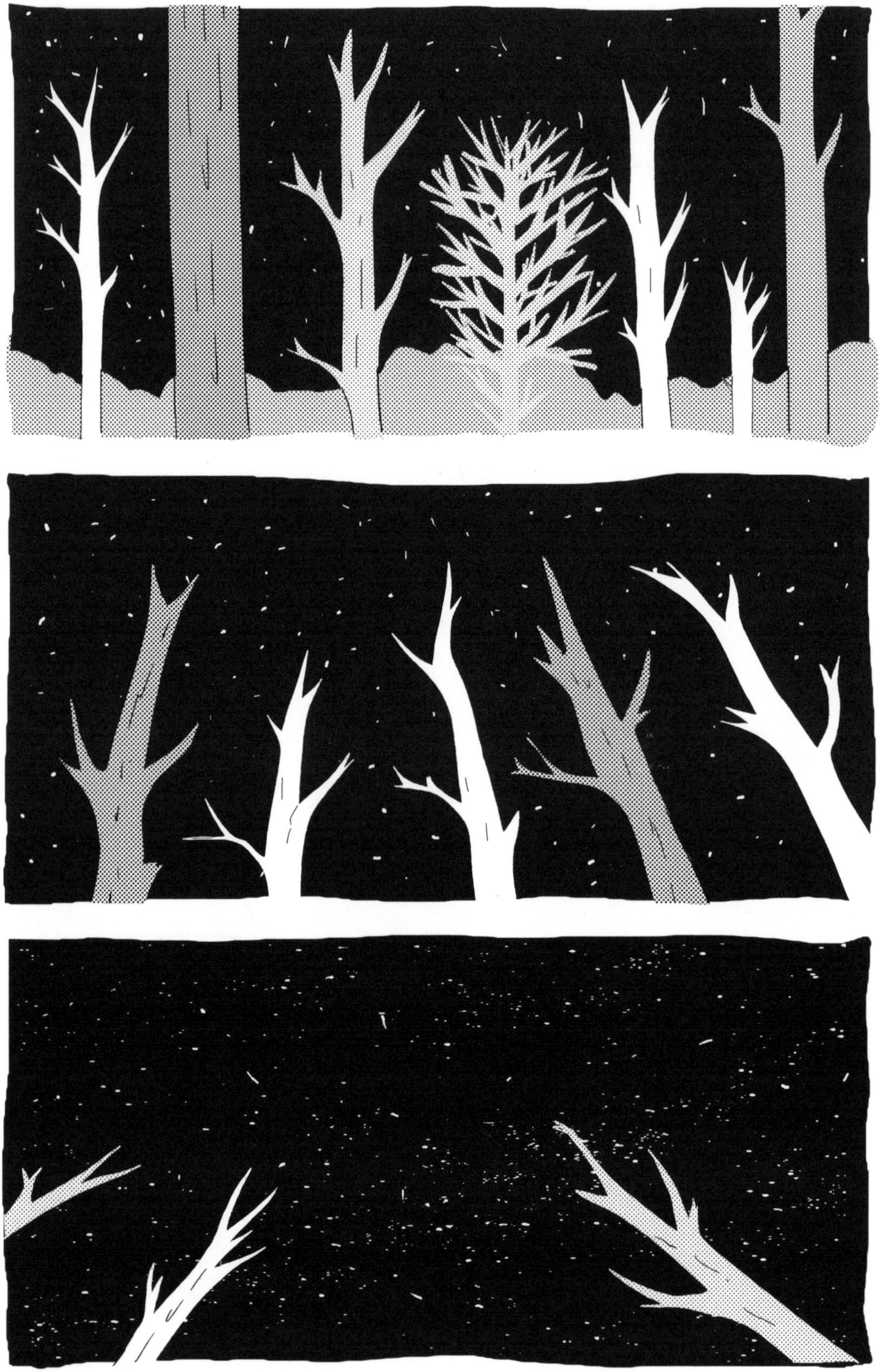

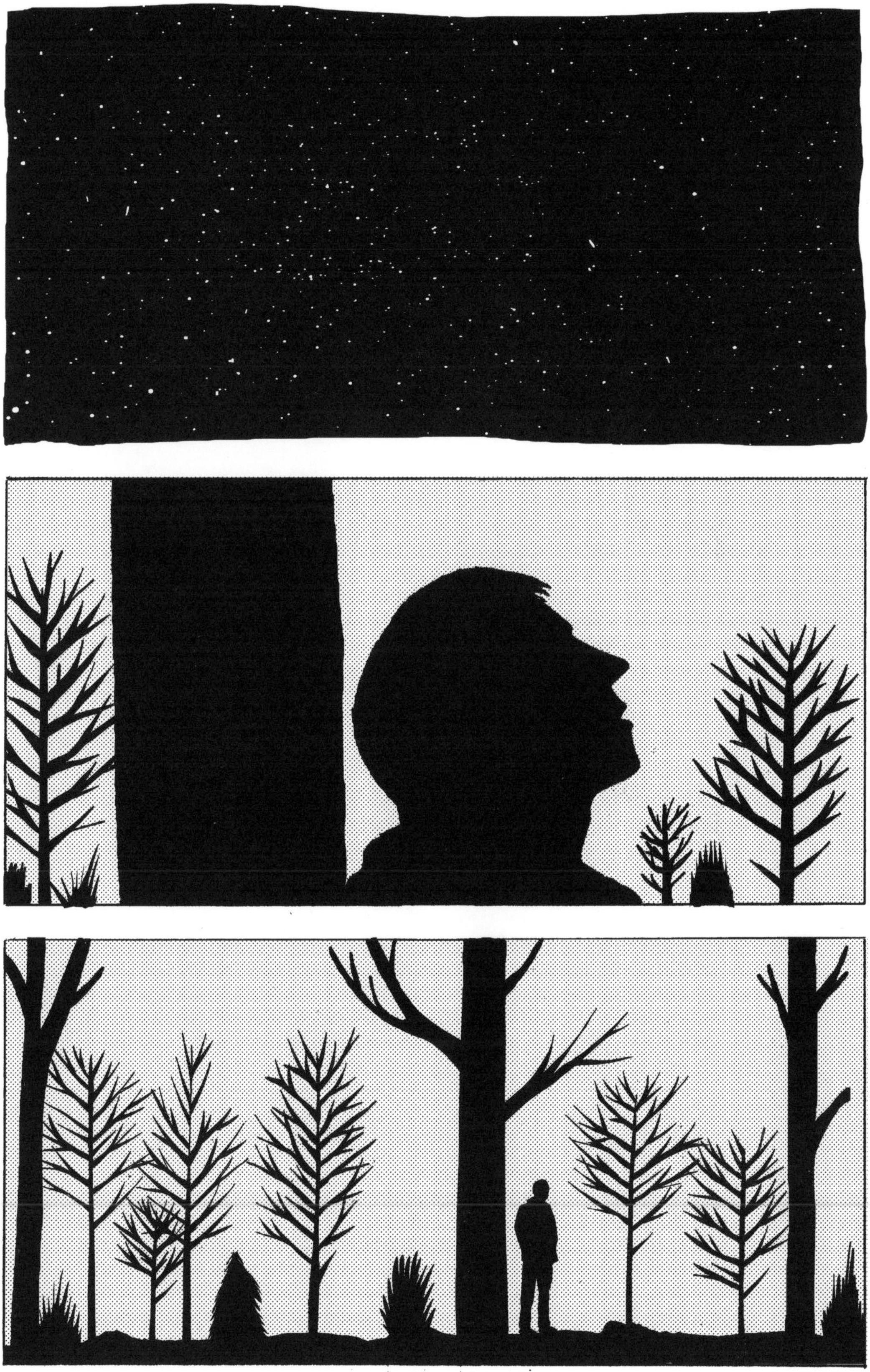

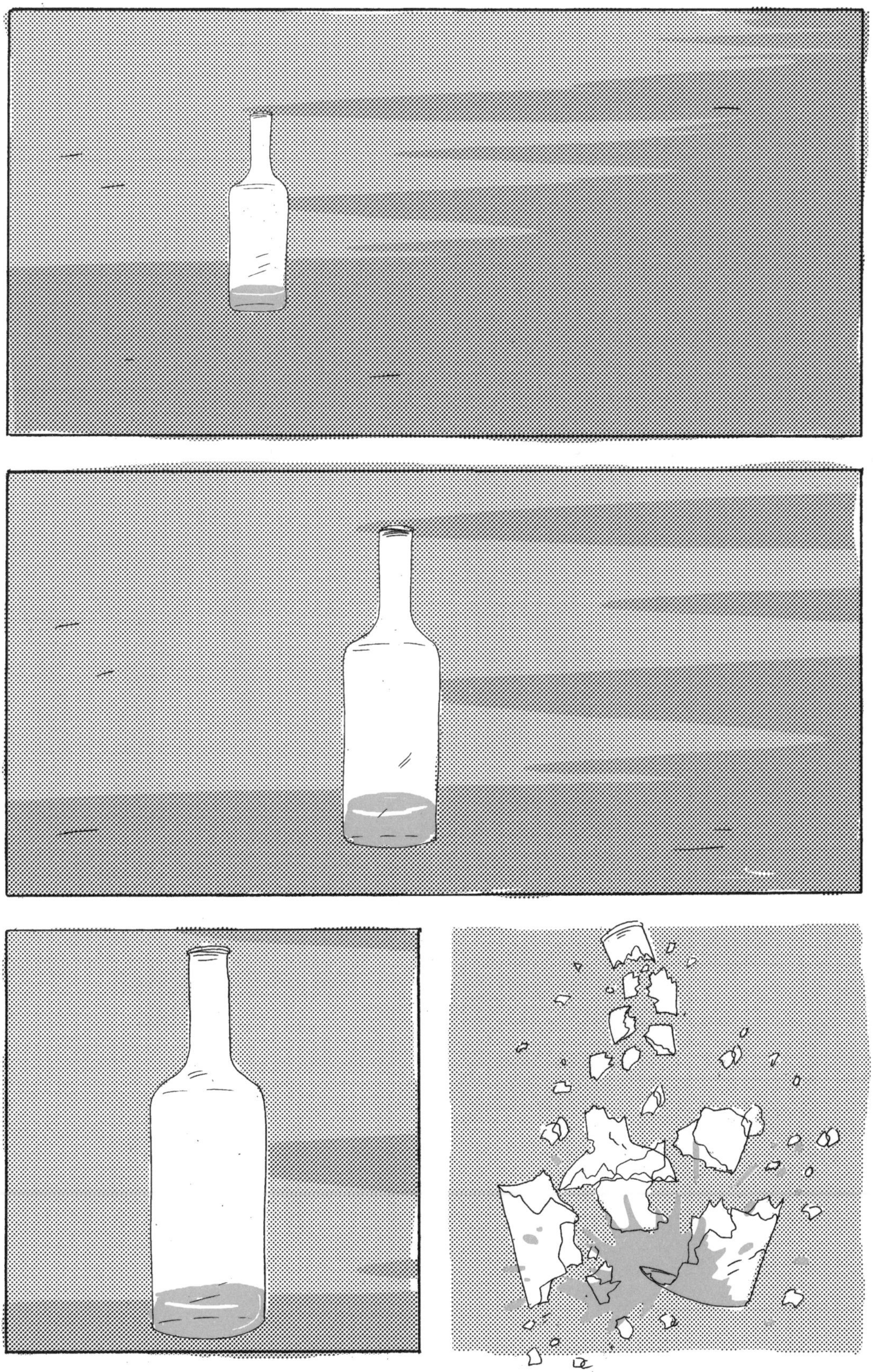

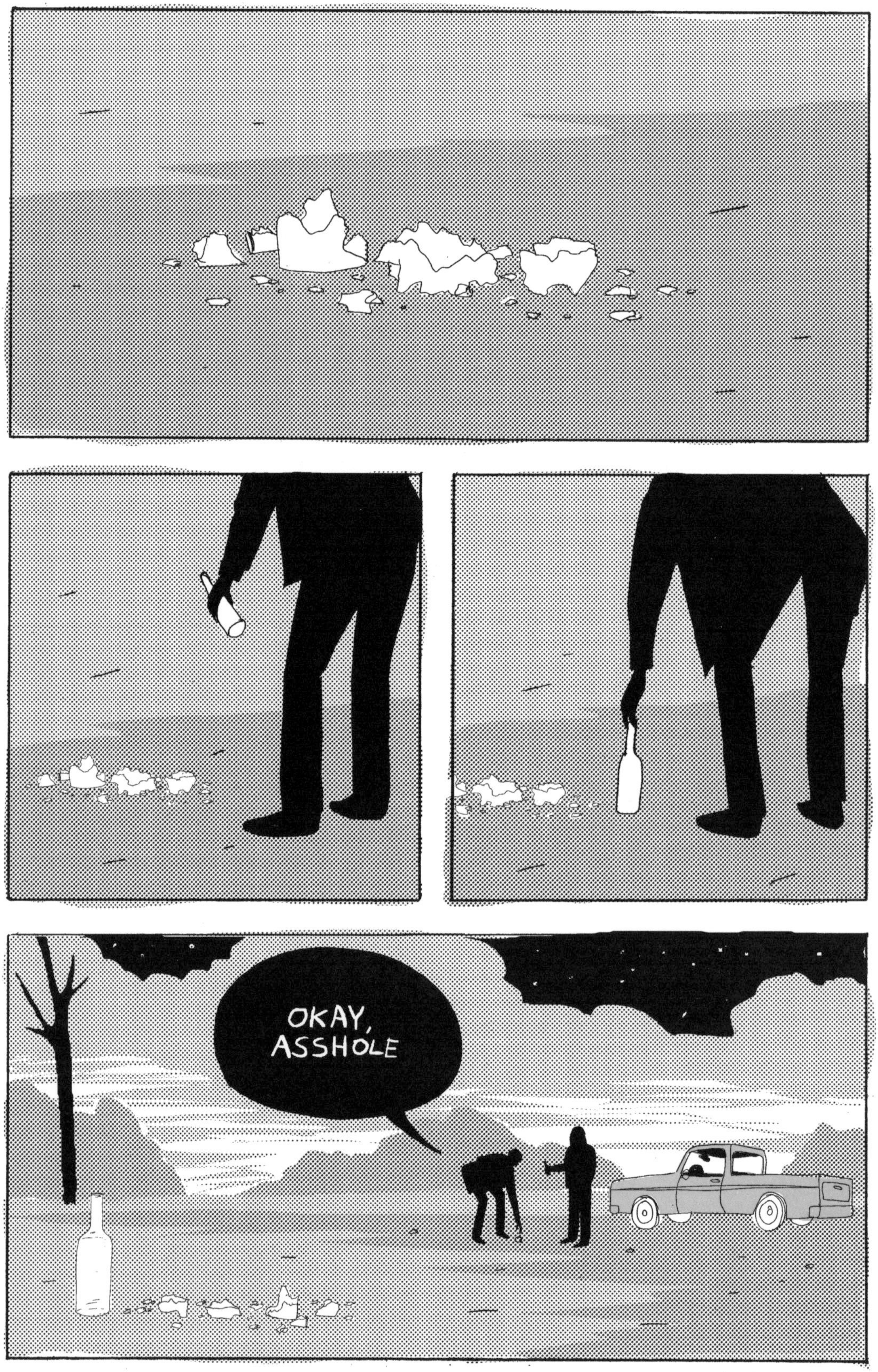
OKAY, ASSHOLE

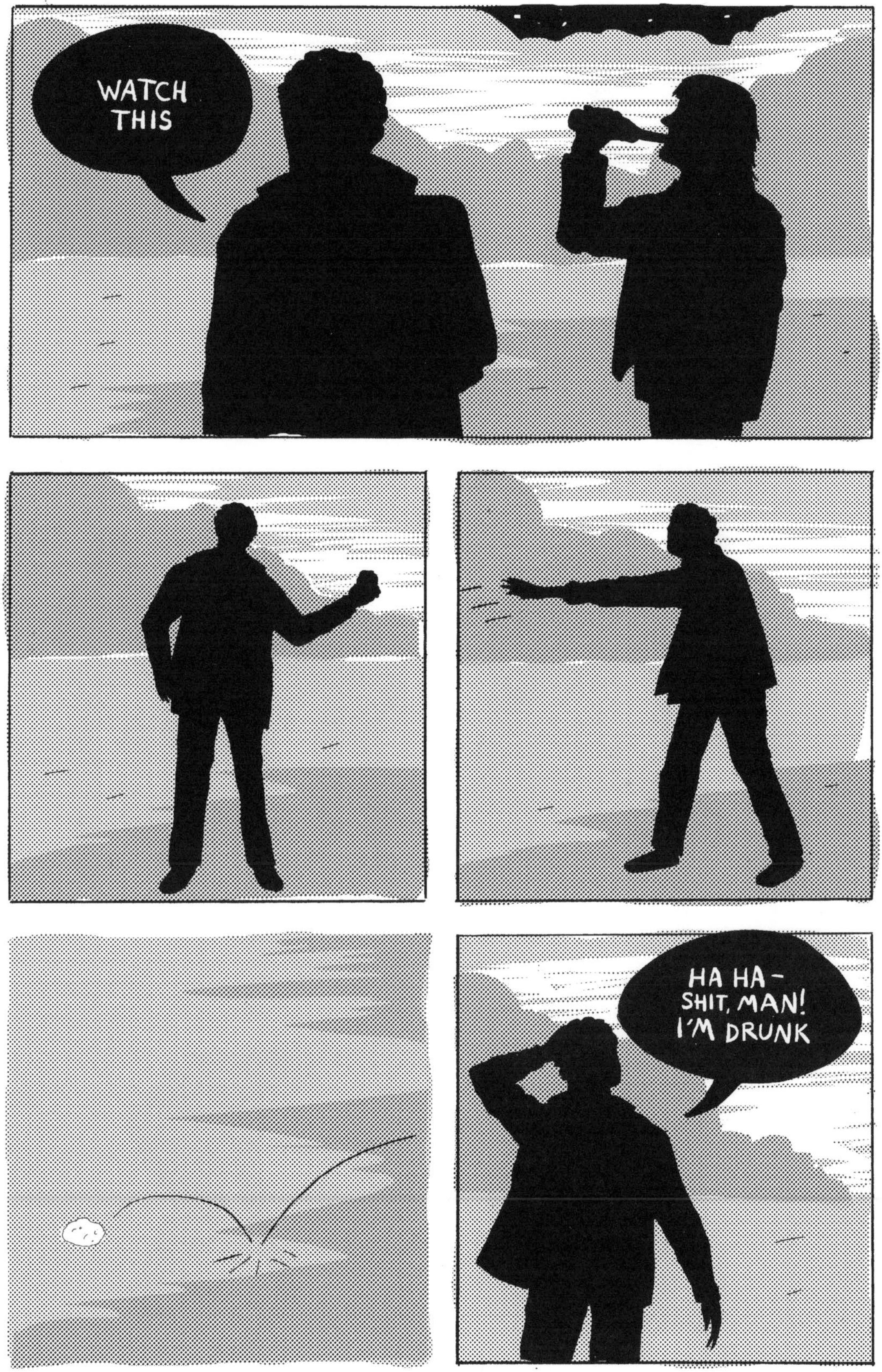
WATCH THIS
HA HA - SHIT, MAN! I'M DRUNK

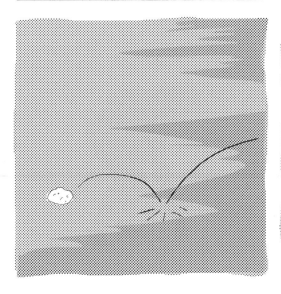

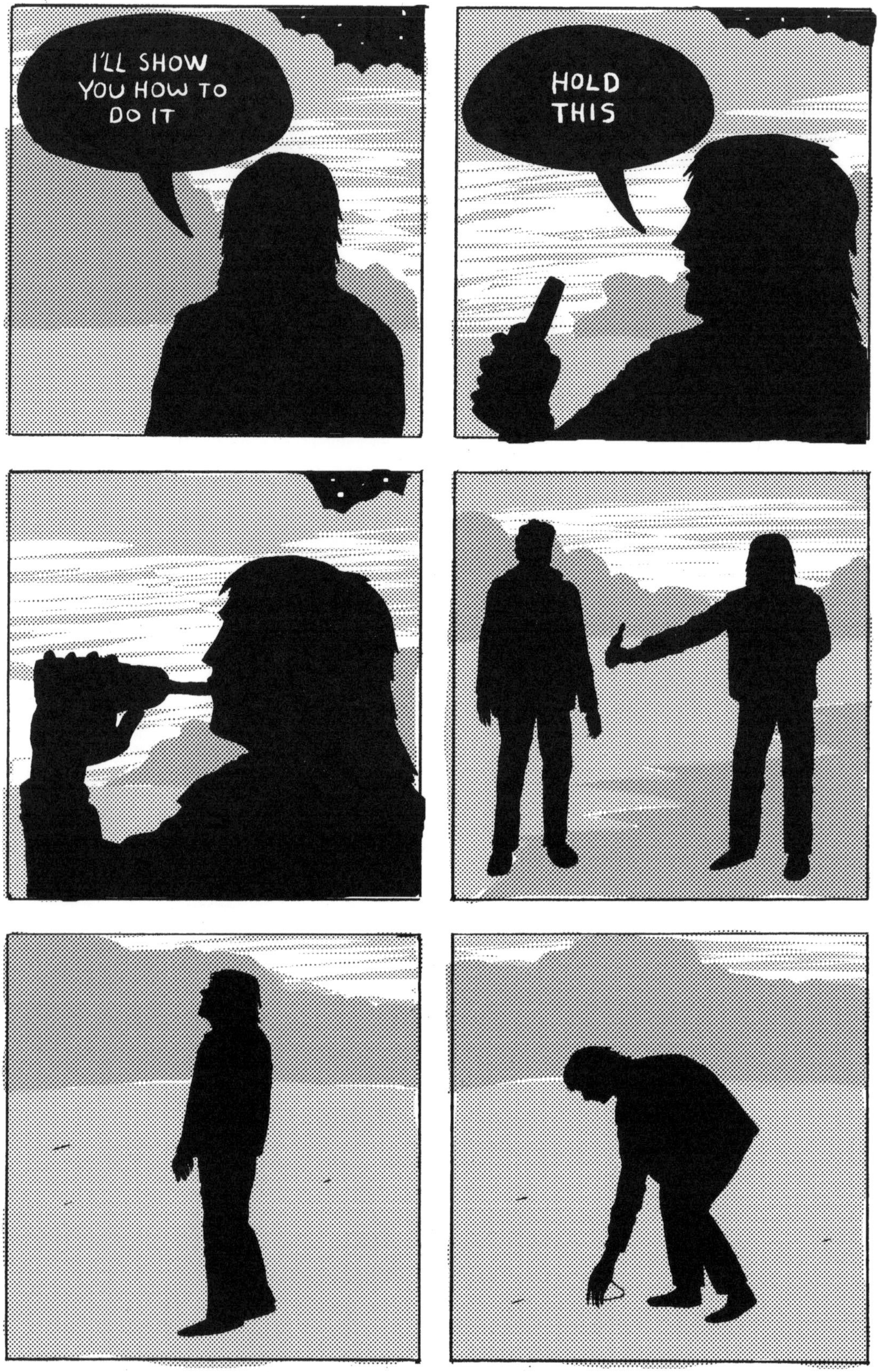
I'LL SHOW YOU HOW TO DO IT
HOLD THIS

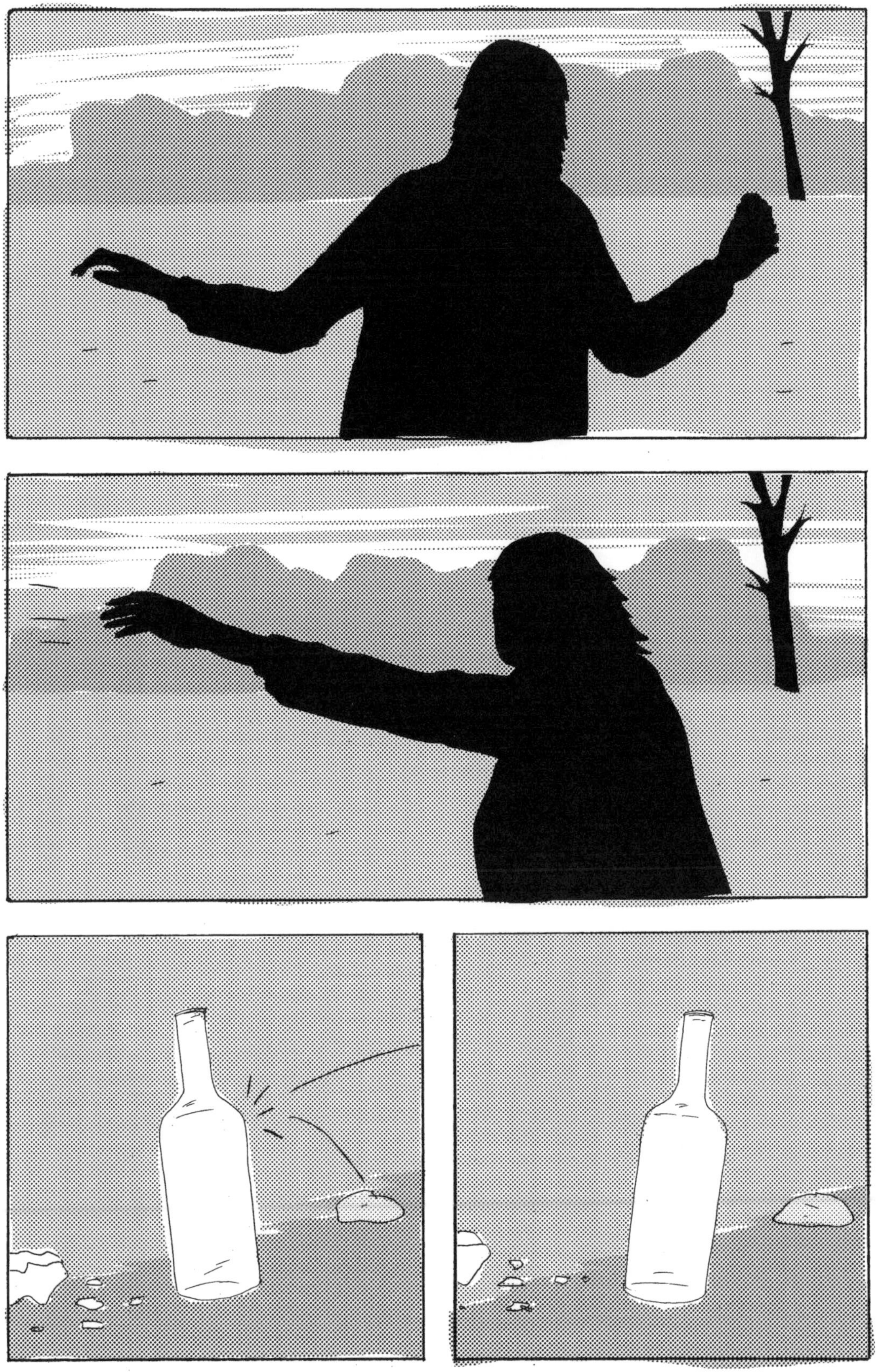

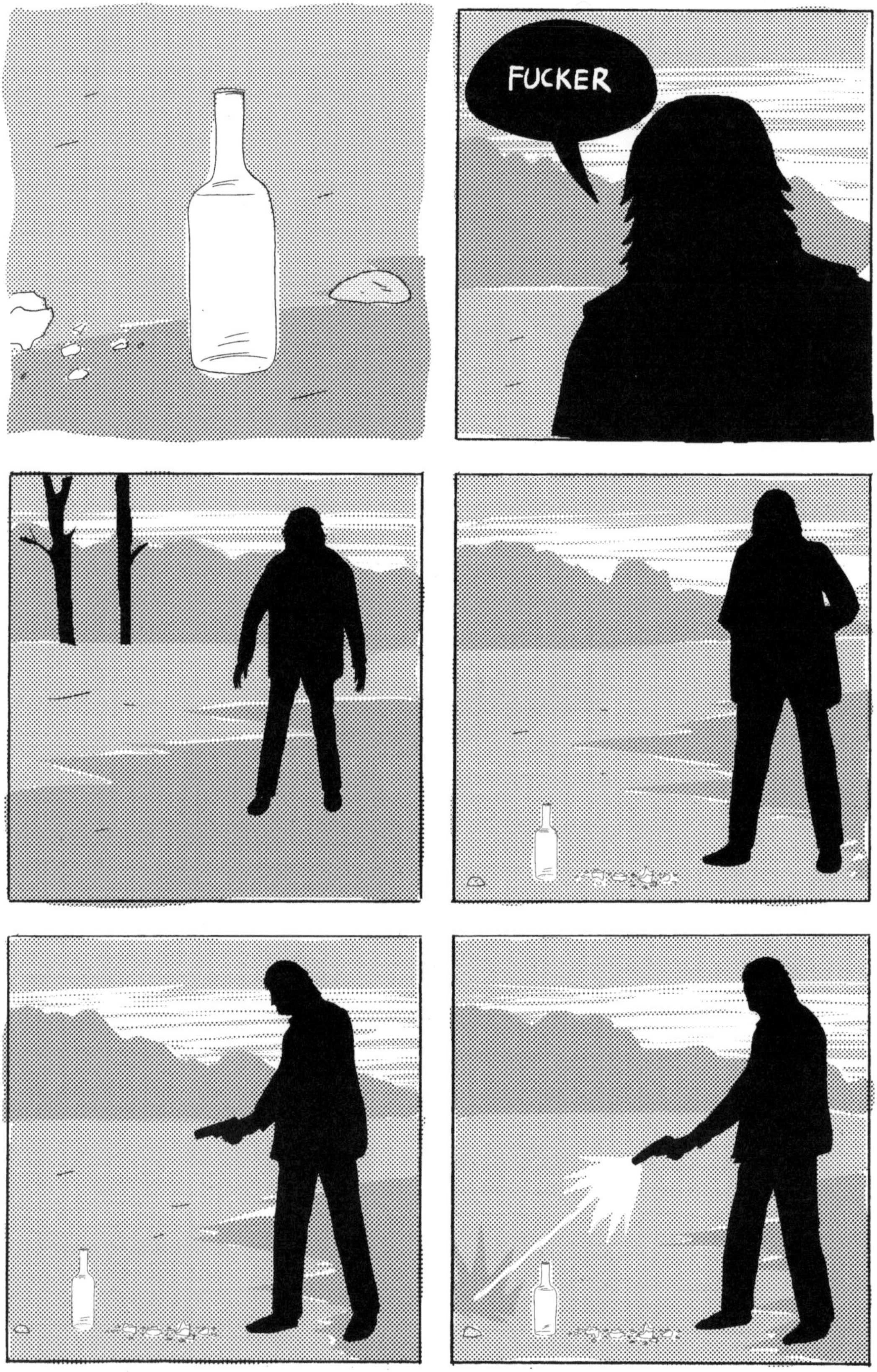
FUCKER

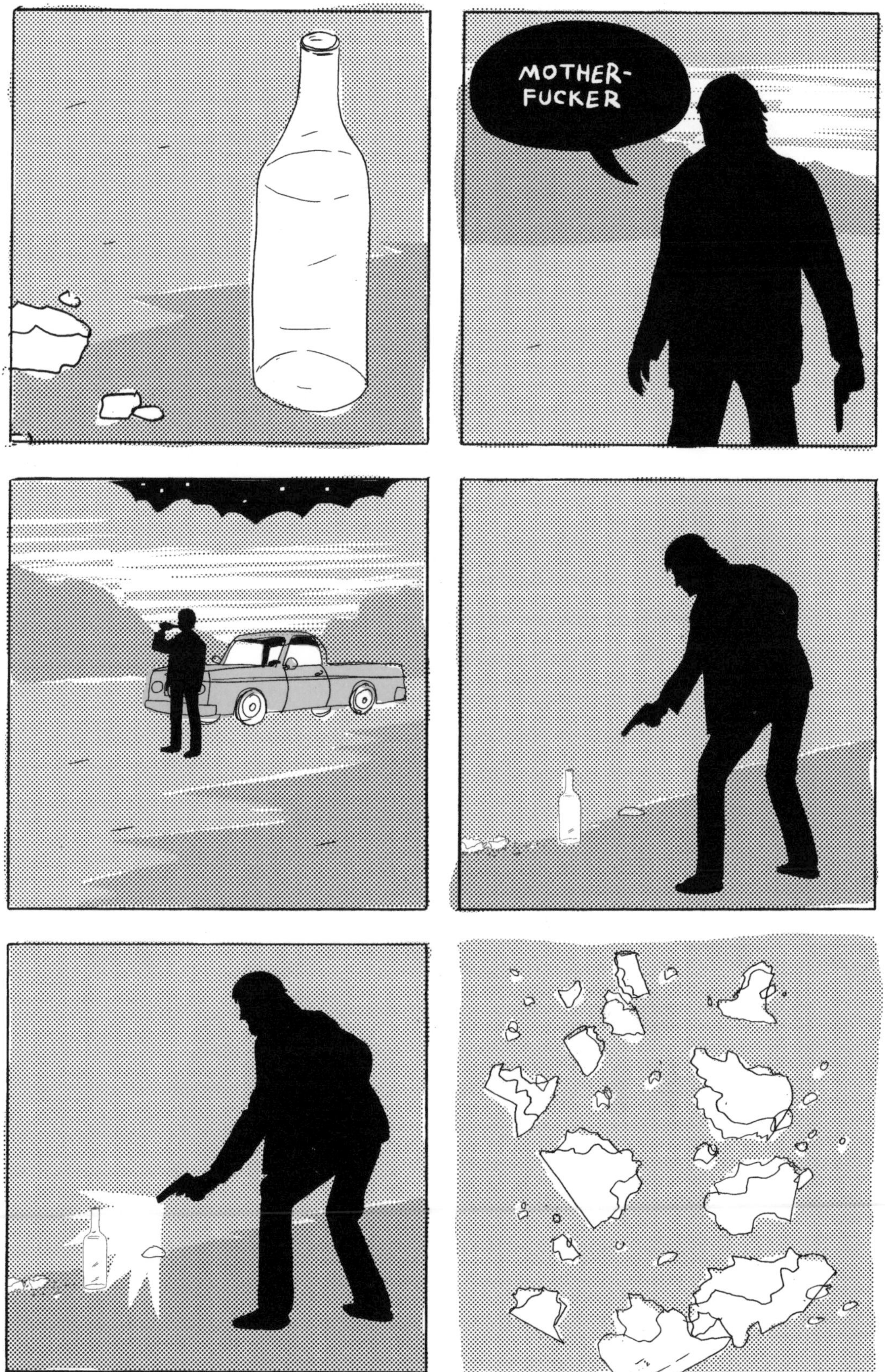
MOTHER-
FUCKER

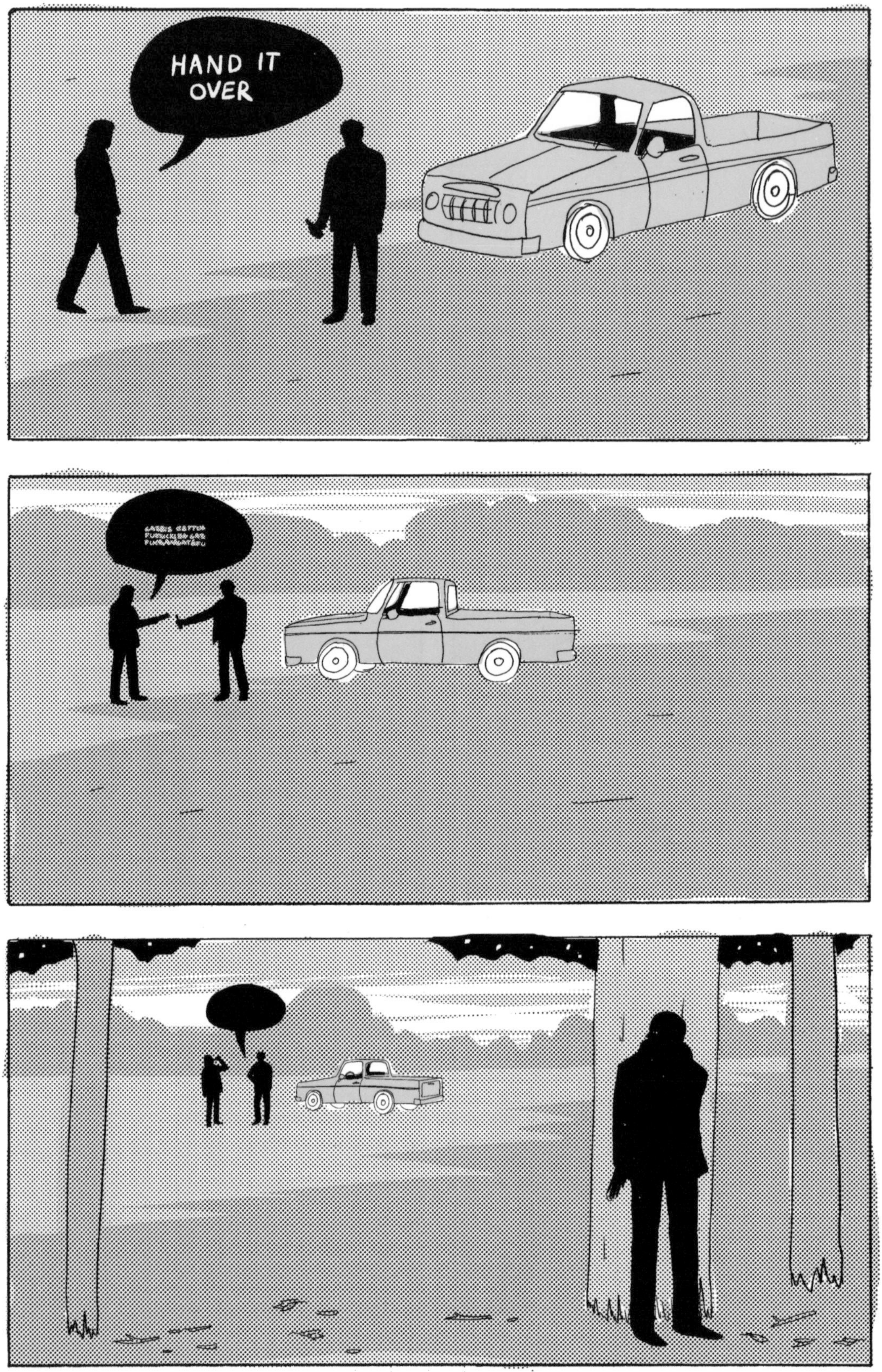
HAND IT OVER

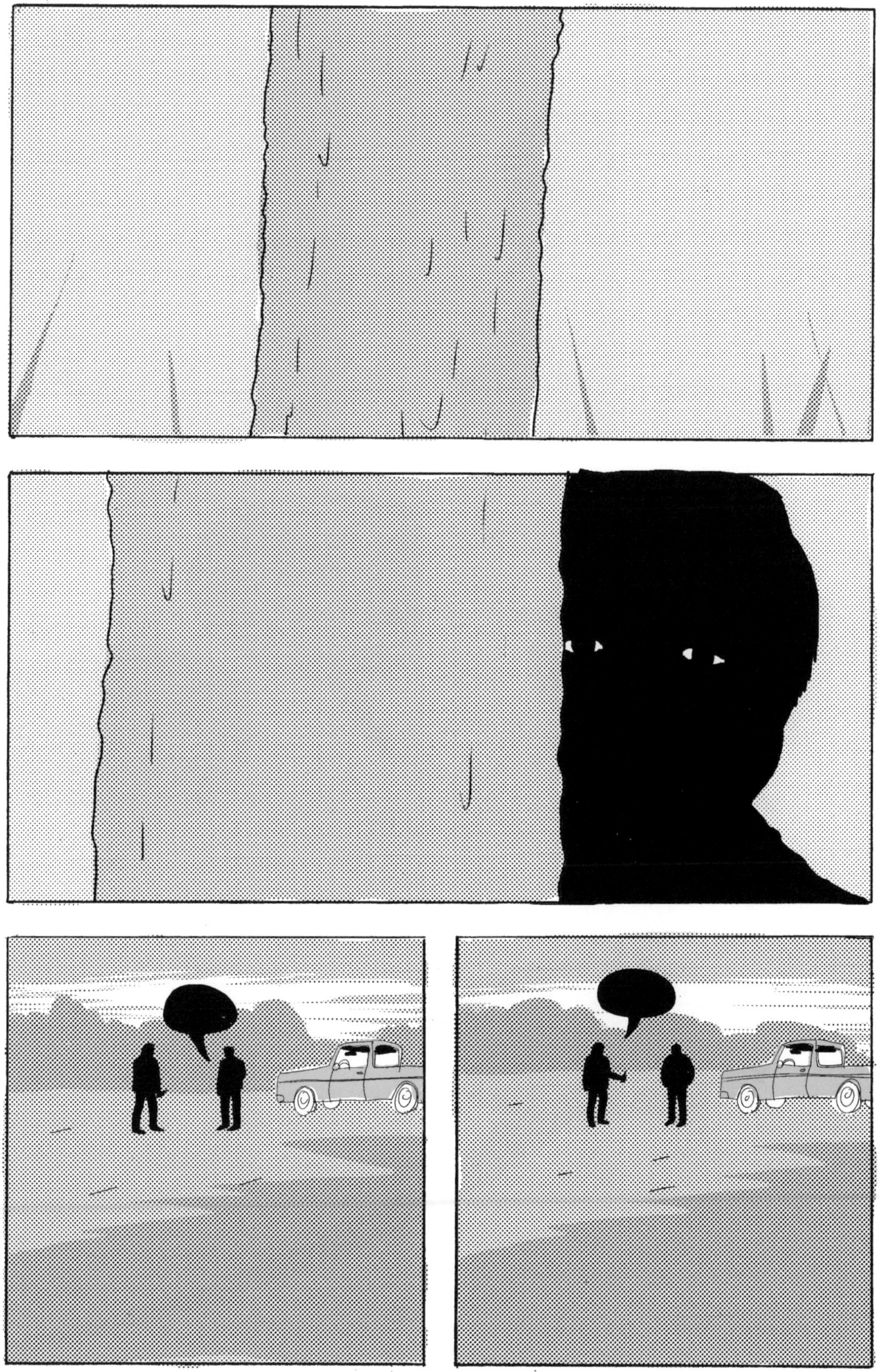

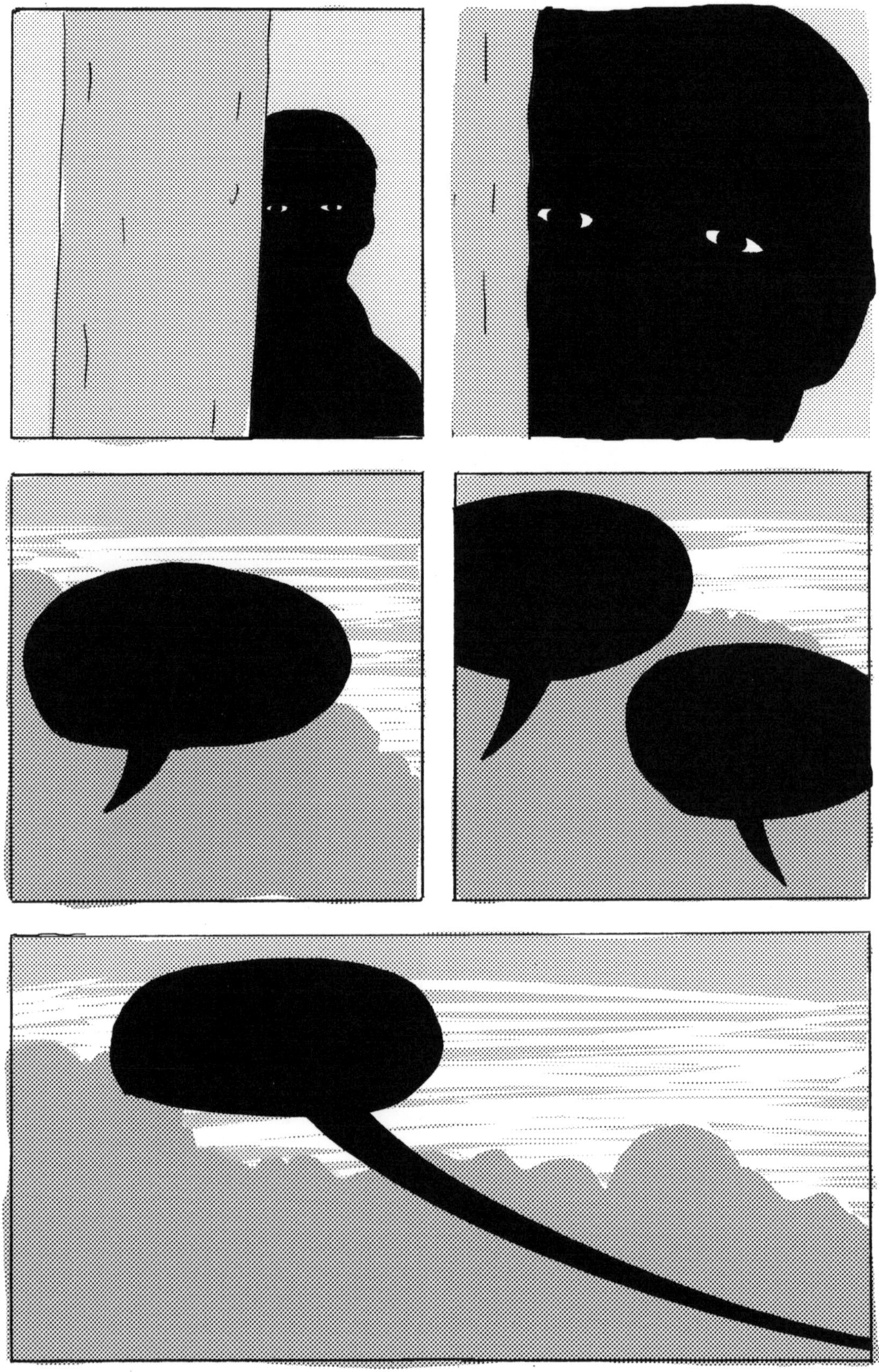

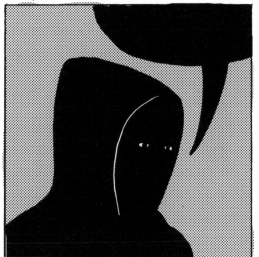

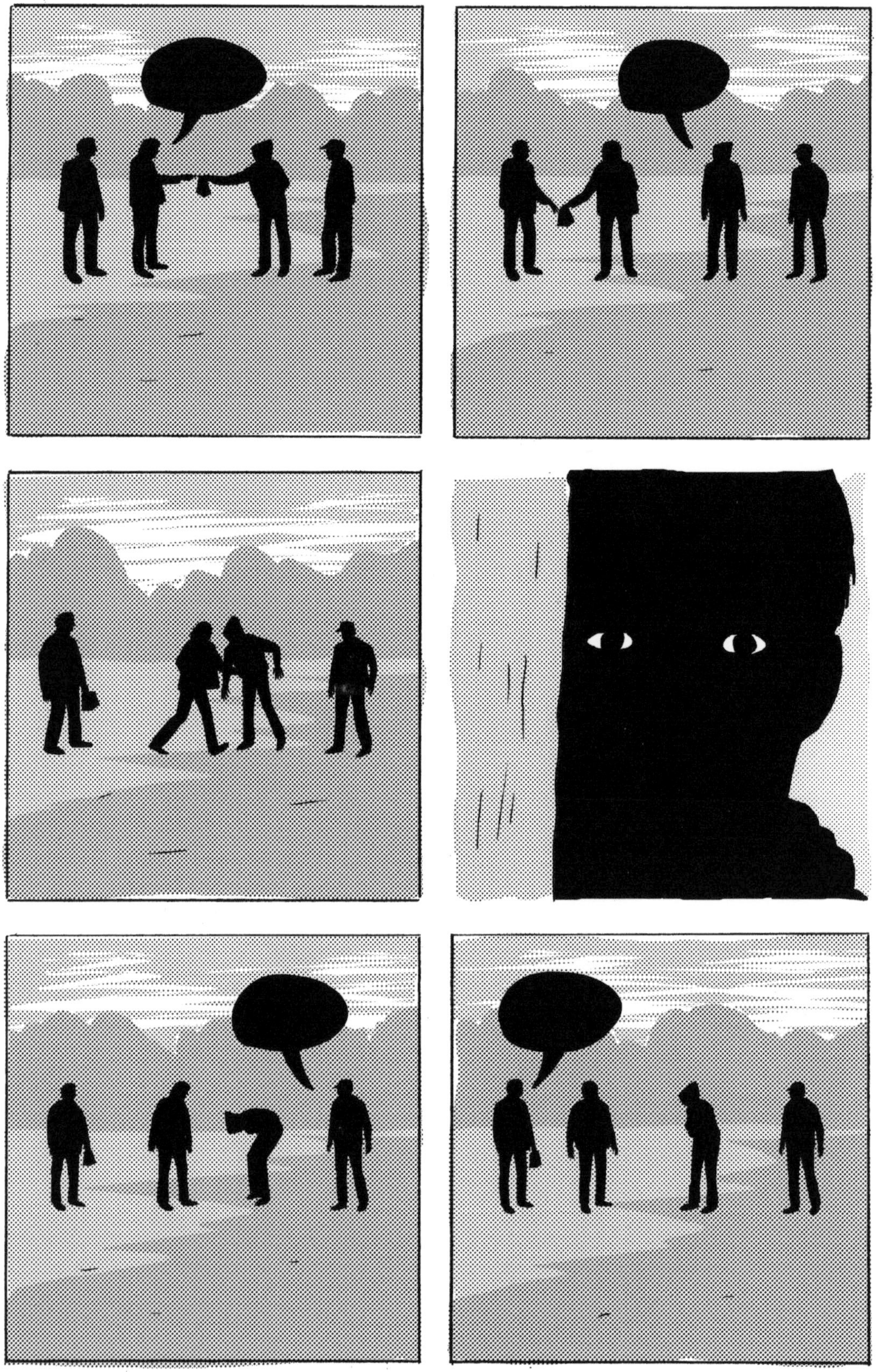

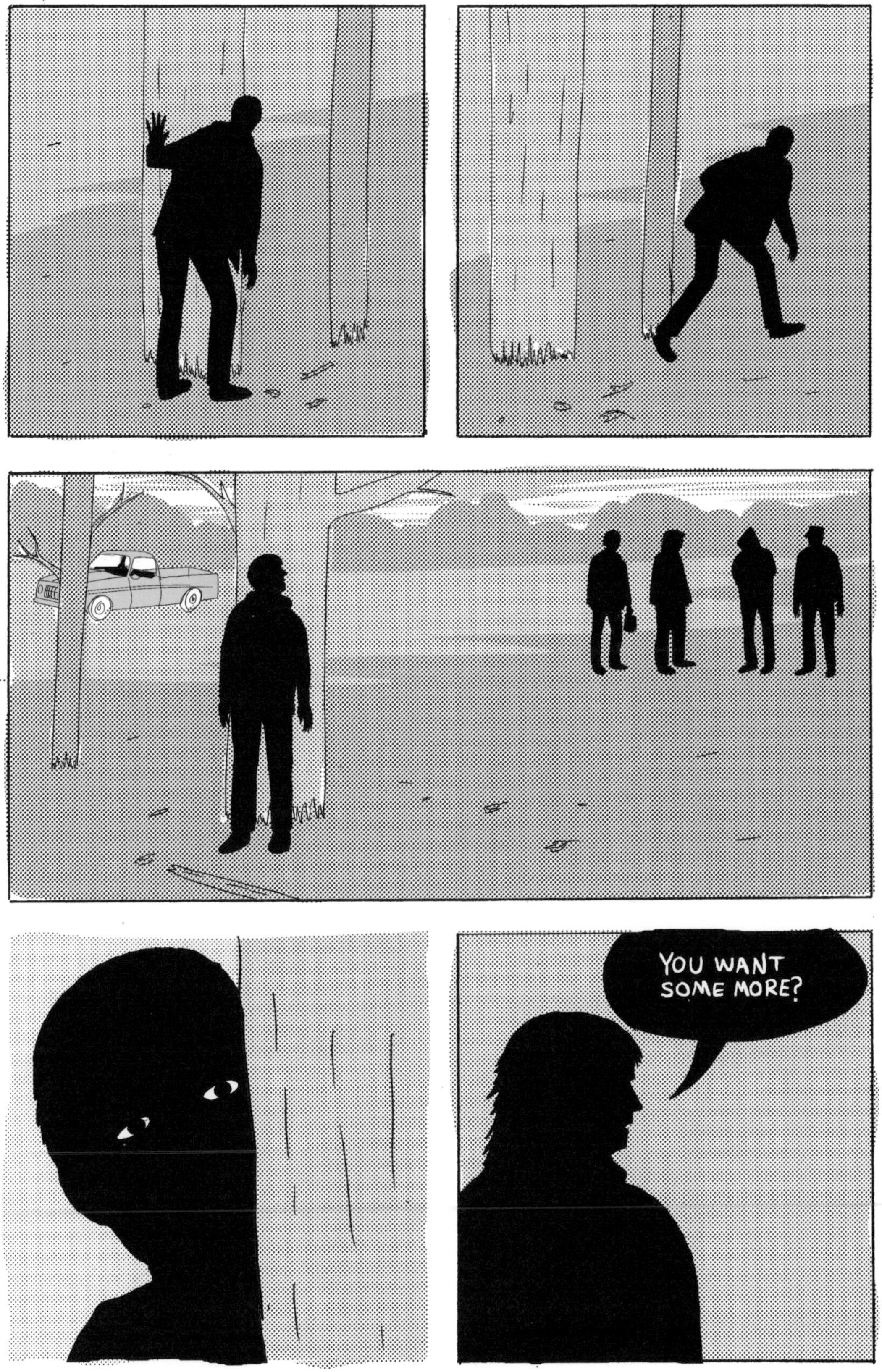
YOU WANT SOME MORE?

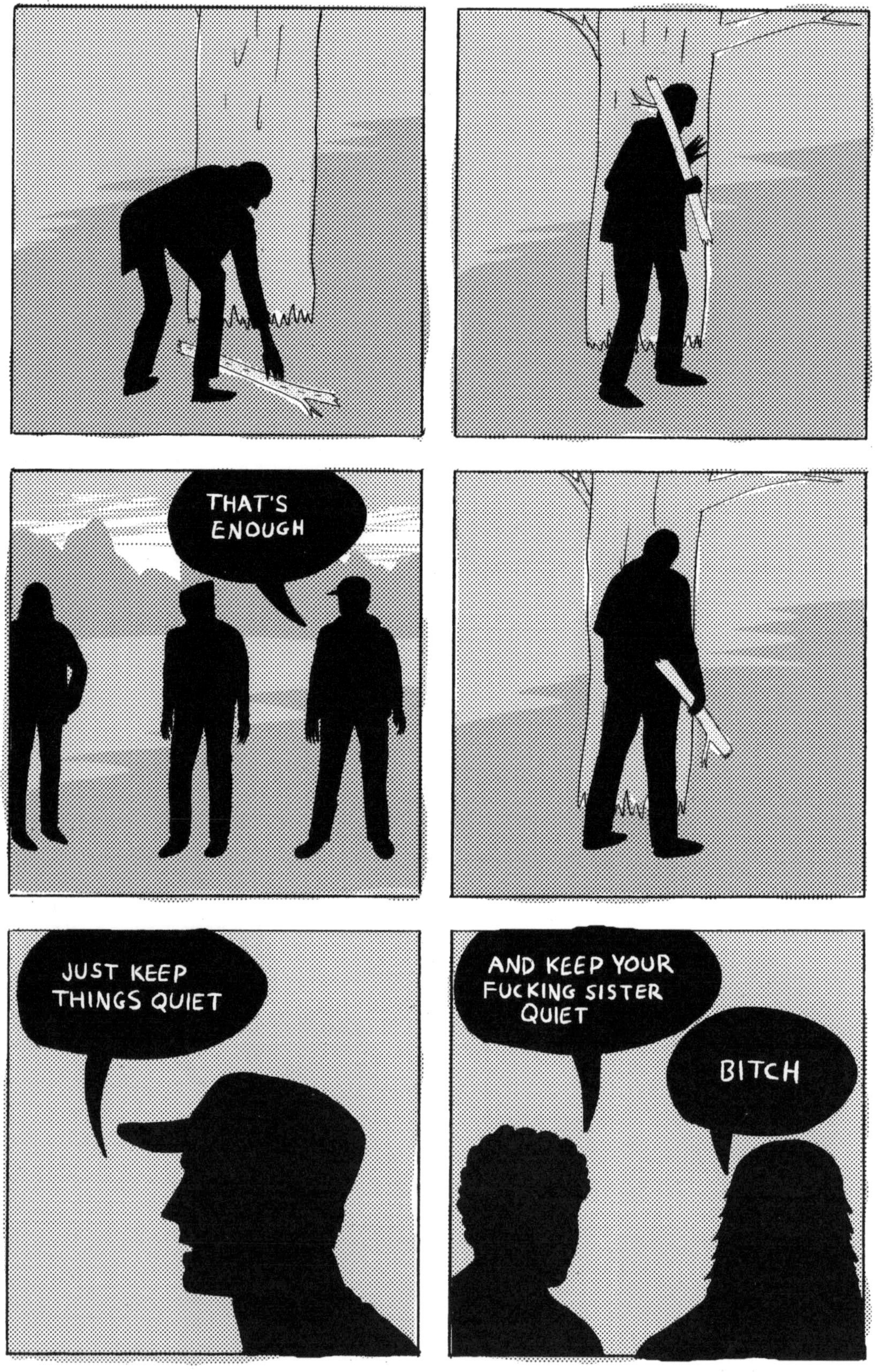
THAT'S ENOUGH
JUST KEEP THINGS QUIET
AND KEEP YOUR FUCKING SISTER QUIET
BITCH

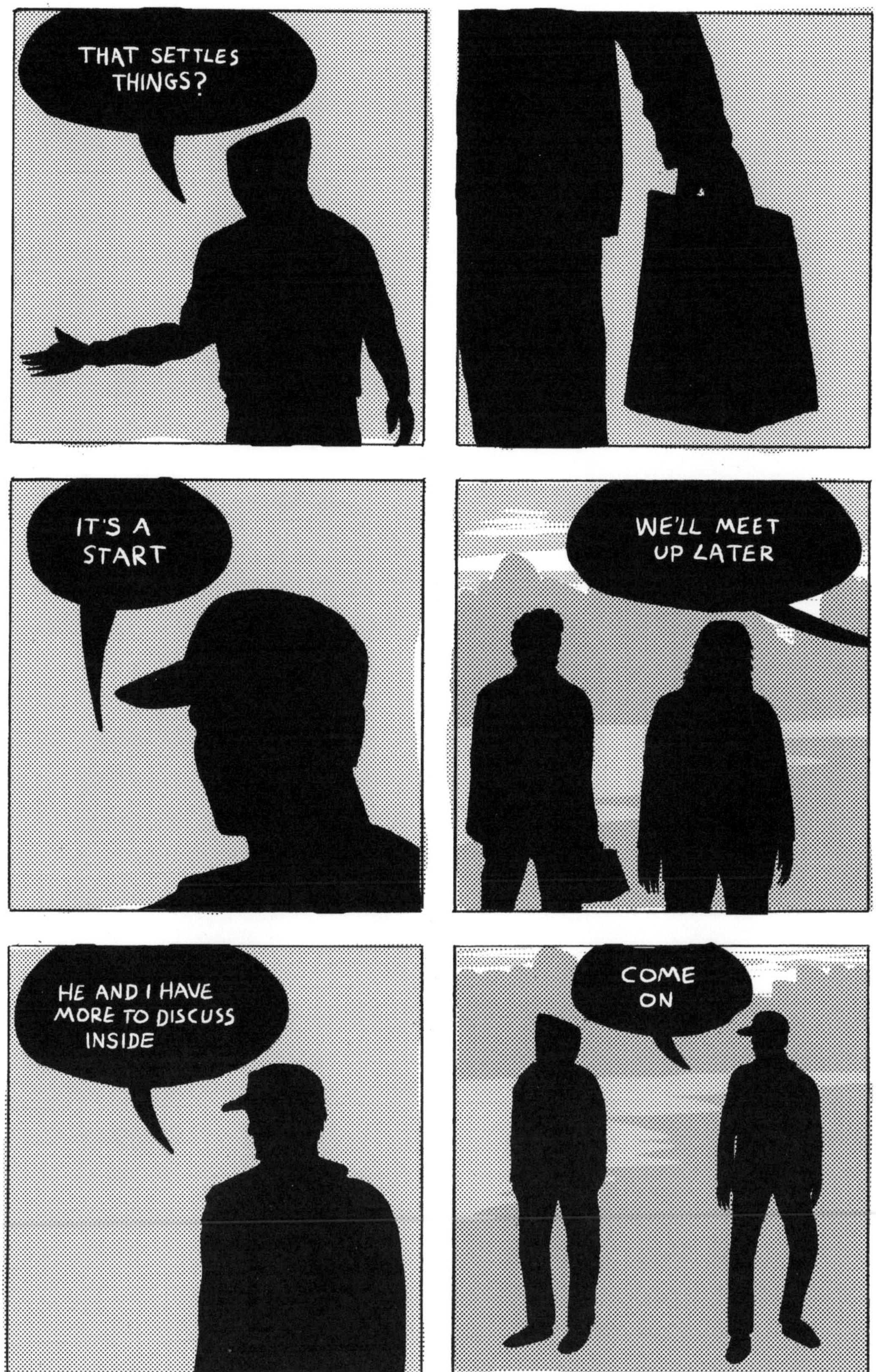
THAT SETTLES THINGS?
IT'S A START
WE'LL MEET UP LATER
HE AND I HAVE MORE TO DISCUSS INSIDE
COME ON

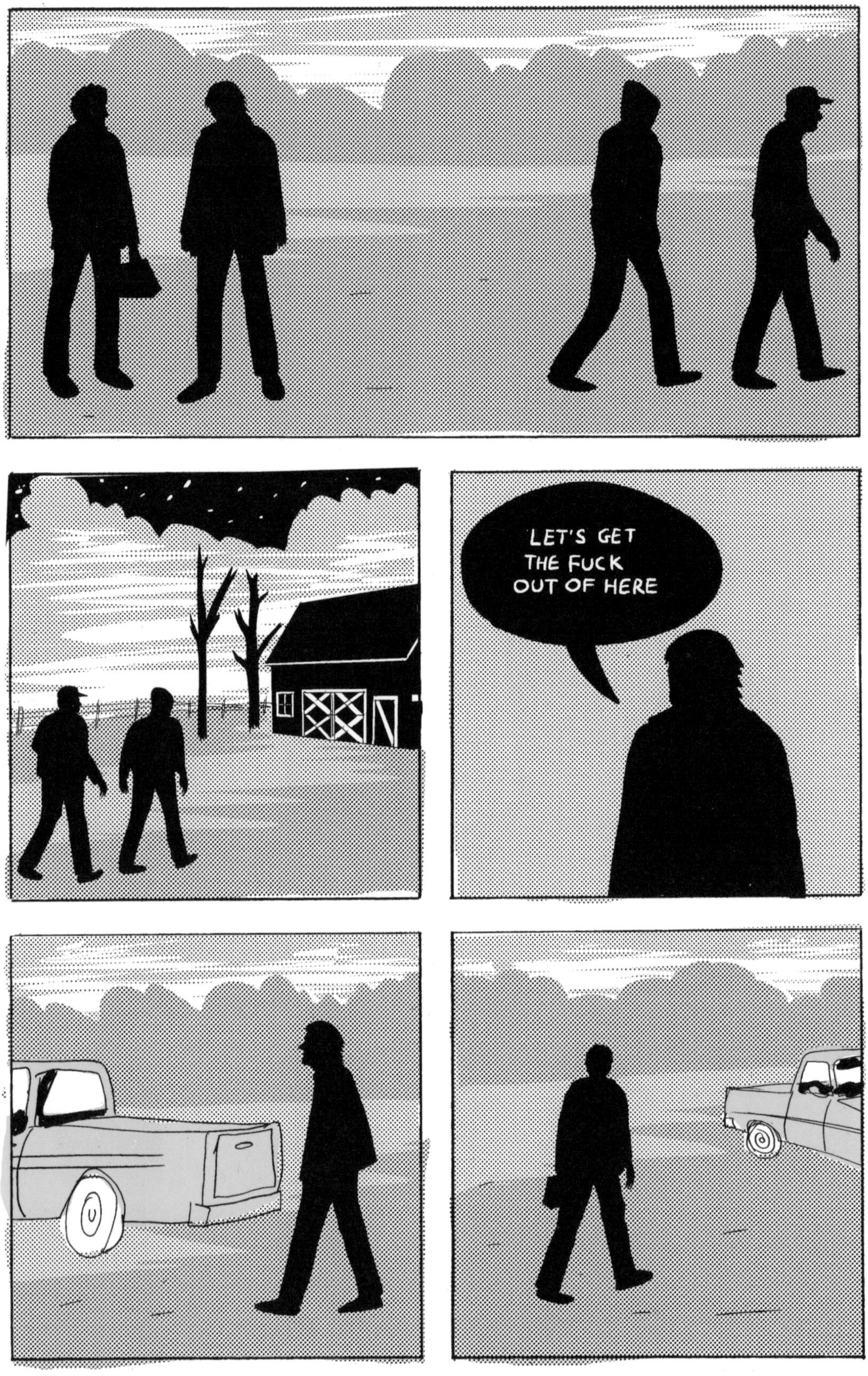
LET'S GET THE FUCK OUT OF HERE

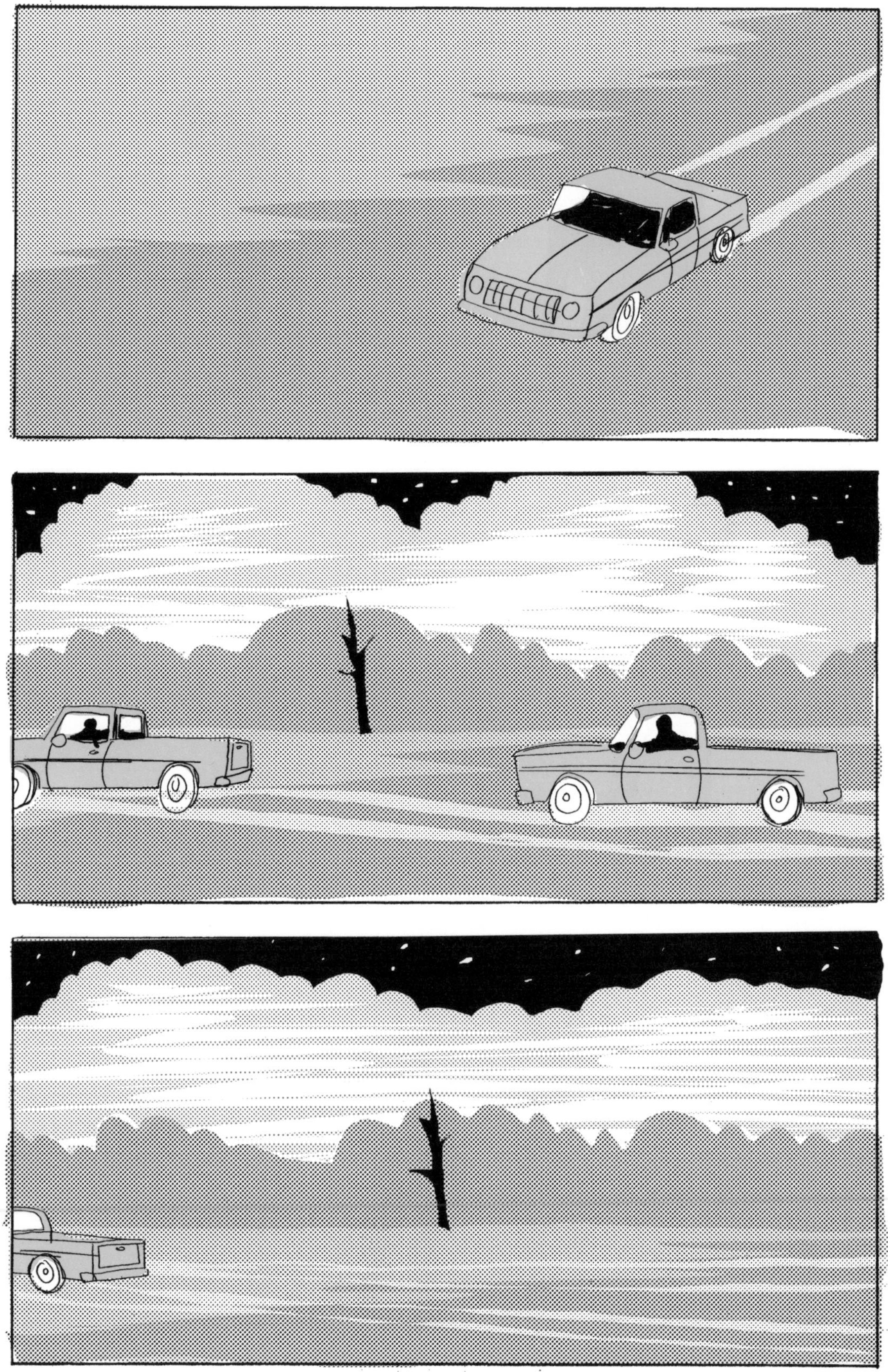

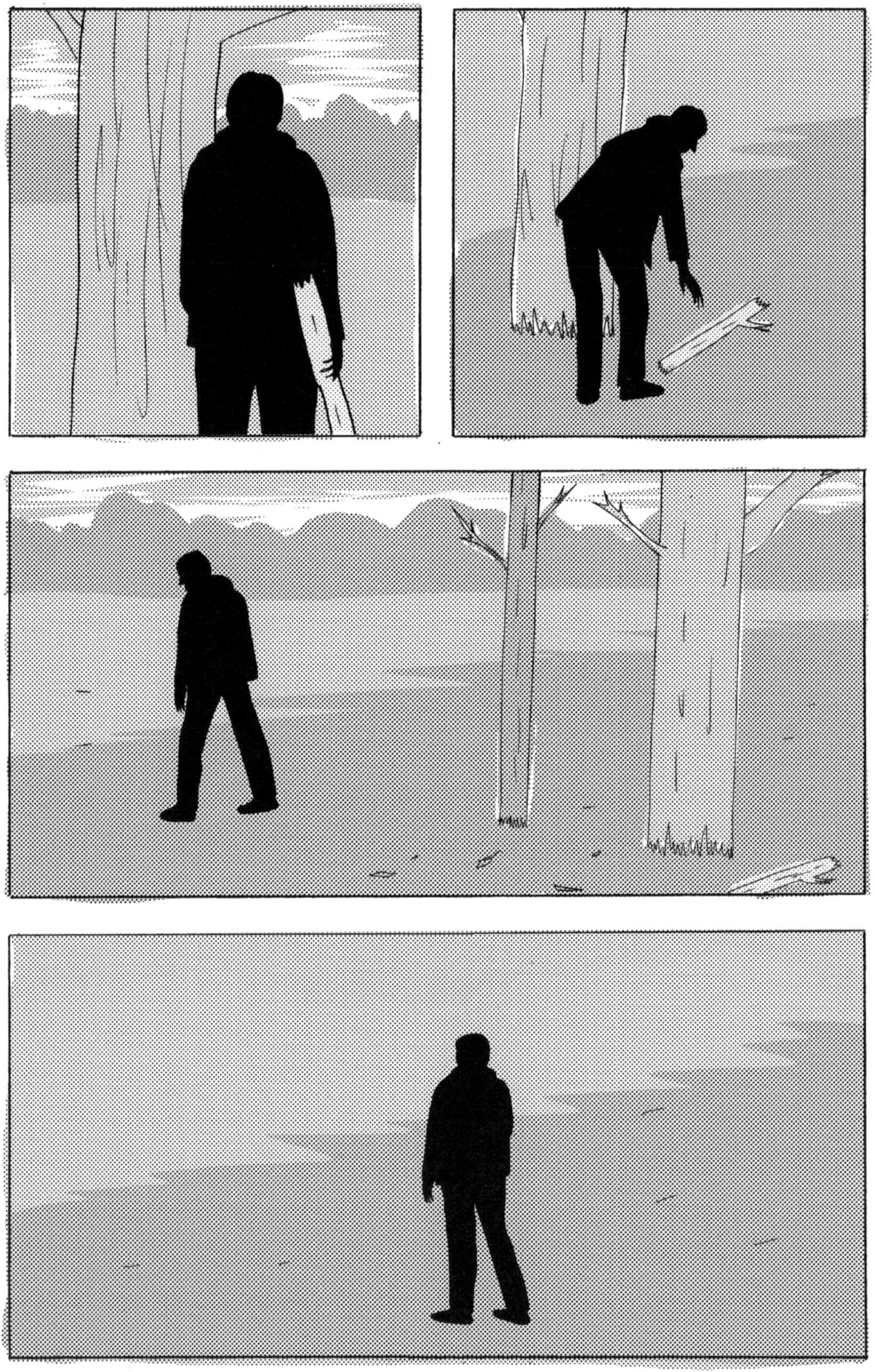

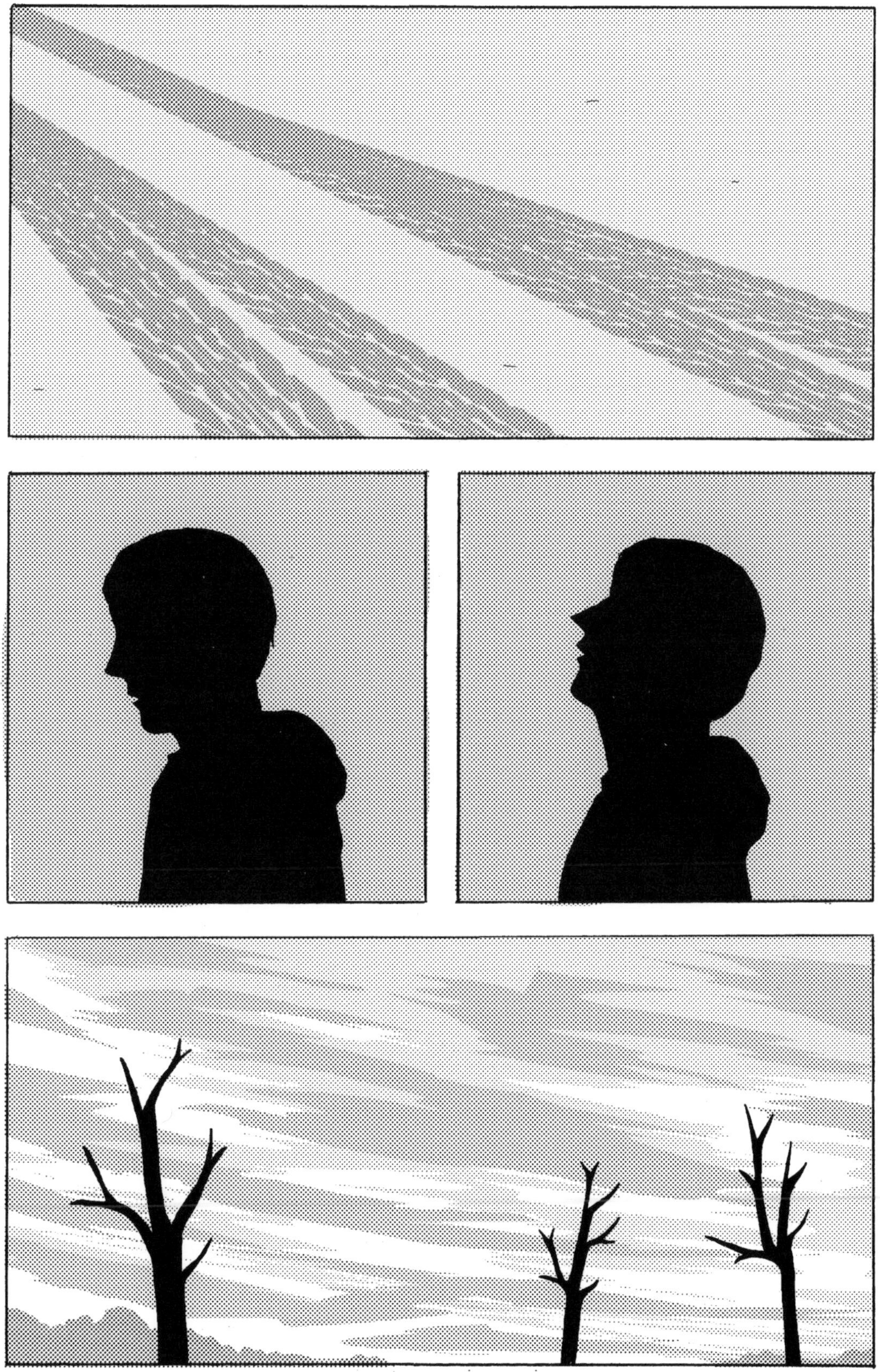

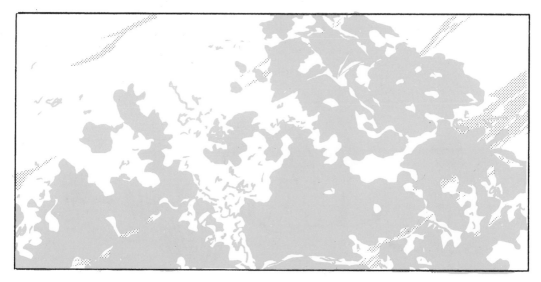

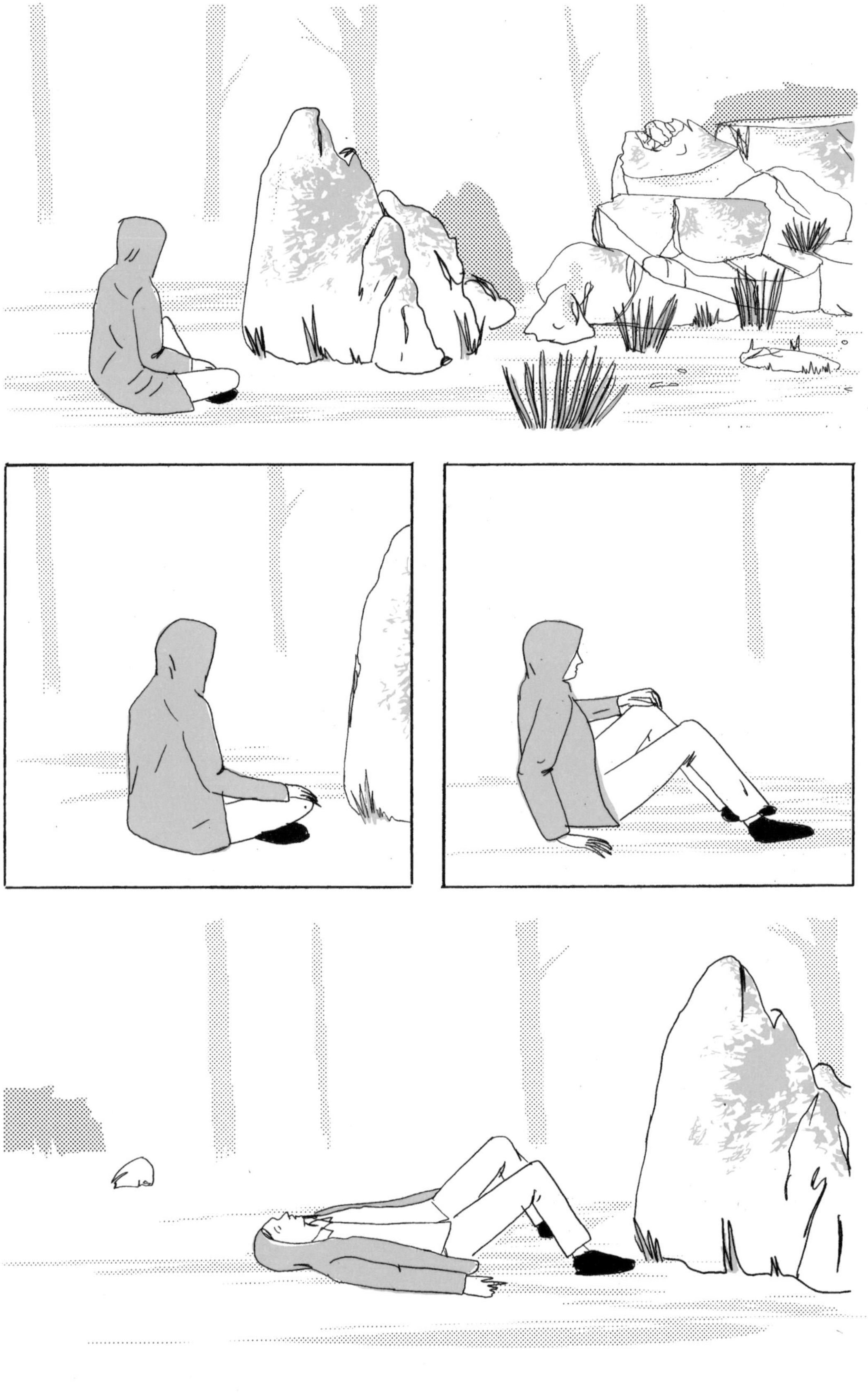

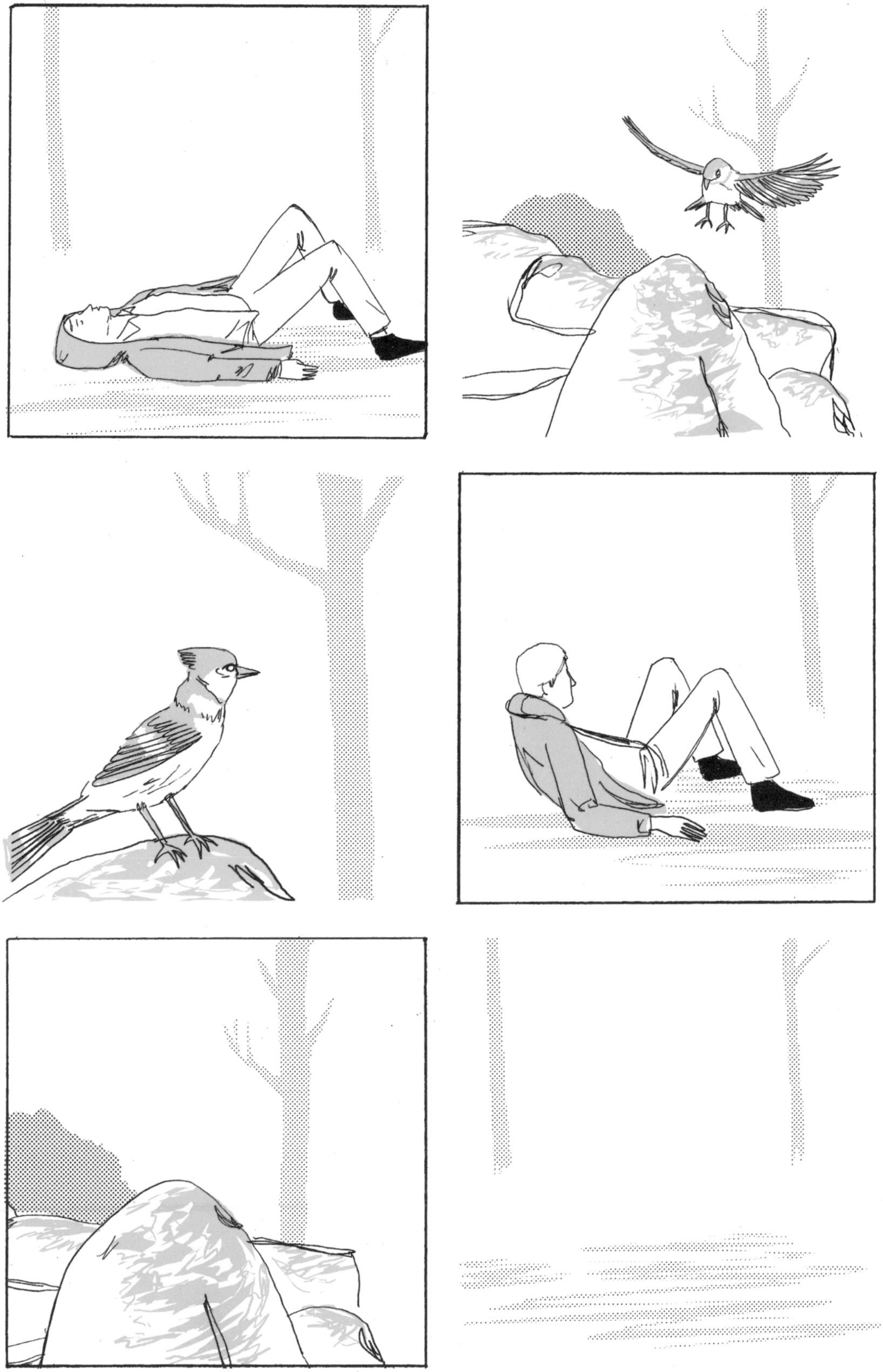

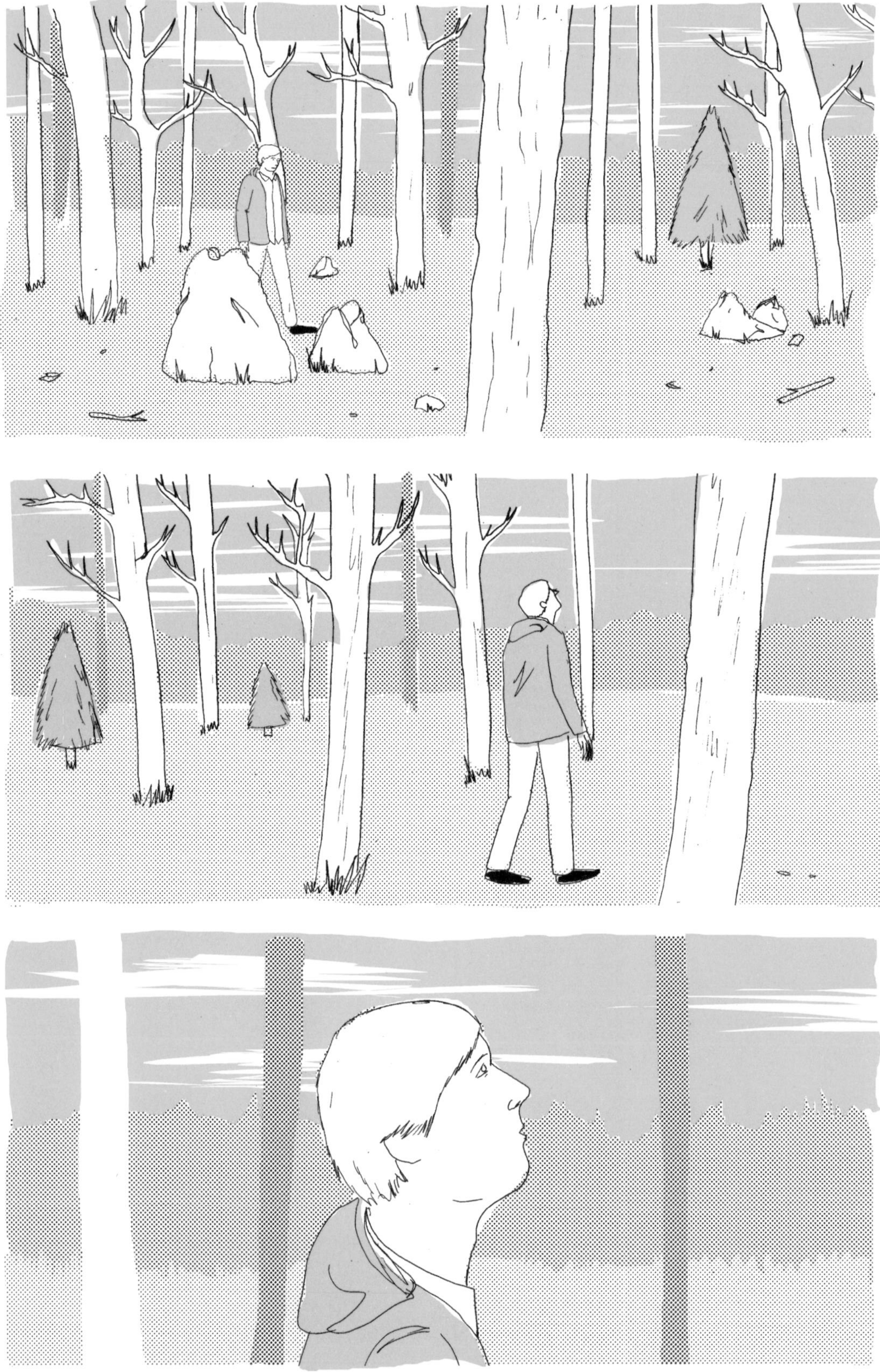

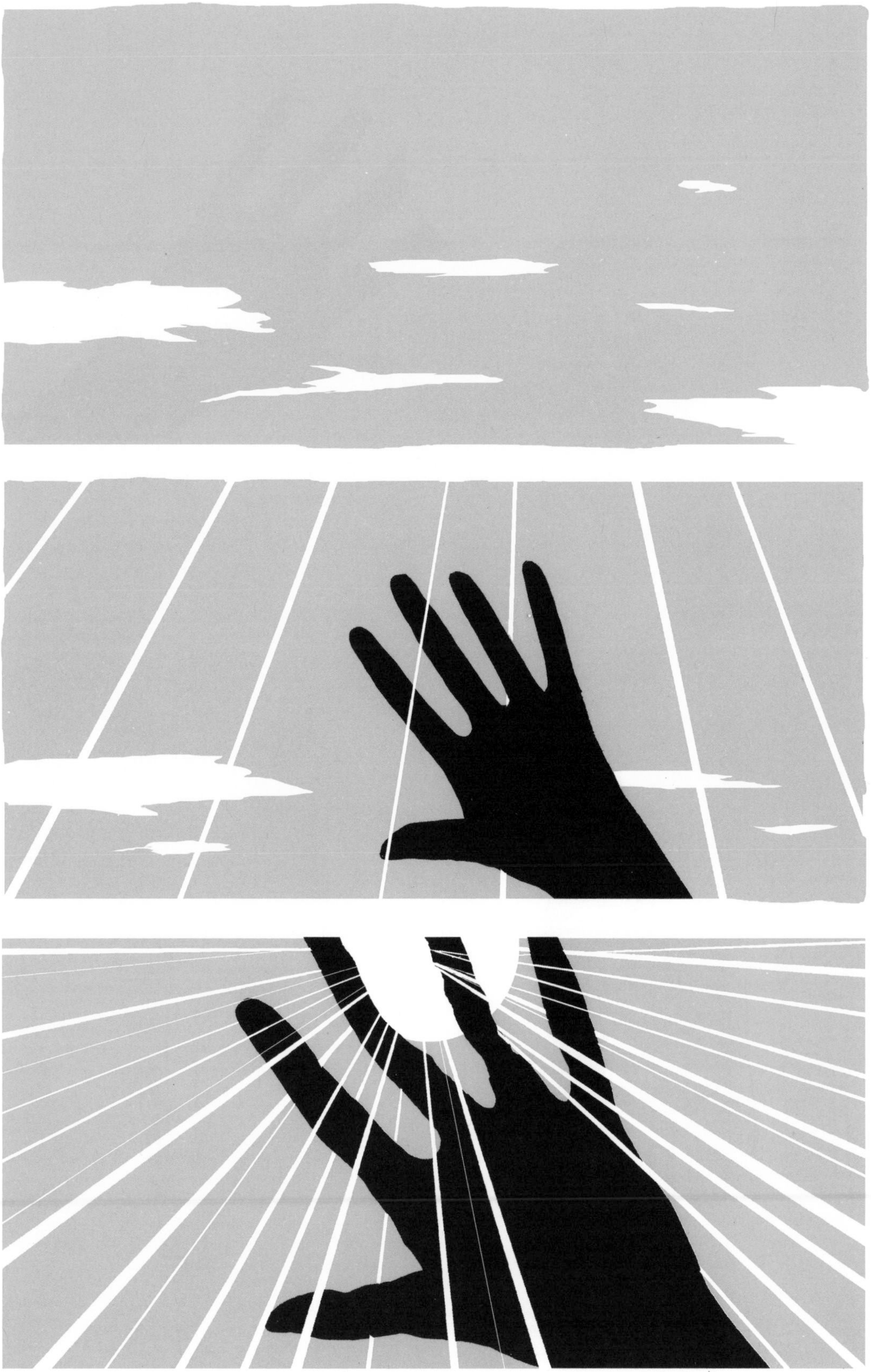

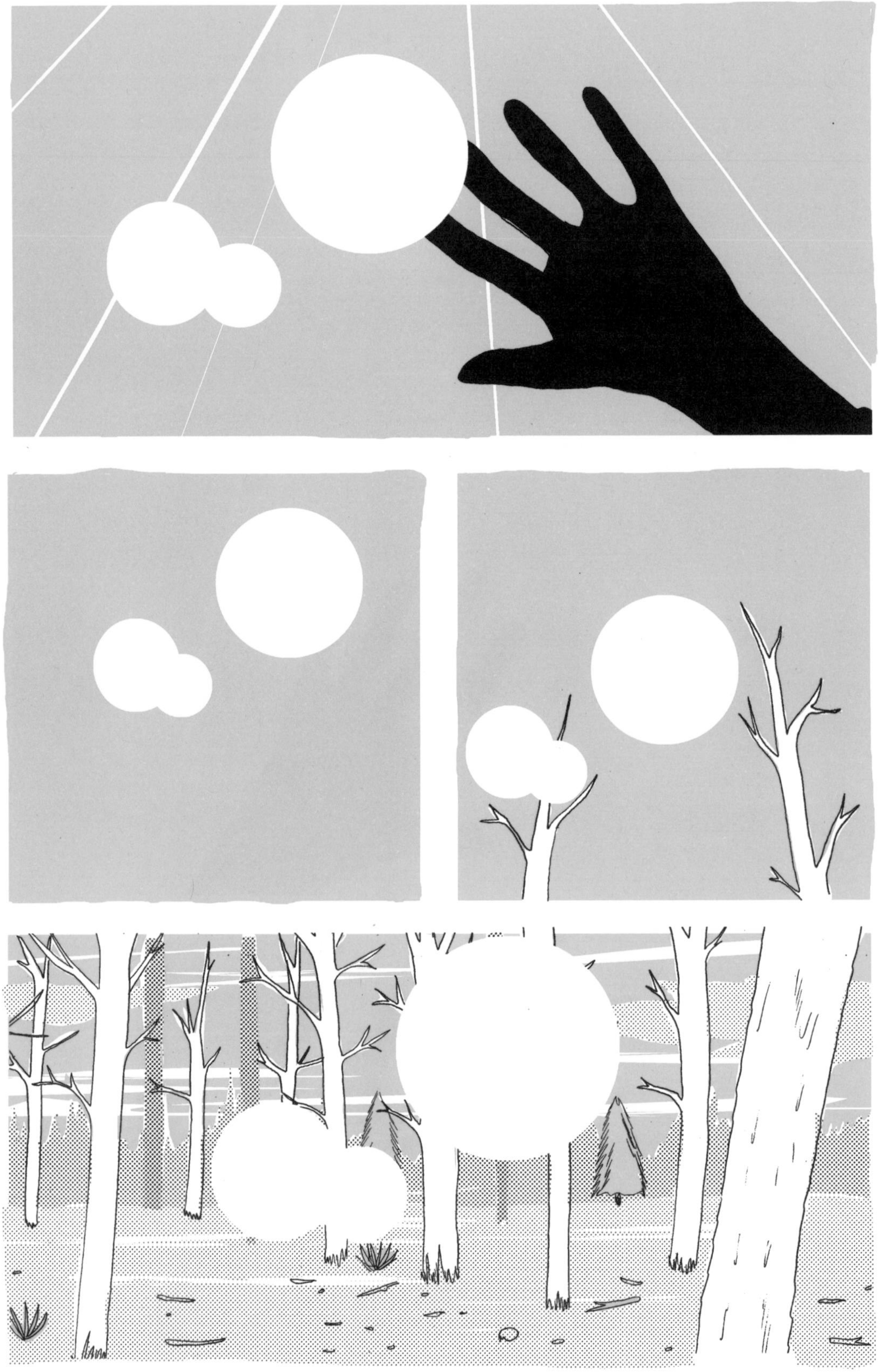

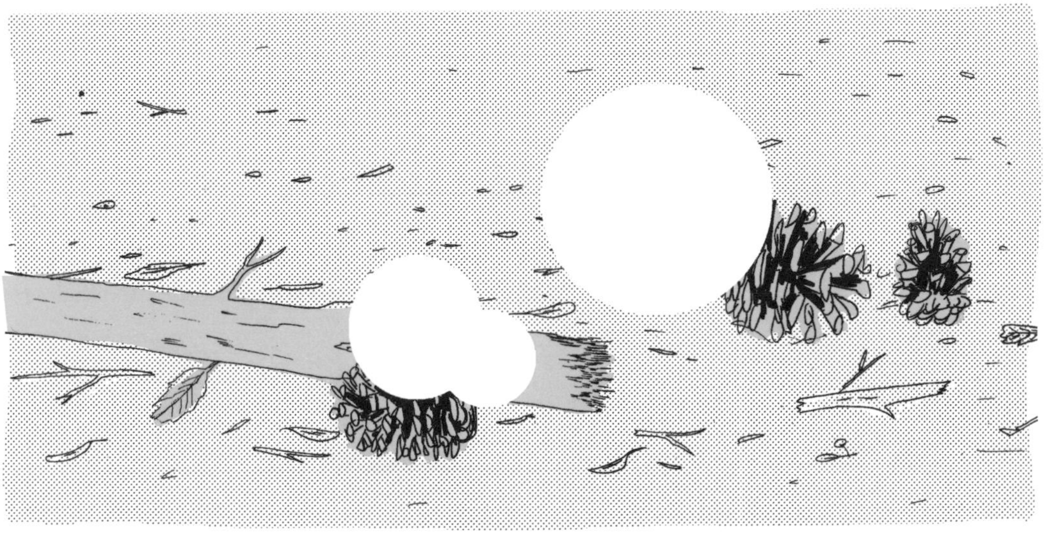
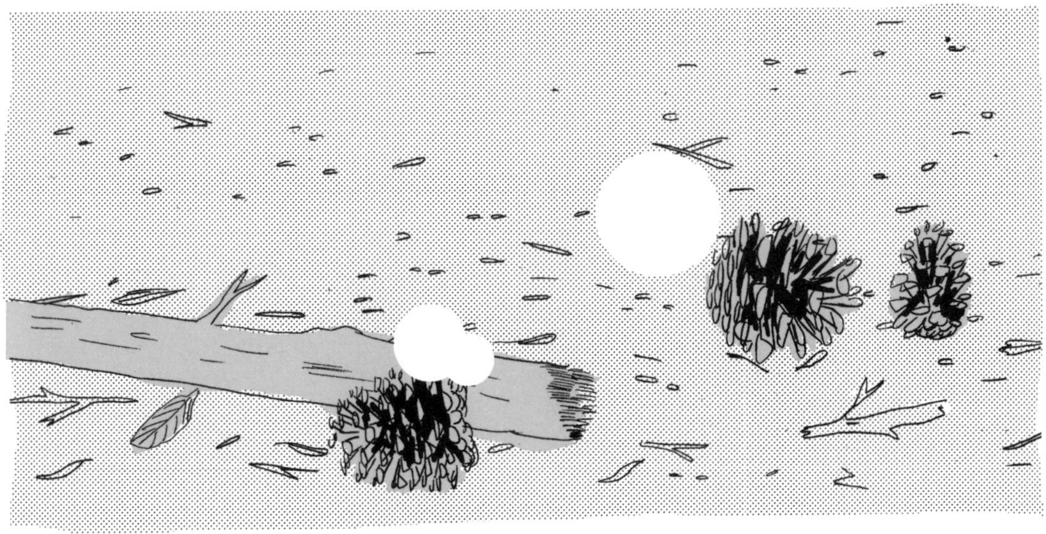
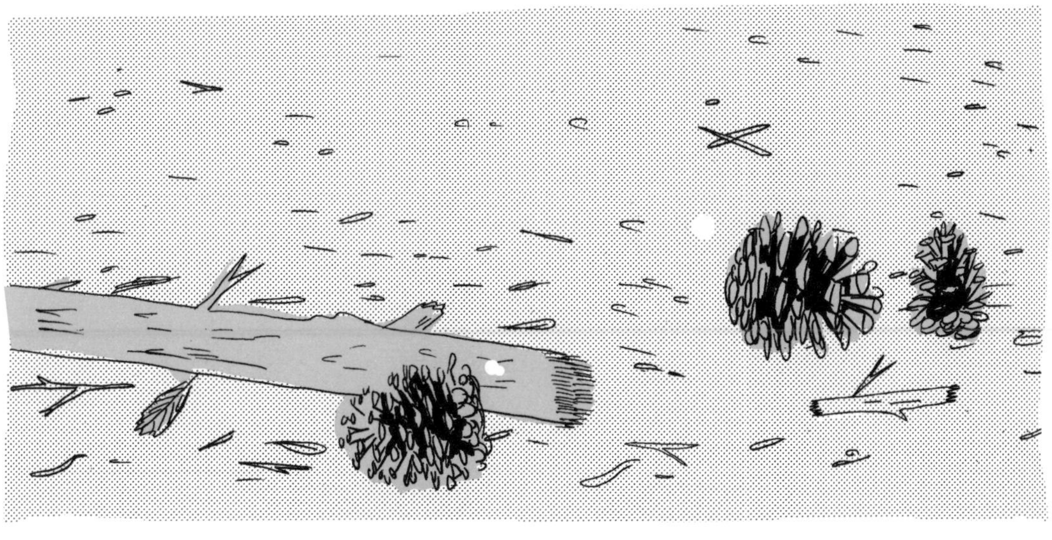

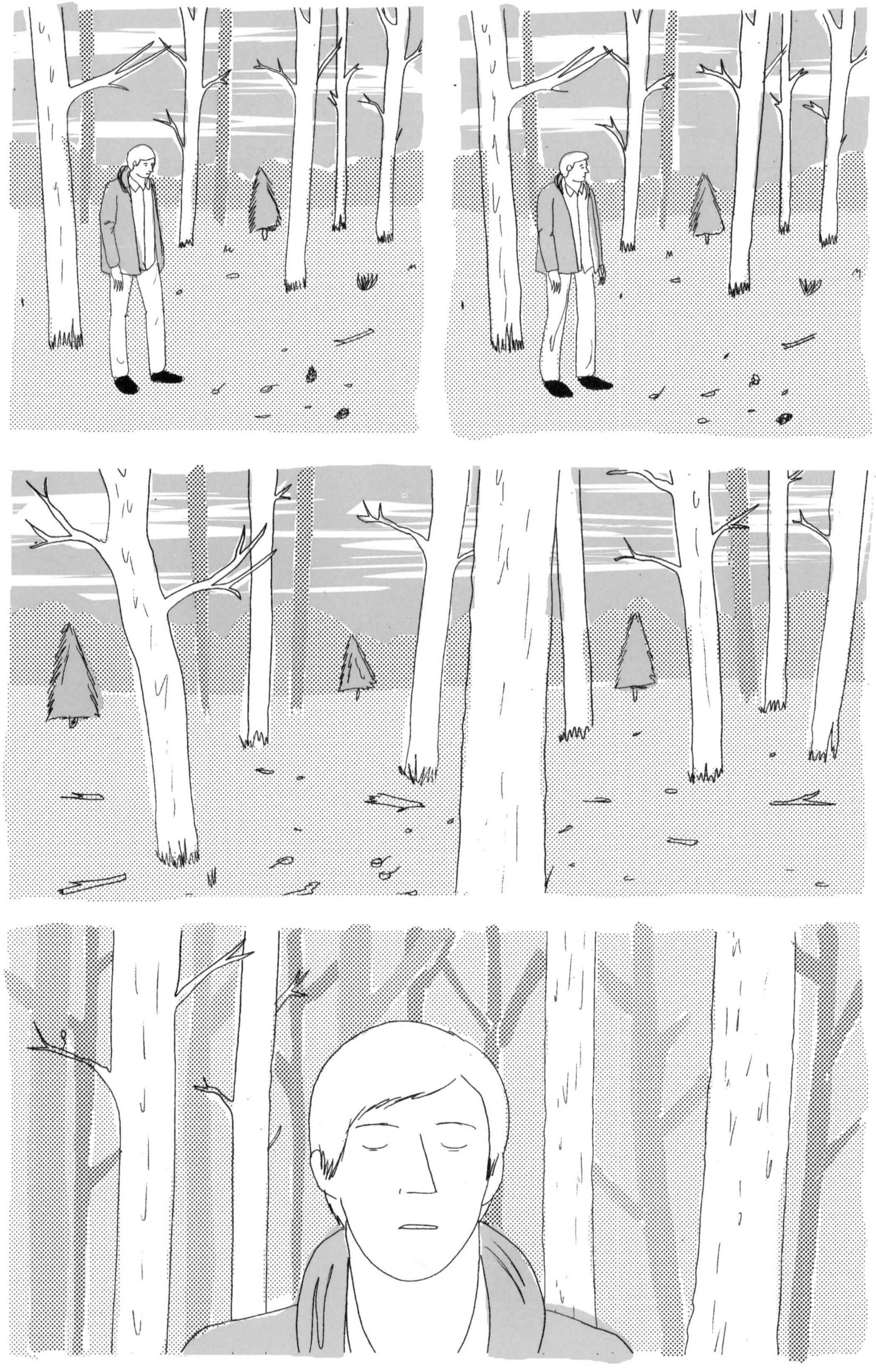

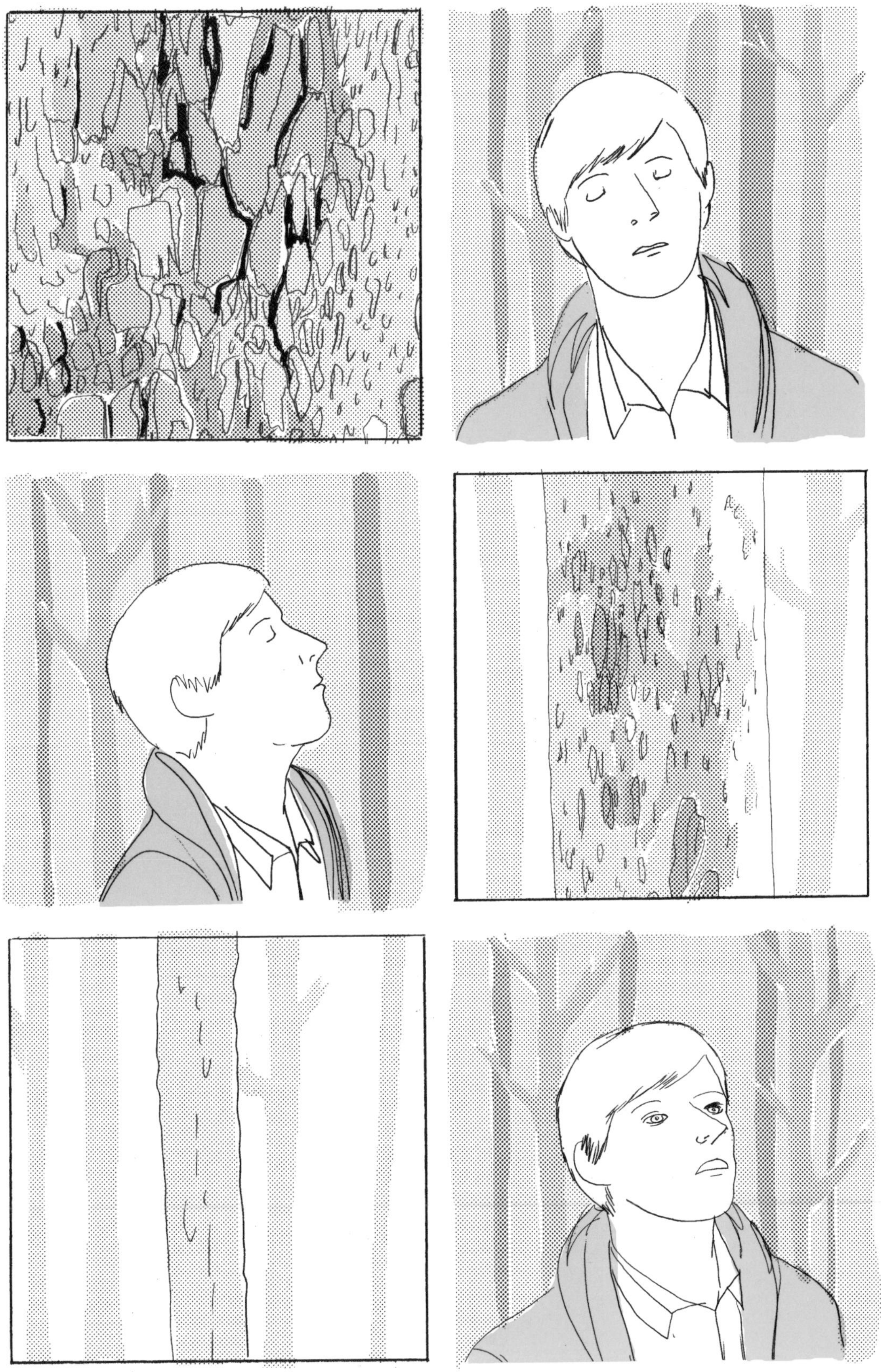

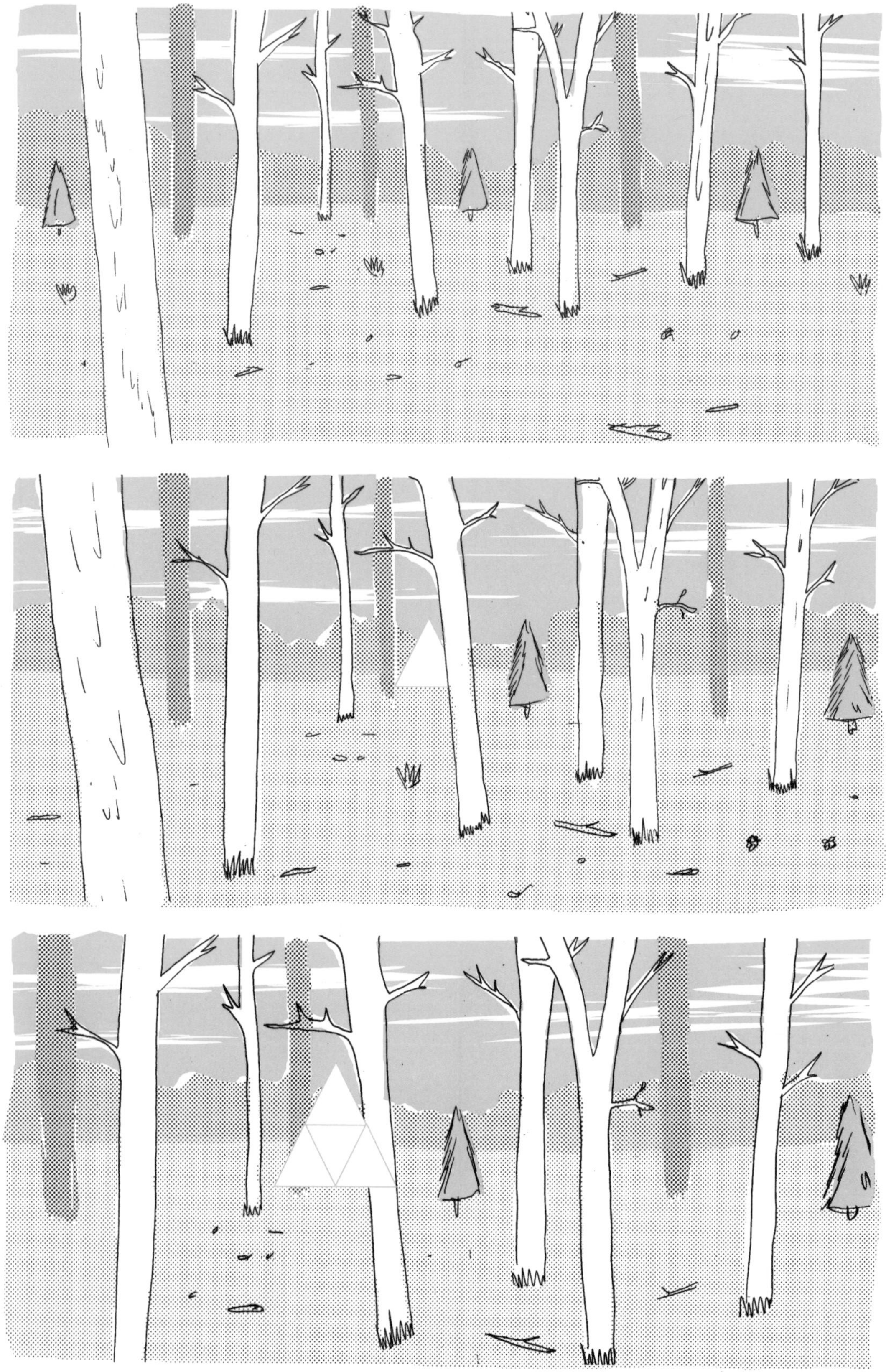

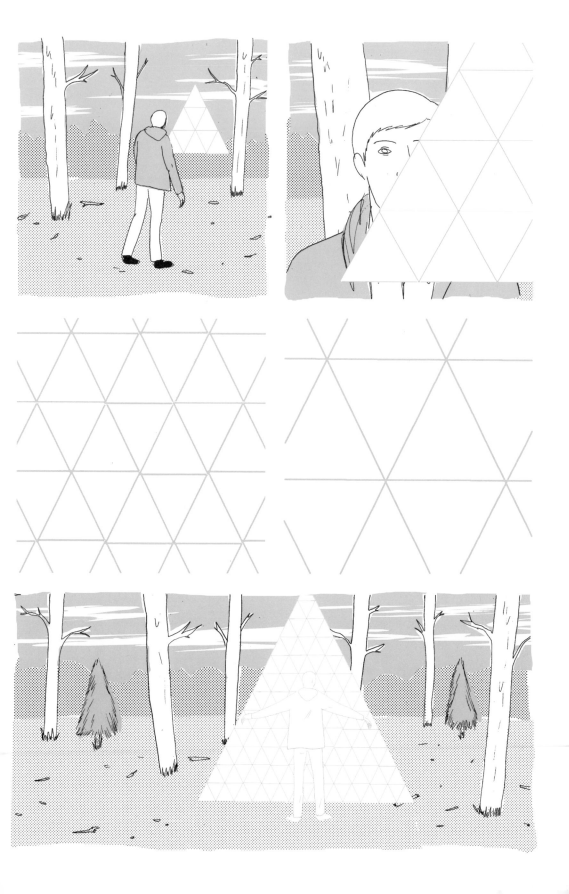

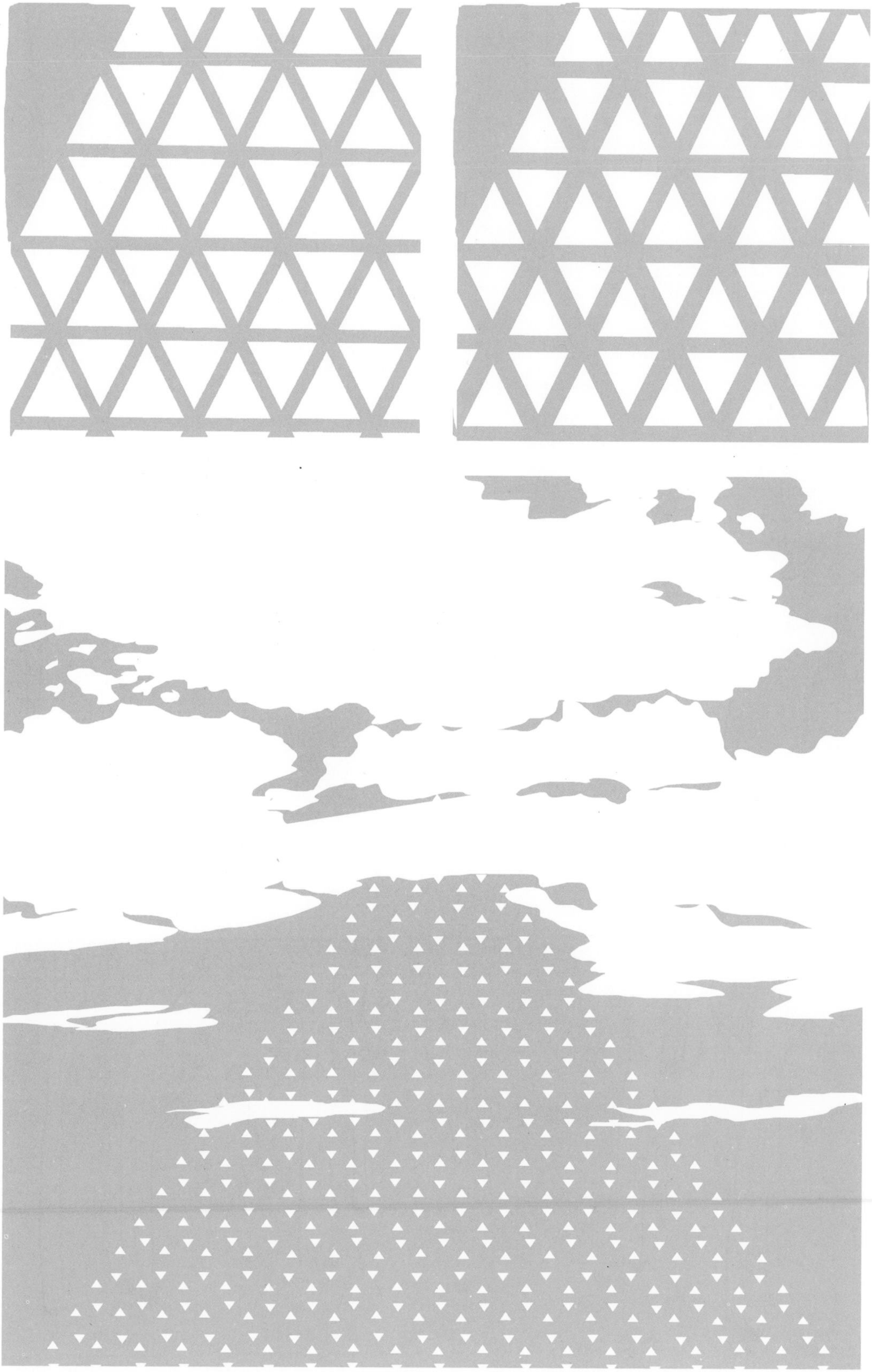

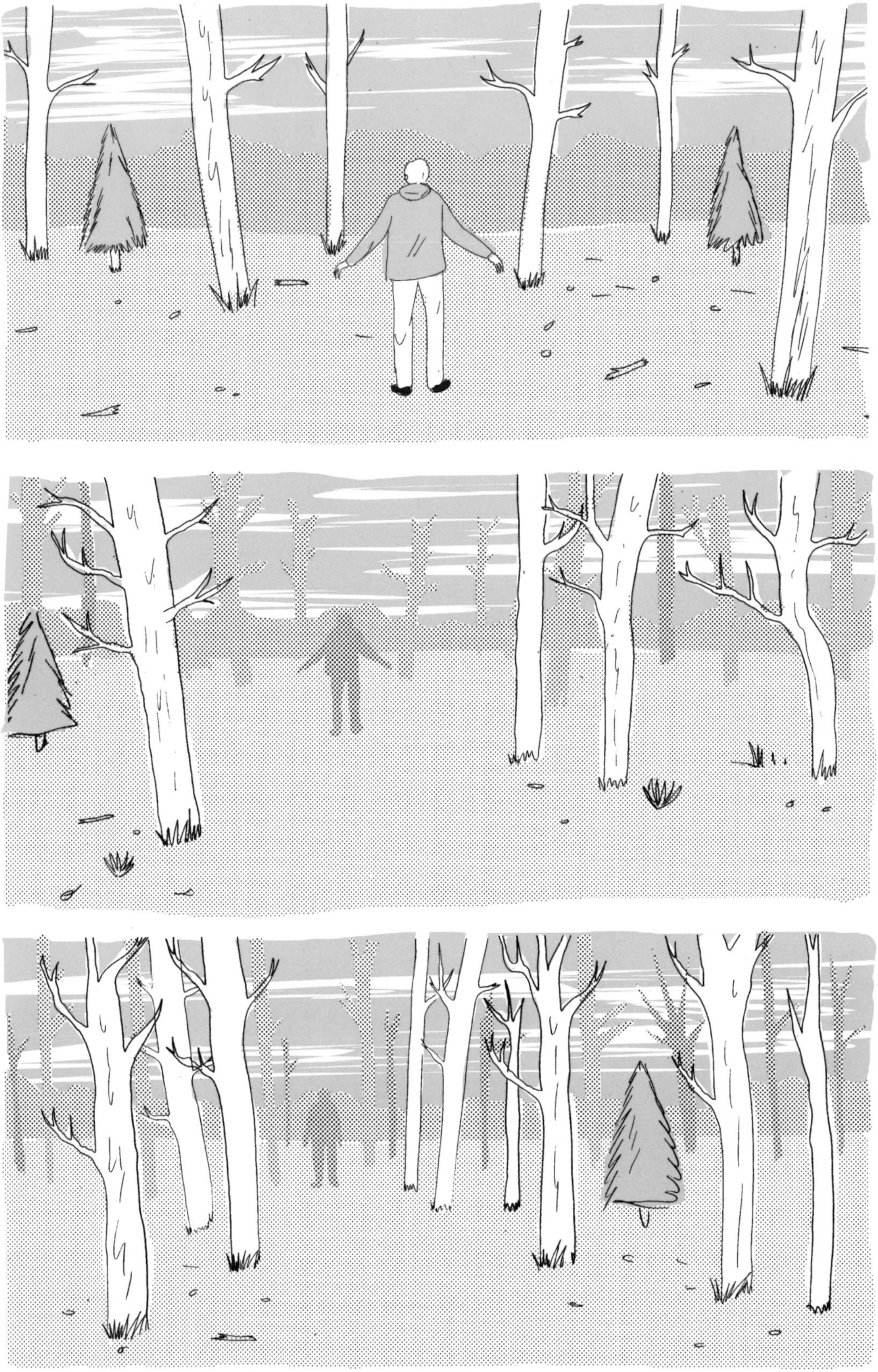

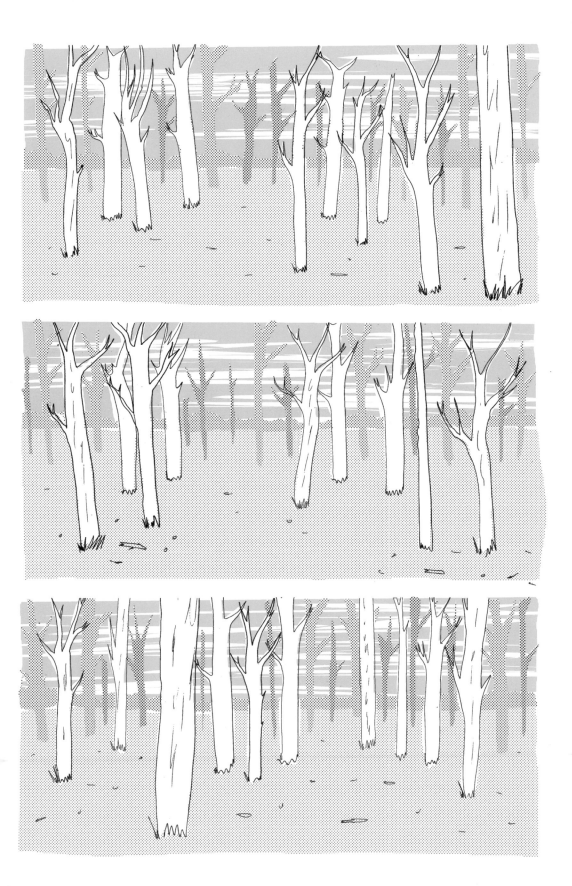

LONE PINE © 2010 JED McGOWAN
ISBN 978-1-935233-07-7

CONTACT JED@JEDMCGOWAN.COM
VISIT WWW.JEDMCGOWAN.COM

PUBLISHED WITH FINANCIAL HELP FROM
THE XERIC FOUNDATION

DISTRIBUTED BY ADHOUSE BOOKS
WWW.ADHOUSEBOOKS.COM

PRINTED IN THE US